RIVERSIDE COMMUNITY COLLEGE
1916

P9-ECT-141

MIDDLE EAST JOURNAL

BY THE SAME AUTHOR

A Bridge Through Time (as Laila Said)

MIDDLE EAST JOURNAL

A Woman's Journey into the Heart of the Arab World

by Laila Abou-Saif

CHARLES SCRIBNER'S SONS
New York

Charles Scribner's Sons
Macmillan Publishing Company
866 Third Avenue, New York, NY 10022
Collier Macmillan Canada, Inc.

Library of Congress Cataloging-in-Publication Data

Abou-Saif, Laila.
Middle East journal : a woman's journey into the heart of the Arab world / by Laila Abou-Saif.
p. cm.
ISBN 0-684-19136-9
1. Middle East—Politics and government—1979– 2. Jewish-Arab relations—1973– 3. Islamic fundamentalism—Arab countries.
I. Title.
DS63.1.A24 1990
956—dc20 89-10394 CIP

Macmillan books are available at special discounts for bulk purchases for sales promotions, premiums, fund-raising, or educational use.
For details, contact:

Special Sales Director
Macmillan Publishing Company
866 Third Avenue
New York, NY 10022

10 9 8 7 6 5 4 3 2 1

Printed in the United States of America

To My Mother

BAHEYA M. FALTAS

(Mrs. Dr. Nessim Abou-Saif)

Contents

SEPTEMBER 1986 *95*

OCTOBER 1986 *179*

NOVEMBER 1986 *221*

Acknowledgments

Special thanks go to Dr. Mamdouh Beltagui for permitting me to carry a press card during my research in Cairo, to my mother for giving me office space and a phone in her apartment building, and to Ahmed Sami Sharara, my close friend, for helping me with the research for this book and also for translating so much of the interviews conducted in classical Arabic. Special thanks also go to Elaine Markson, my stoic agent, to my assistant and secretary, Sarah Abdel Fatah, and to Bradley Davis, my New York attorney.

Finally, I wish to give very special thanks to Robert Stewart, chief editor at Scribners, who guided me skillfully and serenely through this arduous project. I thank him also for never losing his faith in the significance of presenting the Arab world to Western readers. Without him this book would not have seen the light of day.

Introduction

If you're riding in a cab in New York and you glance at the name of the cabdriver on the license card in front of you, it might be something like Issa Mohammed (an Arab name) or Igall Nidam (an Israeli name). These drivers might be in their mid-thirties or early forties. You don't have to stretch your imagination too far to envisage them a decade or so before, facing one another across enemy lines in the Sinai Desert or across the banks of the Suez Canal.

Why are they here driving cabs in New York? The answer is simple. There is instability in the Middle East and the future is uncertain. Unemployment and inflation are some of the problems. But these men, like myself, have lived through at least three wars in the unending Arab-Israeli conflict. Egypt alone has lost 100,000 men in those wars. Its internal problems, such as the population explosion, have intensified. Its population will nearly double to 103 million people by the year 2020. Islamic fundamentalism has pervaded the country, and Islamic extremism, as a result, reflects discontent internally and externally. Islam is disenchanted with the West and especially the U.S. because of its support of Israeli occupation of Arab territories.

Meanwhile, Israel, in the aftermath of the Palestinian *intifadeh* of December 1987, has become polarized. Many Israelis now want a dialogue with the PLO and the restoration of the occupied territory to the Palestinians. Many do not. Especially the government. Israel is the strongest military power in the Middle East, but it is no longer the Spartan state that fought single-mindedly to gain more territory for Eretz Israel. It is a divided nation.

What has changed? It is difficult to say. Maybe both Israelis and Arabs are tired of fighting. Even the PLO wants to sit down and talk. Finally. And maybe the U.S. will listen. But it is difficult to predict.

It is important to realize that the Palestinian problem is still unresolved. And for those of us who live in the Middle East, the Palestinian issue is an integral part of our lives. Our existence is overshadowed by the fact that six million Palestinian refugees are homeless and stateless. It is an Arab problem. But it is also an Israeli problem and therefore an American problem.

How many Westerners realize that Islamic extremism and fundamentalism, responsible for so much of the terrorism in the Western world, is fueled by the Palestinian problem?

Even before World War II, the Society of Muslim Brothers, or the Muslim Brotherhood as it is referred to, began to take political action against the Zionist movement that was taking root in Palestine in the thirties. When Britain ended its mandate over Palestine in 1948, all the Arab countries, including Egypt, declared war on Israel. This 1948 war proved a training ground for the paramilitary organizations of the Muslim Brotherhood who volunteered to fight. To them this war was a holy war, a *jihad,* in which they sought death as martyrs in order to save the Holy Land and especially the holy city of Jerusalem from Jewish domination. That war also proved to be a training ground for young Egyptian officers, such as Gamal Abdel Nasser, who staged a revolution in Egypt in 1952. He overturned the monarchy, making Egypt a republic with a real Egyptian as its leader. Nasser's close friend, Anwar al-Sadat, was also a member of the Society.

Subsequently, Nasser fought two wars with Israel: the Suez War in 1956, and the Six-Day War in 1967. Sadat fought a third one: the October War in 1973. But even after Sadat went to Jerusalem in November 1977 and then signed a peace treaty with Israel in 1979, the Palestinian question remained unresolved. Egyptian territory was returned to Egypt in exchange for peace. But no Palestinian territory was ever returned to the Palestinians.

Thus the Camp David accords and the peace treaty did not bring peace to the area. They alienated Egypt from the rest of the Arab world, which opposed Sadat's peace with Israel. The peace treaty complicated the dynamics involved. With Egypt out of the way, Israel could invade southern Lebanon to liquidate the Palestine Liberation Organization outposts there. But the PLO, though weakened, is alive. More important, there has been a kind of national awakening of the Palestinian refugees. They have revolted. *Intifadeh* means an uprising. It is not the first uprising of its kind. As long as a refugee problem exists, with homeless people living in camps, waiting to return to their original villages within what is now Israel, there will be no peace in the area. The unresolved Palestinian question is behind all the dynamics of the Middle East. It is the source of all the political struggles that have arisen and will continue to arise there.

This is an opinion I share with many of my countrymen and women. Indeed, with most Arabs. For us, the Palestinian issue is not an abstract issue we read about in the newspapers. It is our reality, and it is reflected everywhere in this journal I have kept over the last three years. The Palestinian issue crops up at every twist and turn of my interactions with intellectuals and ordinary people. It is part of the landscape itself. Cairo, like many parts of Israel, is a military area. There are military installations and landmarks everywhere that remind us that still another war may take place. Bayonet-carrying soldiers guard our bridges, and our army rules us. Since Nasser, our rulers have always been military men, men who led Egyptians into battles with the Zionist state. Ours is a military society. So is Israel, so is Iraq, so is Syria.

But the Arabs, unlike the Jews in Palestine, have been singularly unsuccessful at presenting their point of view, lobbying, propagandizing, or even communicating with the West. In the pages that follow, I attempt to get across why the Arabs feel the way they do. The object of these interviews is not anti-Israeli propaganda but an attempt to bridge the gap between the Middle East and the West on this particular issue, simply to give insights to Westerners in order to help them gain a deeper understanding of the Arab-Israeli dilemma.

At the core of the Palestinian problem lies the confrontation of two nationalisms, the Arab and the Zionist, which lay claim to the same land. The Jews had their first contact with the promised land in about 1800 B.C., when Abraham led his followers to the outskirts of the Palestine area. Abraham's descendants went to Egypt and returned in the twelfth century B.C. Saul united them into one kingdom. Saul's successor, David, built the first temple in the city of Jerusalem during the tenth century B.C. This first united kingdom, which lasted for less than two hundred years before dissolving into the kingdoms of Judah and Israel, provided the religious and emotional basis for the Jewish claim to Palestine.

In 721 B.C. the Assyrians invaded the kingdom of Israel and destroyed some of it. The Babylonians attacked Jerusalem in 586 B.C., destroyed the first temple and scattered the people. A second temple was built in the sixth century B.C. when the Jews were allowed by the Babylonians to return. Later the area called Palestine was conquered and ruled by Alexander the Great, the Ptolemies of Egypt and the Syrian-Greek state to the north.

The Maccabean revolt in 168 B.C. resulted once more in the Jewish dominance of Palestine, but this ended when the Romans conquered the area in 63 B.C. Jewish revolts in A.D. 70 and A.D. 135 resulted in the destruction of Jerusalem and the banishment of the Jews.

As the birthplace of Christianity, Palestine gained political significance. It was settled by a Christian majority in the fifth and sixth centuries. In 638, the Christians lost Palestine to the Arab Muslim conquerors led by Caliph Omar, the successor of the Prophet Mohammed. Soon the Christian inhabitants of Palestine became Arabized, as did the small Jewish communities that remained there. In the seventh century, Jerusalem became a sacred Muslim city. Near the spot where the Prophet Mohammed was believed to have ascended to heaven, Muslims erected the Mosque of Omar, otherwise known as the Dome of the Rock.

The Arab domination of Palestine ended in the eleventh century. Subsequently, it fell to a succession of invaders such as the Seljuk Turks, the Crusaders, the Tartars, the Mongols, the Mamelukes of Egypt, and the Ottoman Turks, who remained there until World War I.

During all these invasions, most of the inhabitants remained Arab and Muslim. Meanwhile the hope of returning to the Promised Land of the Old Testament never died among the Jews. The persecution of the Jews in Russia and other countries led in the nineteenth century to the concept of a Jewish state, and the Zionist movement was created. In 1897 the first Zionist Congress met in Basel. A resolution was passed to create a home for the Jewish people in Palestine. By World War I, Jewish settlement in Palestine numbered 80,000.

Dr. Chaim Weizmann, a well-known British chemist, and Nahum Sokolow, a Russian member of the Zionist Executive, lobbyed arduously in Britain for the Jewish state. As a result of these efforts, the Foreign Secretary, Arthur Balfour, wrote a letter to Lord Walter Rothschild referring to the establishment "in Palestine of a National Home for the Jewish People." At that time Britain hoped to gain control over Palestine through its support of a strong Jewish nation.

The British also encouraged the Arabs to revolt against the Ottoman Turks who still controlled Palestine. In exchange, they promised them independence. The revolt broke out in 1916. At this time, the Arabs had two choices: They could cast their lot with the Turks who promised them autonomy, or they could support the allies in the hope of acquiring independence.

They chose the latter. Sir Henry McMahon, British High Commissioner of Egypt, even gave assurances to Sharif Hussein (the ruler of the Hejaz, now Saudi Arabia) that if the Arabs rose against the Turks, Britain would agree to recognize and uphold the independence of the Arab countries. Meanwhile Jewish immigration into Palestine was increasing.

In March 1918, Chaim Weizmann visited Cairo and Palestine in order to dispel fears that the Arabs were beginning to have concerning Zionist political claims.

Furthermore, British and French communiqués were publicized in the liberated Arab territories claiming that the Allies would assist in setting up "indigenous governments" in Arab territories. Emir Feisal, Sharif Hussein's son, even signed an agreement with Chaim Weizmann in 1919 welcoming Jewish immigration to Palestine. This agreement was dependent upon the wartime pledges of the British regarding Arab independence.

After World War I, however, Britain and France chopped up the Levant, or eastern Mediterranean, in the famous Sykes-Picot agreement. This agreement divided the area into spheres of influence or mandates for the French and British. In 1920, Britain received a mandate over Palestine and Transjordan. France acquired Syria and Lebanon. A British High Commissioner was appointed to Palestine.

Between 1919 and 1936, Western Jews invested $400 million in Palestine. The Jewish National Fund purchased Arab land. The land bought by the organization not only became Jewish property but could not be resold to Arabs nor could Arabs be employed on it.

Meanwhile, the Jewish immigrants, who by comparison to the Arabs were highly educated, developed their communities along sophisticated economic, political, and military lines. Thus from the outset, the Arabs, who did not have this steady stream of Western-educated immigrants, were at a disadvantage. The Arabs were also weakened by their own dividedness and religious factionalism.

Outbreaks of violence against the growing Zionist influence in Palestine occurred in 1922, 1929, 1930, and 1936. The Arabs became so alarmed at the extent of Jewish immigration that parliamentary committees for the defense of Palestine were organized in many Arab countries. At this point the

British suggested the idea of the partition of the country into an Arab and a Jewish state. Dr. Weizmann and David Ben-Gurion accepted this idea and so did the Zionist Congress in 1937. But the Palestinians rejected it. They did not want a Jewish state in their midst that would take up their land and dispute their holy places. As the land purchase and immigration increased, so did the agitation. Terrorism was also leveled against the British for their passivity vis à vis the growing Zionist power. The British punished with the death sentence any Palestinian who carried a bomb.

The events of World War II, especially the persecution of the Jews by the Nazis, strengthened the Zionist position in Palestine. Before the war, the British had trained armed Jewish defense forces. These later formed an underground Jewish army called the Haganah. In 1944 the British established a Jewish Brigade in its regular army. These military forces facilitated the smuggling of arms and immigrants into Palestine. Extremist groups, such as Stern and Irgun Zvai Leumi, committed acts of terrorism against the British, who were trying to control the immigration of Jews into Palestine through quotas.

Meanwhile, behind the scenes, Winston Churchill informed Chaim Weizmann that the British Cabinet on Palestine would "eventually recognize Jewish sovereignty in a partitioned Palestine."

In the U.S. both Roosevelt and Thomas Dewey strongly backed the Zionist claim to Palestine. The now powerful Zionist lobby in Congress succeeded in getting thirty-three state legislatures to pass pro-Zionist resolutions. In March 1945 the Arab League was created as a result of the fear of the growing Zionist threat to Palestine. Arab governments began to apply diplomatic pressure on behalf of the Palestinians. In April 1945 the King of Saudi Arabia obtained a promise from President Roosevelt that he would consider "Arab interests and views" in any settlement of the Palestinian question.

After World War II the Zionists found a strong sympathizer in President Truman. He pressured Britain to permit 100,000 Jews to enter Palestine without delay. Meanwhile attempts by the British to solve the Palestinian dilemma in conferences with both parties failed.

The Arabs and the Jews had preconditions before attending a joint conference. In despair, Britain turned over the Palestine problem to the U.N. in April 1947. On May 15, the U.N. General Assembly adopted a resolution authorizing a special committee on Palestine (UNSCOP) to inquire into all questions relevant to the Palestinian problem. UNSCOP proposed a first partition plan that was rejected by Arabs and Jews alike. This plan would have divided Palestine into an Arab state and a Jewish state, with an independent Jerusalem under U.N. trusteeship.

At the end of 1947, the U.N. proposed a second partition plan. Among other things, it was to put an end to the British mandate over Palestine and internationalize Jerusalem. The Jews accepted it joyously because with the ending of the mandate, they would have a legitimate state. The Arabs rejected it because it was perceived as a slicing up of Arab territory. Many Zionists also rejected it because they saw it as a division of "the homeland." Nonetheless, the Haganah was converted to a regular army and Jewish immigration to Palestine was speeded up. Jewish villages were hurriedly constructed in strategic areas.

Meanwhile the Arabs called a strike, and fighting broke out between the two communities. On May 15, 1948, the British evacuated Palestine. That same day the state of Israel was declared and immediately recognized by President Truman. This further embittered the Arabs, who still hoped that once the British left Palestine, the U.S. would finally help them in their struggle for independence.

They felt betrayed by the U.S. History was to repeat itself as the events of the next thirty years were to show. The Russians, who like the U.S. had voted for the partitioning of Palestine, also recognized the State of Israel. But it was to the West, first Britain and now the U.S., that the Arabs had looked for support in their struggle for independence. That may explain why that relationship would never be the same again—a fact that the Soviets exploited skillfully.

Once the State of Israel was declared, a great deal of psychological and military pressure was put on Palestinians living in the area, now Israel, to leave. There were stories of atrocities perpetuated by the Irgun against Arab villagers. On May 15, the same day that Israel became a state, 200,000 Palestinians fled their villages into neighboring Arab countries. Their villages were destroyed by the Israeli armed forces so that they would not return. Thus the Palestinian refugee problem was created.

War broke out. In spite of the combined Arab armies that fought them, the Israelis won a stunning victory because of their military superiority. Moreover, they were able to conquer territories that had belonged to the Arabs as stipulated in the U.N. partition plan. Significantly, they managed to occupy the new city of Jerusalem. And, during the 1967 war, the Israelis also managed to occupy the old city, which they rapidly annexed. The annexation of Jerusalem was perhaps the single most provocative act in the 1967 conflict. It cnraged the religious feelings of all the Muslims of the Arab world. And it gave rise to the renewed political agitation of Islamic fundamentalism and extremism. It also saw an increase in terrorist activity against Israel. The PLO had been officially recognized in 1964 by the Arab League of Nations and by most Arab governments as the organization that represented the Palestinian people. It was headed then by a young engineer from Jerusalem called Yassir Arafat.

After the 1948 war there was more fighting, more rhetoric, more wars, more truces, more ignored U.N. resolutions, and then again more wars.

The U.S. may have made a major breakthrough in 1980 by agreeing to speak with the PLO. But it is difficult to predict.

When I met him in 1987, Arafat was optimistic. He spoke to me candidly and as an Arab. He said he felt sure a Palestinian state would come into existence.

Nonetheless, the Palestinian problem remains as the setting for the tragedy that has been taking place in the Middle East since 1948. No Arab country has escaped being involved in this conflict. I focus on Egypt only because it is the country I know best. And also because it has always been one of the major players in this drama. My life and the lives of other Egyptians—like the lives of the Palestinians and Israelis—demonstrate how inextricably the personal is interwoven with the political.

JULY 1986

JULY 15
Jacob Beach, Connecticut

I am sometimes happy in Connecticut. In the autumn, for instance. That season of "mellow fruitfulness" obliterates everything. Even the loneliness. Or in the spring, when you can hear the birds again and see the buds struggling on the nude branches.

But aside from that I am stranger in this fabricated paradise. Here, where everything is clean and neat, where poverty rarely shows its face. It all seems somewhat unreal. Maybe I've never been in idyllic surroundings before, I tell myself. But the loneliness is real.

I think I am just about tolerated in this waspish New England town with its manicured green. People walk past me as if I didn't exist. Sometimes the police or dog warden comes by. One of my neighbors is complaining that Egyptian dogs bark too much. My neighbor has a cat, and in Connecticut cats are allowed to roam everywhere. My dogs find this inexplicable. Why can't they roam too?

I pay most of my bills on time, especially the monthly mortgage on my house. I teach at a provincial state college where I am also tolerated. They consider my theatrical experience "Arab." Tomorrow, I will return to the Middle East, the Arab world, which I fear I should never have left. I never thought I would ever want to return. Of course, there was the occasional homesickness. But to leave America for a year or so, to go back and live there. Impossible! Especially after the scandal caused by *A Bridge Through Time.* My publishers want me to keep a sort of diary where I will interview personalities, insiders, people who have never been heard of before in the U.S. Of course, they wouldn't mind if I threw in Qaddafi or Arafat.

This isn't an easy assignment. Too soul-searching, maybe too painful. As I look around at the little private beach that I share with some of the privileged inhabitants of this New England town, I wonder if they care what happens in the Middle East.

I shudder slightly with the afternoon breeze and pick up a newspaper that has blown next to me. There is a front-page story about some Israeli troops killing two five-year-old Arabs because they threw stones at them.

The woman sitting opposite me shifts her position and then, picking up a nearby can, sprays herself methodically with insect repellent. She looks bored, middle-aged, and fastidious. Suddenly the tranquillity is pierced by the triumphant shrills of some young boys playing down by the water. "Look, I've got it. I've got it." I sit up and look out. The boy, about nine years old, was poking a stick ferociously at something lying on the beach. I must have looked so alarmed that somebody volunteered yawningly, "The kids have caught a jellyfish." I lean back and observe the scene. Now each of the children seems to have a stick and to be beating at that amorphous lump of life. "I am *torturizing* it. I am *torturizing* it," one of the boys shrieks with apparent delight.

The commotion attracts the sea gulls. They circle the children. The lifeguard stares ahead indifferently from her Olympian heights. An empty box of Marlboros flitters in the breeze. The sea gulls are screeching loudly now.

"Damn," exclaims a man not too far away. His suntan oil has dripped into the sand. It is muggy. I look out at the water. Picking up my few belongings, I walk slowly across the pebbly beach to my car. It is too late for another swim.

Time to go home.

JULY 16
In Flight on TWA

It's 5,000 miles to Cairo from New York. But time flies. My thoughts return constantly to my book. Why am I going back? Loneliness? The yearning for family, sunshine, warmth, and the facile humor of my countrymen? Yes. But there is more. The challenge of providing American readers with the opportunity to see the Arab side. But who am I to attempt such a herculean task? More knowledgeable Arabs have tried. Edward Said, for example.

When I left Egypt in the mid-eighties I was disillusioned and frustrated. Sure, I had become Egypt's first and only woman stage director. But what had I done for women? How was I able to change things? The miseries I lived with remained and would worsen. And to top it all, with the publication of my book in the U.S. chronicling my personal and professional life, I had antagonized my family. I had also antagonized the "authorities."

As I sit in my tight seat on the TWA jet, I wonder if they will even let me into the country. Worse, will they let me out? I ring the bell and ask for a blanket; the air conditioning is so cold. We will be arriving in Cairo in a couple of hours. I wish I could stop thinking.

But my mind continues to churn. I switch on the music channel. An ad for *Business Week.* I switch it off. I heard while in New York that my book has been banned. Whatever that means. Apparently certain personal revelations I made have touched off a storm of outrage. And the rest of the book? The political side? The fact that it is an artist's story? That it is critical of so many aspects of my society? That it is a cry of pain and of love?

"Would you like something to drink?" asks the stewardess mechanically. I decline. Alcoholic beverages are hard to obtain in Cairo. I switch on the music channel. Again an ad for *Business Week.* I switch it off.

I pick up a journal on Arab-American affairs: "Since the death of Sadat, the honeymoon between Egypt and the U.S. is over," writes an American authority. "Yet the great achievement of American foreign policy in the area was that it displaced Soviet influence and brought about a formal peace treaty between Egypt and Israel. The two superpowers had almost had a confrontation in the area during the 1973 war. Because of this, the détente that had been achieved between them had almost eroded." In order to keep the Soviet Union out of the area, the U.S. keeps Egypt: financial aid for the fiscal year 1988 is estimated at $6 billion. Israel gets three times as much. But there are other strings. Uncle Sam gives all this money away provided Egypt "normalizes" relations with Israel. This is what is called bilateral relations between Egypt and the United States. This was all agreed upon in the 1979 Peace Treaty negotiated by President Carter. Israel returned to Egypt all of the territories it had captured in the last thirty years through its various wars against the Arabs, but the Egyptians must have "normal" cultural and trade relations with its enemy of thirty years. Now there's a catch there, I think, putting the magazine down. The Egyptians don't mind the peace treaty. They are sick of war. But do they have to climb into bed with the people who killed a hundred thousand of their young men? Moreover, since Khomeini came into power, there has been a growing wave of Islamic fundamentalism—a movement opposed to the Western presence in the Arab world that started way back in the twenties when the British were occupying Egypt and the French the rest of the Middle East. To the fundamentalists, such contact with a Western country, with Western ambitions in the area, is distasteful. Especially because Israel is still occupying Arab land, the Golan Heights in Syria and the West Bank of Jordan where millions of Palestinians live in refugee camps and cry for independence from their Israeli occupiers. But the Israelis won't relinquish the West Bank, which they claim is biblically theirs. So what's the solution? All of this is referred to as the Palestinian problem. To the Arabs, so long as Israel continues to occupy Arab land (the West Bank was seized by Israel from Jordan in the 1967 war), there will be no real peace. But the Egyptians want peace. Sadat did, and while he was alive he kept a marvelous affair going on between Egypt, America, Israel. He even conned the Egyptians into believing that the peace with Israel would bring Egypt prosperity. And for a while it did. The money poured into Egypt. But it was not channeled properly. We have a lot of corruption and a population explosion. When he was assassinated in 1981 (by Islamic extremists), we discovered that Egypt had severe economic problems. Hosni Mubarak, Sadat's successor, turned to the U.S. for help. The U.S. imposed more restrictions. The peace started to get a little cold. Then Mubarak came over to the U.S. and asked the Reagan administration the million dollar questions: "Why don't you pressure Israel into negotiating with the PLO? Why don't you negotiate with the PLO and settle the Palestinian problem once and for all?" The full reason for the failure of these negotiations was one of the things I am hoping to find out.

Meanwhile, the peace is getting colder and colder. Mubarak fought against the Israelis in 1967 and 1973 as an air force pilot. It is said the Israelis don't like him because in 1967 he flew successful deep penetration air raids into Israel. In other words, he bombed Israel from inside Israel. Still, as he repeatedly states, he doesn't want war. He wants to improve the internal situation in Egypt, continue the peace treaty, solve the Palestinian question—*without* compromising Egypt with Israel. It may be that he wants to avoid Sadat's fate. But it must be remembered that Egypt is an Arab country with economic ties to the rest of the Arab and Islamic world that it cannot afford to jeopardize. Millions of Egyptians earn their living by working in Saudi Arabia, Kuwait, Iraq, and other Arab countries.

The fact remains that the honeymoon is over. What now? Will there be a dialogue between the PLO and the U.S.?

We will be in Cairo soon. I switch on the music channel. The sonorous chords of Beethoven's "Eroica" boost my morale. I could never live in a country where Western music and culture were forbidden. I am being pessimistic again. Wait and see, I tell myself.

"Ladies and gentlemen, if you look to the right side of the

aircraft you will have an aerial view of the pyramids." I am on the right side of the aircraft. I have seen the pyramids a thousand times before, but they never looked quite as good as they do now.

JULY 18
Cairo

Cairo—crowds, crowds, crowds. Fifteen million people live in Cairo, and I thought New York was crowded. My third day—I've been asleep and almost afraid to step outside to that dreaded, beloved reality. My little Chevette, a 1979 model, has a new battery, and I finally moved out of my mother's house in Garden City two days after my arrival. There are new bridges, overpasses everywhere, and the traffic seems to flow much more smoothly with imported cars: Chevrolets, Mercedeses, Fiats, BMWs.

It's a beige city, sand-colored, and people's faces are of the same color, as if they had been sculpted out of the surrounding intertwining desert. Even the refuse is overladen with sand. There are stray dogs in the street and so many, many small children who play on the sidewalks, bedraggled, half-naked, and smiling. Always smiling. And covered with dust. Even the trees are dusty and layered with the golden sand. Cairo is always beige—just like people's faces.

The city is split by the longest river of the old world—the Nile. And it is greeting me now as I make my way to my small apartment in Maadi, a suburb of Cairo.

They say in Egypt, whoever drinks the water of the Nile will return to it. We empty our sewage in the Nile. Maybe that's why it always looks so muddy, so greenish. But the Nile, like my people, is a gentle river, which flows slowly and serenely.

There are so many skyscrapers overlooking the corniche of the Nile I am traveling along. But behind these high-rises are, haphazardly spawned, poor neighborhoods where houses of mud brick have been rapidly erected on patches of green agricultural land. The poor in Cairo always live just behind the rich. I have returned.

JULY 19

My apartment is submerged in dust. On the terrace my tall cactus is still alive. Surely this is a miracle. I gaze at it. It is slightly bent but it holds on unwaveringly, overlooking the Nile flowing below the terrace. In the distance beyond the Nile, on the other bank, a couple of step pyramids show their faces. The sun shines brightly. It pierces through the industrial fog of Cairo's pollution. I gaze hungrily on the impervious river and those ancient burial mounds. Suddenly I know who I am. I am an Egyptian, a speck in the history of this magnificent civilization.

JULY 20

There is so much noise in Cairo. My terrace is glass-enclosed, and yet I can hear the barking of stray dogs, the honking of horns, and the shrieks of children. Even the lament of braying, overworked donkeys penetrates my small apartment on the twelfth floor.

JULY 21

I have finally been able to get rid of the tenacious dust. My mother's manservant, Rizk, did most of the work. Rizk is a Copt. He flung out the carpets fiercely and beat the dust out of them, then he uprooted the cobwebs clinging to the corners with a long broom, and then he swept and swept the rooms, piling the dust in neat corners. Then, with a pail brimming with soap suds, he splashed every corner of the apartment and wiped it bit by bit, rarely stopping to catch his breath. I can breathe now. But the smell of mothballs still hovers in the air.

JULY 22

AT&T has revolutionized the phone system in Cairo. When you dial now, you immediately get your party. There was a time I can still remember when it took as long as an hour to get a dial tone. But that was a long time ago. The Americans are here now.

JULY 23

Busy making lists of all the people I will be contacting for the interviews. Managed to locate Mohammed, a loyal student who promised to help me. "I'll do anything for you, doctor," he had said on the phone and then he added, "And how is 'Amreeka' doing?" "Amreeka" is the Egyptians' customary way of referring to the United States. My first meeting in Cairo: Yussef Idris.

JULY 24

Yussef Idris

Novelist, playwright, and journalist

"Amreeka screws us and then it gives us ten cents and says go and buy a cup of coffee," said Yussef Idris bitterly as we sat in his apartment overlooking the Nile in Dokki, not far from the Sheraton Hotel. He was wearing a white cotton suit and looked very tanned. He had aged and had gained some weight since I last saw him almost ten years before when he came to one of my plays. Not very far from where we sat, surrounded by an assortment of rubber plants and other potted lush greens, was a bust of Idris that made him appear more statesmanlike than he was. The bust reflected the reverence and respect with which he is held by his contemporaries.

Idris's face seems to be sculpted from the desert mountains in the *sa'id*—the south of Egypt. High cheekbones, thick, strong lips, a stubborn chin, and honey-colored eyes that penetrate like a laser beam.

The forehead is wide, furrowed. His hair—a lion's mane—is white, his body thick, his walk and posture confident. This year he was one of the nominees for the Nobel Prize in literature. He is the pampered child—the intellectual, par excellence—of the Egyptian revolution. Yet he wrote a satirical play about Nasser's totalitarianism and vicious articles against Sadat's foreign and domestic policies.

In 1965 I directed a little one-act play of his, *Farahat's Republic,* about a policeman with utopian socialist dreams. We became friends. Subsequently, he supported me and my attempts at reviving a folk theater in Cairo.

When we met we embraced. Idris's loyal wife joined us. She displayed her fully equipped Americanized kitchen with pride. Idris complained about this and that. I was an old friend. He didn't want to talk politics with me—just to socialize. But finally I managed to get him to speak.

As far back as I can remember, Idris was a leftist, but above all, he is an artist, one of those rare artists who live in developing countries, survive repressive regimes, and never compromise their art. His hatred for the U.S. did not surprise me, even though it was and is a qualified hatred. For Idris has often visited and lectured in the U.S. and only recently was a guest lecturer at the von Grunebaum Center for Near Eastern Studies at the University of California in Los Angeles. He was a close friend of the Sadats, too, but also one of their staunchest critics. To him, Sadat sold Egypt lock, stock, and barrel to the West in what was tantamount to treason. But he was soft-spoken when it came to Mubarak, saying that there was more intellectual freedom now than there was before. "If you are going to write a book telling Americans what they want to hear, then don't do it. Say the truth or nothing."

"You really hate America," I commented.

"America is going to ruin the world with its push-button politics. Reagan with his dyed hair is a farce. If we had been screwed by Kennedy or Roosevelt, it might have been bearable, but Reagan . . ."

Idris told me that in 1984 he was invited by the Department of Near Eastern Languages and Cultures at the University of California's Los Angeles campus to give his opinions on the Middle East conflict. "The Americans are saturated with their mass media, which represents the Israeli point of view. When I was in Los Angeles, any news about the Middle East came from Jerusalem—its source is Jerusalem. How come?" The conversation then turned to Jihan Sadat, whom Idris said he likes very much "personally, but politically—I would kill her," he said emphatically. "Because she killed Sadat."

"How did she kill him?" I asked.

"She is responsible for 90 percent of what Sadat did."

"You mean she was too visible?"

"No, she was ruling Egypt in the style of peasants. Sadat was a flexible man—she was in control of things, but he had to face the public. He was responsible to the people. I knew them both well, since 1958, and I know that she had a tremendous influence on him. They were very corrupt; even Sadat. But she was more corrupt than Mrs. Marcos."

"Really?"

"Oh, yes, much more corrupt. She was greedy for money, influence, and appearances."

"Your objections to the Sadats cannot be personal. Weren't you well treated by the regime?"

"Yes, I was not thrown in jail in 1981—I was fired once along with a group of journalists, but that's all. The problem is not only with America, but with Israel—and it seems that we will not be able to deliver ourselves from these ties for fifty years."

"Why do you want to undo these ties?"

"Do you want us to be followers of Israel? As a treaty, it's all wrong. To begin with, we have demilitarized the Sinai while the Israeli army stands on the borders of the Sinai. It's not true that the Negev desert is demilitarized and the Sinai desert is demilitarized. We are threatened—Israel need only make a slight move and it will be occupying the Sinai—because the Sinai has no soldiers. Our army cannot be present except near the canal, and the rest is guarded by security police. How can anyone put their country in such a state? On the other hand, normalization should be a choice—if I make a treaty with you, does that mean you have to love me? Since when?"

"I think what is meant is just a *solh*—peace," I said.

"Solh, yes, but then they don't get Egyptian tourists. Egyptians don't want to go there. Must we be forced to go? As for Israel—it will have no future if it continues to live off the United States. The United States treats Egypt very badly, in the interest of America of course. I don't blame America; I blame the Egyptians who take this kind of treatment."

"Could you explain what you mean by 'bad treatment'? Do you mean economically?"

"Take Russia, for example. When it was here, it established heavy industries. It built the Aswan dam and it made long-term investments in the country. Americans don't do that—with the exception of General Motors, which will be established at the expense of a local industry, which has been Egyptian for twenty-five years. America encourages the private sector. The private sector in Egypt is dishonest, not like the private sector in America—at least in America there are formidable laws which keep the private sector in line—but in Egypt there are no such laws. The 'aid' gets lost. France builds hospitals, Germany erects institutes, but America does nothing at all. It just gives arms to the army for money. And for what? Look at Spain, for example; it has rented out a military base to the U.S. for $2 billion. Why don't we rent them out a piece of Egypt and rid ourselves of the influence of the United States? America has taken all of Egypt for $2 billion. What a cheap price! And then it gives Israel, which has three million people, what it gives Egypt, which has fifty million people! Who locked us into this tight spot and gave the key to the Americans? And then we can't protest. If we do, we will stop getting the wheat and the arms."

"And if they stop the wheat?"

"We will go hungry. We will die of hunger. We only have a three-month reserve of wheat. . . ."

"So the Americans have us by the scruff of the neck? Who put us in this position?" I asked.

"Sadat. Sadat's crime is not Camp David. Mubarak should have started negotiations to alter Camp David—in order to place an army on the borders of the Sinai. How can the country have borders that are unprotected by the army? Our army is standing on the west bank of the canal only, not on the east bank. Before, Israel occupied the Sinai and spent money on it, and now that we have the Sinai, we spend the money on it but the Israelis hold the Sinai hostage and threaten us with occupying it. And instead of developing the Sinai as a national cause, we have lost this cause without really getting back the land of the Sinai."

"Excuse me, but we did get back the Sinai," I remarked.

"I mean ours, to be *defended* by us."

"But there is a multinational force there now."

"Yes, there is a multinational force and there are Israeli tourists under Egyptian protection. When that soldier went beserk and killed some Jews, they came here and entered the military prison and killed him."

"The Jews killed him, really?"

"Yes, they killed him in the prison, just like that."

"I had heard that it was Egyptian intelligence that killed him in order to get out of an embarrassing situation."

"After he was killed, Shamir said that Soliman Khatter was an obstacle [to peace] that no longer exists. That's a major item. I also don't like that Mubarak was called a liar by Reagan—that's bad. Americans only understand violence. At a time when they intervene in Nicaragua and call the war there a war of liberation, the Afghanis are *mujahhidin,* but the Palestinians are terrorists."

"What do you think is the real role of the United States?"

"Imperialists should learn from imperialists. The Americans have learned nothing from the British occupation of Egypt, and Egypt obtained the assistance of the Americans in order to get rid of the British. But the Americans viewed Egypt like the British did: *Egypt is a major force in the Middle East and we must minimize its influence or even ruin it in order to control the entire area.* Moreover, they are keeping the Egyptians on the verge of starvation and on the verge of economical existence."

"Why?"

"Every time Egypt surfaces or gets its breath back, it rejects the West—that has always been the case, since the crusaders. So they [the Americans] want to keep it down."

"To destabilize the area?"

"To destabilize the area—so much so that they have encouraged religious extremism. The religious extremism we have comes to us from Saudi Arabia and comes to us from Sadat who used to encourage the fundamentalist societies in Egypt."

"The CIA encourages extremism?"

"I told them when I was in America, you are playing with fire, you are encouraging religious extremism in Egypt with the hope that it creates a regime like Khomeini's where you keep it busy with people's hands being cut off. No, in Egypt these people would slaughter Israelis and they would eliminate the American influence."

Idris had spoken. As I said goodbye I carefully labeled my cassette with his name. I was lucky to get this interview. Idris does not speak this frankly to everyone. It had been refreshing.

JULY 25

Dr. Mamdouh Beltagui

Deputy Minister of Information

My next meeting was with the Deputy Minister of Information, without whom I would never have been able to obtain press credentials.

Dr. Beltagui received me very cordially at the Ministry of Information and reminded me that he had heard good things about my theater work from many people. He is a suave, good-looking man who speaks fluent French and who has lived in France extensively. He sat behind a large desk in an elegant office in downtown Cairo. Next to him were several phones. They rang continuously. No foreign correspondent or writer can function in Egypt unless approved by him. He also provides the press with the government's official position on all political matters.

As we talked, I felt I was being treated as a foreigner. It bothered me. Or maybe I was just not used to being an expatriate.

The first subject we broached was the Palestinian question.

"We in Egypt believe that the PLO is the sole representative of the Palestinian organizations and therefore there is no rationale for refusing to negotiate with it." He stopped short, as if there were nothing more to say on the subject.

"What is the position of Egypt toward the Islamic fundamental groups?" I asked.

"Socio-politically the Islamic movement in Egypt is old. It dates back to the twenties and therefore it doesn't have that edge of militancy you find in newer movements. I am saying all this because I believe there have been over-generalizations about the political power or the force of these Islamic groups—by the Western media and the American media in particular. They don't seem to be able to differentiate one movement from another, Iran from Egypt. Sunni from Shi'a and so forth." I nodded in agreement.

He lit a cigarette, not before offering me one. The phone rang. He ignored it. "Egyptian society is extremely connected with religion—it has never never abandoned this deep-rooted relationship. And it is a society that bases its social fabric on religious sources and beliefs. And, therefore, the revival of religion in Egypt will not take the same approach as it did in other societies.

"Second, Egyptian society is 'centrist.' It rejects the extremism of the right and the left. We are peaceful people—violence and television do not form a part of our past or our present heritage.

"The impact of these Islamic groups is small and seems to flare up only in times of economic crisis. Once the economic crisis subsides, their influence dies down as well.

"Finally, the Egyptian state deals with this problem through dialogue. We are an open-faced society now, and we accept that they [the fundamentalists] express their viewpoints in our media, on TV, and in the universities. Repression breeds terrorism, and so by allowing them to vent their views, we are also affording them a certain relief. Therefore, these organizations are under control. There is rule of law in Egypt, don't forget," he said, leaning forward, slightly breathless.

"But I have heard that these Islamic groups have penetrated many aspects of Egyptian social and political life. . . . Do you think this to be untrue? Are they not a political force?" I asked.

"But this only confirms what I said," he replied. "It shows that there is freedom in Egypt now, and the present regime is fully capable of defending the state from extremism and/or terrorism.

"I didn't say they were not a political force. I said they are allowed to express themselves but not to practice terrorism. The Western media has absolutely no understanding of this problem and exaggerates it vastly. Egypt is politically now on a new course of freedom—freedom for the press, freedom in multiparty systems—and moreover we are embarking on vast economic projects to improve the situation of the country.

There is work, there is production, and there is democracy. That is what we need to emphasize—and not the negative aspects of our life such as overpopulation.

"From an international point of view, we are on good terms with the U.S. on every level. What I object to is the *stressing* of our religious problems and the population problem," he said angrily. "What the West does not know is that we are doing everything we can to fight the population problem as well as our economic problems."

"But why has nothing been done about the population problem? In China, for example, there are penalties for having more than two children. . . ."

He interrupted me and said, "We do not believe in penalties—or in totalitarian methods. We believe in persuasion. . . ."

"Do we have all that much time?" I countered. "We must keep in line with the Egyptian character, its temperament. Besides, we have an enormous economic potential in Egypt—we do not have a structural problem in Egypt—we can improve and change fast. So you think we can solve all our problems?"

"Yes, I am optimistic," he concluded.

JULY 26

I read the newspapers every day. Today my interest was aroused by an article in which the writer demands the application of Islamic Sharia law to Egyptian law. Among other things, he states that the wife of an Islamic leader should not appear in public without the proper Islamic dress. Obviously an allusion to Mrs. Mubarak. Moreover, she should not have leadership over men in any ceremony on any official or unofficial occasion.

The article also asks whether it is the prerogative of the leader of a country to have many homes or guest houses, where the majority of the people live in mud huts or tin homes threatened with collapse.

The writer then demands that the leaders of Egypt should

build their relationship with Israel on the basis of its historical oppressiveness. Israel, he writes, will continue to practice oppression and we should not forget this even though we have a peace treaty with it.

Islamic fundamentalism and the Palestinian question—these, surely, are the main issues I must concentrate on. But I am also eager to meet old friends, supporters from the Sadat days. People like the Mansour Hassans.

JULY 30

Mansour Hassan

Minister of Culture and Information and Minister of State for Presidential Affairs, 1979–1981

When Saad al-Din Wahba, the Deputy Minister of Culture, closed my Wekalat al-Ghouri theater in 1979 for showing a play that was against polygamy, Mansour Hassan, the Minister of Culture, arranged for the play to continue.

Mansour Hassan was one of Anwar al-Sadat's closest aides and friends during the last three years of the president's life.

"Why did Sadat's popularity wane? I mean after Camp David?" I began.

"During the negotiations, Egyptians began to feel disappointed and frustrated with the Israeli response because Egyptian public opinion was that as recognition and security were offered to Israel, Israel would be ready to give up the occupied territories in Sinai and the rest of the Arab occupied territories. But of course the negotiations were very difficult; Israel was showing that they were reluctant to do that, and this created a lot of frustration. Concerning the rest of the Arab rights, the West Bank, Gaza, Jerusalem, the Golan Heights, the Palestinian problem, Israel was showing that they were not trying to concede anything on that level. So this created disappointment, frustration; and this frustration created some sort of instability in society between public opinion and the [opposition] political forces. Therefore, Sadat was put in that position. I have to admit that I learned quite a lot from him, and I believe that real politics have to do with human values. There is no contradiction between politics and values. In fact, I believe that politics should be the most sacred activity in life because it is the activity that influences an indefinite number of people, not only society as it is, but generation after generation and, therefore, it has to be sacred, it has to be ethical. And a very important ethical value in life is personal loyalty—without cowardice."

"And that is when his popularity began to wane, in your opinion?"

"That is, in my opinion, the start of it. The start of the differences between Sadat and the political forces that he had helped to bring back into action. Sadat, in my opinion, was put in the corner while his objective was still not achieved because he had to continue liberating the land and waiting for complete Israeli evacuation. At the same time he had this instability starting to [manifest itself] in society. Now obviously when you are faced with such a situation, you expect that there will be certain counteraction from the opposition, and, therefore, the situation will start to develop and to climax. [On] the fifth of September, the president felt that the tension was becoming too much in society and that this would create a strong instability the consequences of which nobody could evaluate. [Sadat] especially [felt] that this might give the Israelis a reason—which I firmly believe they were looking for—if not to go back on their commitment to evacuate, at least to delay it as long as they could. Therefore the whole country would have defeated its objective. Not that I approve of the measures that were taken. I am just explaining that this, in my understanding, was the situation. This is why he decided to confront the opposition. . . ."

"By jailing them?"

"To put them into jail. And it is my opinion that this action—and what preceded it—[left] Egyptian society puzzled with President Sadat because it was a very ironical situation. He was the man who started his career by proclaiming the rule of law and allowing political dissension and trying to accommodate it as much as he could, which built his popularity with Egyptian society. The same man at the end of his life became a person who opened the jails again, trying to ban political parties, and not feeling comfortable with dissension. And then the assassination took place. So, I think, this explains why some people say that he was unpopular. I think they are looking only at the last part of his years, and they are unfairly forgetting all the eight or nine years when he was the hero of the country."

"Does that explain why President Sadat was not mourned inside Egypt?"

"We have to admit that President Sadat was *not* mourned inside Egypt as would have been expected and as was due—for the great service he has done his country. I think that as time passes, Sadat will be reevaluated, his great achievements will be quite evident, and they will definitely outweigh all his mistakes—and he will be forgiven that last year of tension. And I think he will go down as one of the great leaders of Egypt in modern times, in addition to being recognized as an international leader by all Western society."

"In your opinion, is Sadat an American creation, a puppet of the United States who was out of touch with his people as his critics claim? Or was he genuinely a popular president who made mistakes, was criticized by his opposition, and never really lost his popularity?

"You were a very close friend of Sadat's and you were part of his government. What was your official position?"

"I can't say I was a close friend; my role being Minister of Presidential Affairs, I was more in touch with the president, of course. Now concerning being an American creation and whether he was popular in his country, well, in my opinion, with due respect to anyone who carries this point of view, being an American creation cannot be more than a fallacy created by illusions. I don't think any political analysis would lead to such an erroneous statement, or it's nothing more than illusion if it is anything. Briefly, if you take Sadat's political activities and political role even before 1950—during the thirties—he was definitely very much involved in the Egyptian nationalist movement and played a very important role there aboveground and underground. Inside the army officer cells and outside with the civilians. And then, if you take his development from 1951 until he became president within the revolutionary command, being one of the leaders of the revolution, such a character or such a person cannot be said to be the creation of the West. He is the creation of his own society. And now, if he during one period or the other, in order to serve his objectives, if he would align himself, here or there, then he would be more using these allies as tools. Of course, at a certain point it would be very difficult to see who is using whom, but you have to analyze the whole character of the man and to analyze his whole history in order to find out, even in gray periods, who is using whom and for what purposes."

"Could you tell us why he chose to ally himself so strongly with the United States?"

"His idea, I imagine, would have been this: Since he took office as president in 1970, what has Egypt's situation been? Egypt was—and this is the most important factor at that time—Egypt was in a state of *defeat* from the 1967 war: Sinai occupied, the economic situation deteriorating because the country was overburdened by a war budget and expenditure, tourism nil because no one would come to a war zone, the Canal closed because it was part of the war theater. That was the state of Egypt! So what would a national leader have on his mind except liberating his homeland? Who was the occupier? Israel. My assumption was that he thought: So many wars have taken place between Egypt and Israel that this problem is becoming unsolvable; there are not enough means to see the future in the course of war. Therefore his strategy was that we should have a war in order to liberate the land and after that be ready for peace. Now when you enter into the peace stage, how could you have peace with that country you have never had any normal relations with before? So probably you must create what would act as a common front. Who would be better and stronger than the U.S. to play that role? And I think this is where the link would come. It was purely a pragmatic arrangement and had nothing to do with ideology."

"What about the critics of Camp David who say that Sadat made too many concessions and did not hold out enough for Palestinian autonomy, and that we all lost on Camp David because the Palestinian problem remains a problem?"

"Okay. Okay. When someone says he gave too many concessions—when you enter into negotiations, obviously both parties have to make compromises. In any deal. When you negotiate and you have to make compromises that means you have to give concessions and you have to accept concessions. Now whether you have given too much or too little is always a relative situation depending on what your objective is, depending on what the circumstances are, depending on what means you have in order to fulfill all your objectives without making concessions. Above everything else, I think it is much easier to judge an important event in retrospect and assume that this and this could have been done. But if you put yourself in the exact circumstances and the exact pressures and the amount of means you have, you can never say whether he gave in too much or he took less." Mansour Hassan paused. "What is important is: Did he achieve his goal? Now here I can say that in my reading of President Sadat, his goal was to achieve a comprehensive peace. That means that his goal when he started his peace negotiations was total Arab rights in exchange for peace and security for Israel. This I believe was his grand strategy and his grand plan."

"Then he was not interested in making a separate peace?"

"Definitely no. He was not interested in making a separate peace, although at the end it *appeared* as though it was a *separate peace.* But if you follow the negotiations, you will find, ninety-nine times out of a hundred, whenever the negotiations came to a standstill, and they were almost going to do that, it was always on the Egyptian insistence on what is called Arab rights more than concerning problems on Sinai. I mean there were never severe problems between Egypt and Israel on Sinai itself. The Israelis were ready to concede on that, but the hard negotiations were on what to do with the rest of the Arab rights, the West Bank, Jerusalem, the Golan Heights, and the Palestinian problem. If Sadat did not care about these, and if he had been ready to give any concessions on these, I think he would have been able to achieve more."

"Then he was popular after Camp David?"

"Sadat was definitely popular among the Egyptians, in my opinion, and I also became one of his admirers. If we can just very briefly give the background on all this: When he took over, Egypt was a defeated country—the economic situation was deteriorating—the country was neglected in the political arena, on the international level, a country which had very bad relations with the other Arab regions. In Egypt at that time, we had a one-party system. Out of all this, Sadat comes and the first thing he declares in 1971, just about one year after he has taken over, is the rule of law, and with it, the declaration of the establishment of democracy. We had a one-party system and then he declared that the one-party system is not a healthy political situation and therefore we should have a multi-party system. He declared that all political detention prisons will be closed. . . ."

"Excuse me, Your Excellency, in fact, political prisons continued to function throughout, did they not?"

"No. I don't think they did . . . that is why the fifth of September was such a shock.* In fact from 1971 to 1980 there

* On September 5, 1981, Sadat had rounded up practically all the various leaders of the opposition, both on the right and on the left, and had them jailed. A month later, on October 6, he was assassinated by a young militant whose brother was one of those jailed.

were no political prisons. Absolutely not, as far as I know. But people tend to forget these things. . . .

"Sadat was the one who made the decision [to launch the 1973 war]. He was the one who mended fences with all the Arab countries before entering into the war, and that is how Egypt got the Arabs to take a unified stand for the first time, using the oil weapon, as it was called in 1973, to support the war. After that, he opened the Suez Canal. After that, he invited international investment and local investment, giving security to Egyptian entrepreneurs in order to get money back into the country and to start them developing their country. And then we enter into the grand step toward peace—Camp David—and his initiative visiting Jerusalem. You remember how the people received him when he came back? And so, during all these periods I think Sadat was popular and in fact building his popularity here more and more. There is no doubt about it."

"What happened?"

"Now what happened after that, I think, is that the negotiations with Israel unexpectedly were really very frustrating and disappointing. [The negotiations] affected public opinion in general because they [the Egyptians] didn't expect the Israelis to be so hard and arrogant and to play the game as if they didn't care about the peace initiative. Now I think this started to create unrest among the Egyptian public, especially among the Egyptian intellectuals—and society became restless, frustrated, and disappointed. This started a chain reaction that culminated in anger. Now, as a leader responsible for internal security and at the same time responsible for achieving his goal—the liberating of Sinai—he had to do what he did."

"Jail people?"

"When you are dealing with a restless society, you have to take action, and this meant a confrontation with the opposition, which culminated unfortunately in the September 5 arrests."

"Your Excellency, as we have been talking, I get the impression that you don't think there is much difference between the policies of Sadat and of Mubarak and that if Sadat were alive today, he probably would have pursued the same economic policies that Mubarak is pursuing—tightening the belt, so to speak, more austerity in the economic open-door policy. You also seem to think that even though there is an Islamist movement in the country, that does not necessarily mean that there is an Islamist takeover or that there will be such a takeover. Do you see *any* discernible differences between the two regimes?"

"Which regimes?"

"Mubarak's and Sadat's."

"Well, obviously when we have two different people in command—and as we all know, human beings have to be different—each one would have a different style, would have a different emphasis on one subject or the other. What is more important is the circumstances in which each one of them thinks and acts—which are, of course, quite different. So you must expect differences.

"But what I was saying," he continued, "and I am just objecting to the thought that President Mubarak might on purpose, as you were saying, be de-Sadatizing Egyptian society: In my opinion that is not true. President Mubarak is not de-Sadatizing Egyptian society because on the important strategic aspects of policy, he is still adhering to the principles: He adheres to peace, and he is working for it as much as Sadat was doing and as much as circumstances allow."

"But do you think Sadat would have been so tenacious on the Taba dispute? Isn't that an obvious if not dramatic difference between the two?"

"I don't think so. I don't think so. Because here the matter does not just concern the president, whether he is Sadat or Mubarak. It concerns Egyptian public opinion. And no society in the world can be expected to be flexible when it comes to giving up national territory. So that is out of the question."

"You mean flexibility on this issue is out of the question?"

"Out of the question. As a matter of fact, and you may think this is a joke, but Sadat was the kind of person who, if he could have got Jerusalem in return for Taba, then maybe he would have been flexible!"

"What do you think of the role of the United States in the area? There are some who say that it is trying to destabilize the area in order to better control it."

"I think the role of the United States in the area has gone through different phases naturally, let us say, since the U.S. became a superpower in 1945. The U.S. started in 1947 and 1948 by being completely biased on the side of Israel for reasons which we all know, because of the Zionist movement and its influence in the United States and also maybe because of Arab weakness. The U.S. could afford to ignore the Arabs in that period and sided completely with Israel. As far as the American image was concerned, the U.S. was definitely losing ground among the Arabs, even given all the forces *for* goodwill in the late forties and the fifties. Until, of course, this all came to a head in the 1967 war, in which the Arabs were defeated. Naturally the United States was, quite correctly, blamed for a major part of that defeat, because they helped Israel all the way."

"They helped Israel even in 1973?"

"Until 1973, but after 1973—a new page was turned by President Sadat, and this was part of his greatness. He was able to reach out to what was previously considered—let us say—a supporter of his enemy and to hope that the United States could play, at least, an even-handed role and become more objective and more conscious of their national interest in the area: to try and gain the friendship of both the Israelis *and* the Arabs. We have to admit that during that period, the United States, relatively speaking, was able to play that role. And it helped achieve what was achieved of peace during that period. But we have found again now that we are entering into the third phase, that after the Egyptian-Israeli peace agreement and after the Israeli evacuation from Sinai, the United States has gradually returned more and more to its previous position on Arab rights and, therefore, the U.S. is not playing as active a role as would have been expected of them. At least, that's our feeling."

"How is that?"

"It is losing sight of the major objective: achieving a comprehensive peace."

"Which includes the Palestinian solution—Palestinian autonomy?"

"Not only includes but is basically directed toward, because that is the *core* of the problem. And it is very unfortunate for the United States to do that, in my opinion, because not only might peace be an unfinished work, as horrible as that might be from a historical point of view, but what is even more dangerous is that what the Americans have sacrificed, because they have put a lot of effort into it, and what we—and even the Israelis—have sacrificed in order to achieve [this partial peace] would be jeopardized in the future and would be wasted . . . if the final objective [comprehensive peace] is not achieved. That means that if you do not have a comprehensive peace based on justice for all peoples, you are not going to have stability in the area."

"What do you think of the idea of a confederacy of Israel, Jordan, and the Palestinians?" I asked.

"I don't think that it is practical to try and put human societies into preconceived political forms, because here you are directly in contradiction with the basic human right of self-determination. If you try to impose institutions and preconceived international forms in any area on any people, I don't think it will work because these institutions can't live unless they are supported by the will of the people. That is why the right of self-determination has been [seen for] a long time as a basic human right. So, first of all, we have to have self-determination, and the people have to decide, based on the circumstances they are in, what type of political confederation they want, with whom, and in what way it could develop."

"So you believe there should not even be a Palestinian confederation? That that would also be an infringement on the rights of the Palestinians?"

"No, as long as the Palestinians accepted it and it was shown that they had accepted it, then it would be in accordance with their will—so that would not be an unnatural situation."

"So you think that might be a solution?"

"Obviously that could be a solution. But to try to say that it definitely has to be between Israel, Jordan, and the Palestinians, then you are overreaching yourself and imposing some unnatural forms. Maybe it could take place in the future, nobody knows, but it has to be done through a process of self-determination."

"What advice can you give the United States in its role in the peace process?" I asked. "Would you suggest that, for instance, they negotiate directly with the PLO? That they coerce Israel into doing the same—if that's at all possible?"

"I don't think that anybody has the right to coerce any country on how to deal with another country. We cannot say that the United States has to coerce Israel, or to coerce the Arabs, because that is not practical in international relations, but we can definitely say, from a logical, practical point of view, if the United States is sincere and willing to be active in achieving its objective of a comprehensive peace, then obviously that means they should be working toward achieving Palestinian political rights as part of that peace . . . and this, in itself, logically, means that you cannot work to achieve the political rights of the human society within a framework of a comprehensive peace, without, first of all, *you* recognizing and having direct communication with these people."

"With their representatives?"

"With their representatives."

"And the PLO is their representative?"

"And as long as the United States does not recognize the Palestinian political rights and deal with the political representatives of the Palestinians, then they will be unable to carry forward the peace process because they are not negotiating with one of the partners."

"And in your opinion Arafat is a legitimate representative?"

"Arafat and the PLO are the recognized, legitimate representatives of the Palestinian people, as everybody in the world knows so far. It's only the United States and Israel [that don't recognize the PLO]. And I am saying *only*, specifically, the United States and Israel because even the Atlantic allies of the United States—and they are Western powers—have admitted that [the PLO is the] de facto [representative of the Palestinians]."

"Can you tell the American reader not to associate Arafat with terrorism? This association, unfortunately, does exist."

"Well, of course, we know that there are forces in Israel and in the United States that have a very deep interest in making that association—and in strengthening it and deepening it. Because that serves their purpose. It's quite understandable."

"Excuse me, Your Excellency, what purpose do you mean?"

"It helps their purpose in not conceding any rights to the Palestinians on the basis that they are just terrorists as they claim. But in reality, we cannot deny that there are some Palestinian individuals and maybe some Palestinian organizations that have taken the role of terrorists or adopted terrorism as a means. But admitting that, obviously, is no reason for us to generalize on the Palestinian people as a whole. Definitely it is no excuse for us or anybody to use it against them and deny their human rights. Because terrorism in any society develops out of frustration, and therefore we have to analyze why these splinter movements in the Palestinian society have adopted terrorism."

"Why?"

"Because they have got more frustrated, or quicker so than the rest of society, because they are denied their political rights, which are given to every human being in the world. Now, if we take this as an excuse for denying the whole Palestinian community, that means we are helping terrorism to grow and to continue and we are not fighting terrorism."

There was a pause in our exchange, and then I took up another topic with Mr. Hassan. "Could you share with us any anecdotes about your personal relationship with Sadat? What kind of working day did you have? Did you meet on a daily basis? What kind of advice did you give him? What things did he depend on you for? What kind of rapport did you have with Sadat?"

"Minister of Presidential Affairs—officially that portfolio means that the person is the minister in charge of coordination between the president's directives and the cabinet's work. Now this entails the minister attending almost all the president's meetings that have to do with the affairs of the state and, at the same time, conveying to the members of the cabinet any directives the president has concerning the policies of the state. I was greatly honored and, I believe, favored by fate to be in that position, because it meant I attended a lot of meetings with the president; I was able to know his ideas and his thinking about most of the policies that were going on. During these meetings we participated in discussions on all issues."

"How many meetings? Did you meet him on a daily basis?"

"There were routine meetings on a daily basis. . . . The president was active almost every day, and I met him either alone or with members of the government almost every day."

"What do you think were his concerns the last days of his life? His major concerns?"

"Well, the major concern, I think, was to achieve the Israeli evacuation and to liberate the Sinai. Of equal importance—and if we say it was secondary, it's only because the other had a deadline and this didn't—was the development of the society, solving the economic problems, trying to increase production, trying to alleviate poverty. These are long-term objectives that had no definite date."

"In spite of the dreadful opposition you knew he was facing? I was even told you warned the president. Especially about the opposition on the left."

"Warned him in what way?" he asked me.

"Told him to reckon with it. In spite of all this opposition, was he secure in his power, or did he have any feelings of insecurity?"

"Well, there was no doubt that the president could have held a dialogue with the opposition forces. And I believe that he had credit with all opposition forces that should have given him a chance to reckon with them and to reason with them. And I did not believe that the differences that existed at that time warranted a confrontation at all. But really, there were other facts of the situation that were communicated by different members of the opposition. And finally, he was a decision maker, and he had to weigh the two possibilities that he had for dealing with them. Maybe he opted for the other possibility for the time being."

"You mean the jailing of the opposition?"

"But knowing him, I think that would have been temporary, and after April 25, when the Israelis were to evacuate [the Sinai], I am sure he would have made another attempt at coming back to the road of democracy and dialogue instead of confrontation."

"So you think basically he was a moderate and not a dictator? His detractors say he was always a dictator. Always autocratic."

"Well, I think people can differ on that subject, and the right to differ is everybody's right. But I wouldn't say that he was dictatorial by nature and that he was opting for that style of government; as I said earlier, when he started his presidency he was not like that, and he took action that was contrary to that. So he had proven that he could be democratic and tolerant."

"In the past?"

"For eight years. That doesn't show that he is dictatorial by nature. He inherited a dictatorial regime that was very stable—remember, in 1973 nobody would have thought of speaking about democracy or the need of democracy. Nobody was able to pressure him onto the road to democracy. It was *his* initiative. So how would he take an initiative on the road to democracy if he was dictatorial by nature? That's my question."

"It's a good question. The fact that he lost touch with the people? You don't think that's true?"

"What do you mean?" he asked.

"For instance, he wouldn't wear a bulletproof vest. . . . By the way, were you there when he was . . ."

"No, I wasn't there. After the assassination, I went to the hospital."

"You don't think it indicates something—that he wouldn't wear a bulletproof vest? He didn't feel threatened. He felt the people were on his side one hundred million percent?"

"Being assassinated, in my opinion, is not enough proof that he was out of touch with the people. Not wearing the vest does not mean that he was out of touch with the people: in fact it might mean something the other way around. If you *know* that you are hated by the people, then you start to wear a bulletproof vest. So, if he knew that he was doing something against the people, he would have been more on guard. That's natural. And the fact that a group of three individuals would conspire to assassinate a person, that doesn't mean that he's out of touch with 99 percent of the people. When President Kennedy was assassinated—that doesn't mean that he was out of touch with the people because some fool came out and assassinated him."

"Your Excellency, you were the head of the National Democratic Party, which is the official government establishment party. After the assassination of President Sadat, other parties surfaced and are much more vocal. I am told there is much more freedom. They are allowed to express their opinions in their own papers . . . and I am told that the domination of the National Democratic Party, your party, is no longer supreme. The question is: Do you think there is really more freedom now for the Egyptian opposition? Like the Labor or Right Wing Party of Ibrahim Shoukri; the Progressive or Leftist Party of Khaled Muhhiedin; the Wafd of Serag al-Din; or the Independent Liberal Party of Mustapha Kemal Murad . . ."

"There is no doubt," Hassan replied, "that everybody inside Egypt and outside can see that Egypt is witnessing an era of political freedom. At the same time everyone can see that sometimes this freedom is being misused by the party in government and by the opposition at the same time. So now the hope of any democratic believers is that this misuse should gradually come to an end."

"What do you mean by misuse?"

"I mean by misuse that freedom, political freedom, is a human right, there is no doubt. But it is a human right that should serve the interest of society and not work against it. That means we are all for freedom. But we are free to live together in an orderly way. But that does not mean the freedom to become chaotic. I don't think this is allowed anywhere, even in the United States. And that is why in the United States, whether they are democratic or not, you still have a political system, you still have the police, the army, because freedom does not mean that everybody should do what they like, even if it's contrary to the national interest. Now the misuse is that both the ruling party and the opposition party might go off on tangents that do not concern the national issues that are the concerns of the real public opinion such as economic problems, subsidies, better housing, better infrastructure, better education, all these things. As long as freedom and debate are used to find the better path and the better measures in order to fulfill these objectives, then it is constructive freedom."

"But I assume that you would like to see the emergency laws abolished, the Laws of Shame?"

"There is no doubt, there is no doubt, there is no doubt. Whether these laws were warranted or not, due to certain circumstances. But at least we can all agree now that these circumstances have changed. Then some emergency laws that might have been necessary then, obviously, will have to be changed now, if that is the will of society."

"How would you like to be identified in this interview?"

"Identified like what?"

"Should I just say you were like a national security advisor to Sadat?"

"I was a Minister of Presidential Affairs and the Minister of Culture and Information from 1979 till September 20, 1981."

"About two weeks before the death of Sadat, you resigned? You resigned on account of the confrontation, as you put it?"

"I don't want to say that. It's not that I resigned, because officially and practically, the president and I agreed that I should be relieved of my post because he obviously felt that I was unable to go along with the measures that were executed during that particular time."

"I think it's wonderful, even extraordinary, that you are still sympathetic and loyal to Sadat."

"I think he is due that. First of all, because he gave so much to his country, and I believe that everybody should be evaluated objectively. At the same time, I have to admit that having worked closely with him, in spite of any differences of opinion we might have had at one time or another, in spite of any personal inconveniences an *adjoint* would have in such a setup . . . definitely I respected him. He was a great leader."

AUGUST 1986

AUGUST 7
Afternoon

"You've lost weight," said Lewis Awad, one of Egypt's leading intellectuals, as I entered the Meridien Hotel lobby. He is an agile man in his late sixties, whose quick eyes and sharp movements make him seem as if he were afraid someone might attack him from behind. Awad was persecuted as a dissident. But he has never made an appeal to the West. He would consider that to be unpatriotic. Besides, he is vehemently opposed to U.S. policy in the Middle East, as he told me in our two-hour interview. He was beaten continually when he was jailed by Nasser on charges of being "leftist." He still recalls the humiliation. And now his latest book—a linguistic study of the philosophical influences on Arabic literary language—is banned by Al-Azhar (Cairo's theological school) for its "heresy." They claimed that Arabic is a language that has not been subject to foreign influences, since it is the language of the Koran and the Koran is the word of God.

AUGUST 9

You can buy Israeli cantaloupes in Cairo. Maurice, a student of Coptic background, told me that he refused to wait on a table of Jews when he was a waiter at the Hilton Hotel. "I watched them blow up my home in Ismailia," he said. "How can I forget that?"

We were having drinks at the Meridien. Another student, now a professional film director, told me that he wanted to emigrate to America because he couldn't earn a living in Cairo even though both he and his wife work. The price of the Israeli cantaloupe is about a dollar, almost the same as in the U.S. If I were still teaching here, my monthly salary would be less than two hundred dollars. A pound of meat is about two dollars, and it costs about three dollars for a local bottle of wine if you can find it.

I still do not have my "permit" to be employed abroad. I am worried knowing that this permit is a security precaution and also a way of keeping tabs on Egyptians working abroad.

I had a brief interview with an official in the Ministry of Information who kept me waiting for forty-five minutes while he made a phone call on my behalf to the Press Center. He then spent ten minutes with me. He was curt, though proper almost to the point of clicking his heels, but I could tell he was angry. I asked for an interview with Mubarak and was told that he was unavailable. But I will be granted press credentials. Meanwhile, I think I will start interviewing anyway. I need to find out more about Islamic fundamentalism; I must get to their leaders.

AUGUST 10

Zeinab al-Ghazzali

Supreme Guide of the Muslim Sisterhood

Zeinab al-Ghazzali is clad in white. From head to foot. Only her face and hands indicate that there is a motherly figure beneath her clothes. A kindly yet powerful matriarch with keenly intelligent eyes.

Few would imagine that this woman with her outstretched hand and friendly smile was the *murshida* or "Supreme Guide" of the Muslim Sisterhood—an offshoot of the Muslim

Brotherhood organization established in 1927. That same organization from which the splinter group al-Jihad emerged—the assassins of Sadat.

It was not easy to find Zeinab al-Ghazzali. Although she lives in a comfortable dwelling in suburban Cairo, secrecy surrounds her whereabouts. But one of my former theater students was able to locate her for me and set up the appointment. He never told me how he did it. I suspect that he must have known someone who was a member of the organization.

She received me, even though she must have known I was a non-Muslim. I had been told that she never gave interviews to the Western press or non-Arabs. While Sadat was alive, she boycotted his regime because it was "secular." Yet it was Sadat who freed her from Nasser's jails where she had been incarcerated since 1965—often in solitary confinement. Subsequently her publications have become the manifestos of the Muslim "feminists." It is said she has a following of over three million women. She was one of the principal underground forces that reorganized the Muslim Brotherhood in the 1960s after they were all thrown in jail by Nasser for attempting to assassinate him. Zeinab was sentenced to twenty-five years of forced labor—she survived seven years of it. The smile she gave me as she ushered me into a carpeted and wood-paneled study revealed strength and endurance.

"Ask me any questions you want, but we must record our interview. I have my own equipment for recording," she said, indicating a nearby tape recorder. I nodded silently, and the interview began. Our eyes often met during this formal interview. She seemed to warm up to me as we went along. After all, we were both women—we had that in common, her eyes seemed to say. And sometimes: Maybe you will see the light, doctor—one day.

The interview was conducted in the classical, literary (not spoken, not colloquial) language of the Koran: the Arabic of the sixth century A.D. I have tried to reproduce this formalism in my translation of what follows. In this translation I was aided by Ahmed Sami Sharara.

* * *

"What is the role of the U.S. in the Middle East conflict, in your opinion?" I asked.

"In the name of God the Merciful and the Compassionate, the role of America in the Middle East is an unjust role, for the U.S. is totally prejudiced in favor of world Zionism. And when that happens, the matter becomes very, very critical and dangerous with regard to the achievement of any understanding between the U.S. and the people of the Truth."

"What in your opinion is the worst thing about the negative role of the United States? I mean in addition to its support of Zionism. For instance, what would you say are the adverse effects of the U.S. on Islamic and Arab culture?"

"If there are any shortcomings or defects with regard to our culture, we do not ask America about them, but we ask our Muslims. But the question that we do ask America is: Why doesn't she admit usurpation of the land of the Palestinians, and why doesn't she admit that it is a crime? We ask America: Did the Palestinians go to the Jews in their homes and take them away from them, or was it not the Jews who went to the Palestinians in their homes and seized them, killing their children, their young and old, their fathers and mothers?"

Ghazzali spoke emphatically, but not excitedly.

"How does the Islamic *umma* or nation propose to treat or deal with non-Muslims or religious minorities?"

"When the Muslims came to Egypt under the leadership of 'Amr-Ibn-Al-'As they did not compel Christians to abandon their Christianity and embrace Islam. When they came to Egypt [in the sixth century], they saved the Christians from the yoke of the Romans, the despotism of the Romans, and they even declared that those who had escaped from their priests and the men of the church should return to their homes and their churches. This is the Caliphate in Islam. The Caliph lives a slave who obeys Allah's commands and is just to all his subjects —he is no different from them. The early caliphs did not demand or accept differentiation [of the minorities] from their other subjects. And those of us who are trying to restore the

Caliphate hope that it will be like it was at the time of Abu-Bakr, 'Uthman, and Ali, and the just caliphs who came after them.

"Egypt was ruled by Islam because Islam was victorious and liberated the country from the Romans. Islam allowed the minorities full freedom in all matters. The *djizia* [capitation or poll tax] was imposed on them and the djizia in Islam is like the *zakat* [a tithe on a man's property]. The Muslim presents the zakat and the Christian the djizia in return for the protection that the Islamic army offers to the land, the wealth, and the people.

"So, how did it happen that Christians embraced Islam in great numbers? When they realized the absolute justice in it, when they discovered that the Muslims are supremely truthful and just, they came to realize that what Mohammed preaches is what Jesus, son of Mary, preaches. Mohammed believed that Jesus is the slave of God and the son of Mary, and not the son of God, but he is a Messenger, with a message, just like Mohammed. They saw the truth in all this and they embraced Islam of their own volition; they did not enter into Islam by force or by the wish of the Muslim ruler. They converted consciously and rationally. And after that, the Christian minority lived with the Muslims, ruler and people as cherished brothers, and they enjoyed all the same rights as them. We do not differentiate Muslim and Christian subjects or Jewish and Muslim subjects. The Muslim ruler gives the Christian subjects their full rights as human beings."

"Do you think that Western culture has corrupted Islamic youth? In your opinion does such corruption exist? For instance, in music or other manifestations of modern life?"

"We Muslims have a standard that we apply to ourselves—everything that happens in life is organized by Islam. Islam does not leave anything out. You ask about music."

"As an example."

"In itself, music is not forbidden by Islam. But Islam forbids things in degrees. What is absolutely forbidden and must not be committed is the *makrouh*, the hateful. So if you add to music the drinking of alcohol, gambling, singing, and dancing—

if they are all performed in unison . . . then this is absolutely forbidden. But if it is music alone that is heard, and I repeat, alone, then it is all right, but it is not advisable to become too absorbed in it. Because Muslims must not allow themselves to become absorbed by their senses, and a Muslim satisfies his appetites only out of sheer necessity, because he is human, and Allah wishes to preserve life and to maintain it in accordance with the principles of God, always giving man space to satisfy his appetites, his animal instincts, so that his human life may be moral and righteous.

"In other words, a Muslim can be intimate with a woman or a woman can be intimate with a man, but this intimacy can only take place within marriage. Therefore marriage is there to accomplish a necessary thing for a human being: the replenishing of the world with humanity."

"How about the mixing of the sexes? In the university, for instance? Is there any objection in Islam to that? Can a female sit next to a male in the classroom?"

"The mixing of the sexes is under investigation. What the Prophet of God practices remains our model. Women sat beside the Prophet in the mosque and in the society of men, but there was a system which was adhered to. The men sat before the Prophet in the front rows and the women sat in the back rows, where they listened, learned, and absorbed. So, if a woman sits in the back rows of a classroom, there is no objection. If she sits on the right of the class and the men on the left, or the other way around, there is no objection, provided that she wears long, loose clothes and she is veiled. All of a woman's body is private except her face and her palms, and therefore her clothes should be loose so as not to delineate the contours of her body. There should be no makeup on her face or anywhere else. If a woman appears thus, in this dignified and virtuous manner with the knowledge that her body is shameful, except for the face and the palms, and the face and the palms are devoid of any makeup, then she may sit behind her brother, man, or to his right or to his left, leaving a space between them."

"But if there is a non-Muslim woman among them, can she sit next to the men and not be veiled?"

"She must sit in the ranks of the women out of respect to the prevailing order and out of respect to the Islamic umma [nation]. When a woman does not respect and maintain this appearance, she is not a woman and her value diminishes."

"It is said that you are at the head of a women's organization which includes more than three million Muslim women."

"I am just a soldier in the ranks of the society of the Muslim Brotherhood. I am no more than a soldier who is commanded and who obeys. That they consider me a mother to them because of my age and my seniority in the calling is something that honors me and makes me their faithful servant. Because women, too, are the soldiers of Islam and also work toward the restoration of its state, its nation, and its Caliphate."

"Is one of the organizations devoted to the teaching of Islamic women?"

"The Muslim Brotherhood and the Muslim Sisterhood are an undivided whole because there is no distinction in Islam between the regulations governing men and women. As the Koran says: 'Muslim men and women. Believers men and women.' "

"Could the Muslim Sisterhood or Brotherhood have existed had it not been for the leadership role you played?"*

"I am a soldier of Islam. In 1965 I established the Center for the Society of Muslim Ladies, and I was a soldier in the ranks of the Islamic calling the day that Gamal Abdel Nasser issued a decree to dissolve the Center. And a soldier the day I entered prison. I consider myself a soldier loyal and truthful to what I

* Mrs. Ghazzali, who is known as one of the leaders of the Muslim Brotherhood organization, had a network of sympathizers and contacts among members of the Brotherhood in the late fifties and mid-sixties when they were rounded up and jailed by Nasser for attempting to assassinate him. Her Muslim ladies acted as a link in the secret reconstitution of the organization of the Brotherhood that had been formally dissolved in 1954. In 1957, she re-launched the Muslim Brotherhood with Abd al-Fattah Ismail, and in 1965, when sweeping repressive measures were taken against the Brotherhood, she was jailed once again on charges of conspiracy.

believe in and in what I strive for. If Allah, may he be Exalted, accepts me as a loyal, truthful soldier, I would be very happy and I would have fulfilled my hopes in life. And what I long for is to see the Islamic Caliphate established, and the first thing that I am willing to sacrifice for it is my blood. I am of the belief that it is happening, but when? I don't know."

"Do you consider Sayid Qutb's book *Sign Posts* [Ma'alim fi'l Tariq]* the manifesto of the Islamic movement?"

"The programs or the ideas in *Sign Posts* are an Islamic program derived from Al-Kitab al-Haneef. The manifesto of the Islamic movement in the Koran. The manifesto of the Islamic movement is the *sunna* [traditional teaching supplementing the Koran], the sunna of the Prophet of God. The manifesto of the Islamic movement is all that is written in devotion by Muslims. Sayid Qutb was devoted the day he wrote his book, and it falls under the banner of Islam and the sunna. We examine our books under the scrutiny of the Koran, and if we find them in accordance with the Koran, we accept them. If they are at odds with the Koran, we reject them."

"I believe that the religious establishment, I mean Al-Azhar, singled out this book for attack."

"We stand with the Koran and the sunna. We are not employed by the government, and we speak what Allah wills and what his Prophet wills."

"It is said, and was recently written in a book by a Westerner,† that the Islamic movements are political and contain a utopian element. Can you comment on this?"

"All of Islam is *mithali* [idealistic]. However, it is also within the reach of people as long as a human being lives with simplicity and freedom. Because in Islam, there are no rituals, no heresies, no bigotry. Islam is a religion whose principles flow directly from the hands of Allah, the Truthful. The con-

* This is an influential book on radical Islamic groups, or *jama'at*, in Egypt in the seventies.

† Gilles Kepel, *Muslim Extremism in Egypt*. Berkeley: Univ. of California Press, 1985.

queror Islam is a comprehensive system, which is also a political system, a social one, and a military one."

"How is the issue of jihad or holy war conceived in this kind of a system?"

"The concept of jihad is, as Mohammed says, 'continuous in my nation until the day of judgment.' This means that jihad will not come to an end in the Muslim world until the day of judgment and the final hour. What is jihad? Al-Jihad has a purpose—the preservation of the borders of the land of the Muslims. Al-Jihad is to enable and to empower the Muslims to inform the entire world of the call of Islam. And that is why the Muslim armies stood at a distance from the borders of Egypt, to give you an example, in order to invite Egypt or to tell Egypt, 'I invite you to join Islam.' So if they, the rulers, allow Islam to be explained to the people, they will not fight them. But if the rulers forbid them from explaining and clarifying Islam, they will fight them."

"In the West and particularly in the U.S., the meaning of *jihad* is synonymous with violence and terrorism. To the Westerners it is exemplified in the assassination of Anwar al-Sadat. Can you comment?"

"The one responsible for the assassination of Sadat is Sadat himself because he angered the people and made them rebel, and the wise ruler should not provoke his people. I am not condoning assassination, only jihad. I believe in confronting the ruler with his mistakes, and that is why I say what I think in total frankness. But the assassination of the ruler does not resolve the cause. Assassination does not solve the problem and it is not in the interest of Islamic movements. Those who established terrorism in the Middle East are the world Zionists."

"Can we talk a little about the veil? Do you impose the *hijab* on Muslim women?"

"No, I do not impose the veil on Muslim women. This is not for me to command. But I can persuade her [the Muslim woman] to practice her beliefs. I have to convince her that there is only one God and he has no partner and that Mohammed is the slave of God and his Prophet and that Abraham is his slave and his Prophet, Noah is his slave and his Prophet, Moses is his slave and his Prophet, and Mohammed is his slave and his Prophet. Then she will be convinced that she should wear the veil. And, moreover, for the Muslim it is forbidden to commit adultery, drink alcohol, gamble, fornicate, slander, indulge in calumny, commit murder and all the other vices, and, therefore, for those of us who are the advocates of Islam and its servants, we need to convince the person that there is no god but the One God, and Mohammed is the Prophet of God."

"Before we speak about your personal life, could you tell us what is needed for the establishment of an Islamic umma in Egypt?"

"We are not concerned with the establishment of the Islamic cause in Egypt alone or even in the Middle East. The Islamic cause is a world cause and must triumph all over the world.

"As it triumphs in Egypt, it will also be triumphing in Pakistan, Malaysia, Indonesia, Syria, Jordan, Palestine, Lebanon, America, Russia, France, and Germany, and all over the world. For this to happen, Muslims must be allowed the freedom to communicate their call."

"When will this happen?"

"When Muslims have their state. A state which is ruled with God's *sharia* [Koranic law] and which declares with courage, strength, and power inspired by Allah that Islam is the *final* religion of God."

"How can such a state be established without military means?"

"Praise be to Allah, the Almighty and Glorious [*Subhan Allah Tabaraka wa Ta'allah*]. It has been permitted for those who fight in the name of Allah to carry arms and weapons. But for what purpose? Not for assassination. That is rejected by us, and those who declare that we are assassins are liars, because our cause cannot be solved with the assassination of any individual or any people. The cause will triumph only with the assassination of evil and injustice. We believe that legitimate war can be waged between two equal forces. Therefore, military warfare for us has to be delayed until we are a nation with an army. We must have an official army to confront another official army. We will struggle a thousand years until we establish our nation, our army, and our order, which will have been established by the will of Allah and the commandments of the Koran and the sunna. Then we will go to war. All that has been said about us, that we are assassins, these are lies spread by the agents of American and Russian imperialism."

"So you are against terrorism and the use of terrorism?"

"I do not recognize terrorism, but I recognize jihad. And I call for it. The first thing I would sacrifice for it is my own life."

"Can we speak a little about your life? How were you mobilized for the Islamic movement?"

"Allah, the Blessed, Exalted, and the Glorious, mobilized me. My father was educated at Al-Azhar, and when he graduated, he refused employment as a government official and became a merchant. I was the fifth child after four boys, and therefore, I was the source of great rejoicing when I was born. My mother, who was also an only girl, and her mother wanted a girl badly, so they were as happy with me as they were with the first-born. While I was still a suckling infant, my father had a vision: He was bearing me in his hands and I was wrapped up in white swaddling clothes, but, suddenly, I fell into a mud pond. He was taken aback, thinking I had been immersed in mud, but then an impressive gentleman picked me up and gave me back to my father, saying, 'O Ghazzali, take al-Sayida [Lady] Zeinab.' My father took me back and found no traces of the mud on my white clothes. 'Who are you, sir?' he asked the man. 'I am her grandfather, Caliph Omar Ibn al-Khattab,' replied the gentleman. Later, when my father awakened from his dream, he declared that the Caliph was really my grandfather and that I would play a momentous role in religious life. He believed that.

"So, when I started to talk he taught me rhetoric, made me memorize verses from the Koran and from the *hadith* [sayings of the Prophet], and he forbade me to do housework. For instance, we had a rural peasant home, with a big farmyard, and my grandmother had a cook called Badrawi, and every day a woman from the household would go to the kitchen to help there, and if my mother took me there my father would get very angry. He even went so far as to summon the cook one day to warn him: 'If Lady Zeinab should ever enter the kitchen, I will punish you severely.' When my mother would ask him why he gave such orders, he would reply: 'She was created for other things.' He began to teach me that I was created to be a soldier of Islam. He said that I would become a pioneer of the pioneers of Islam, and he also used to tell me stories about the female companions of the Prophet who used to fight alongside him. He also told me stories about Huda Chaarawi [first Egyptian feminist of the twentieth century] and the poet Malak Heffni Nassef [Bint al-Badawiya]."

"Did he admire these two?"

"He would tell me stories about Huda Chaarawi and Malak Heffni Nassef and stories about Nassibah bint K'ab al-Maziniyah—she was a leader of Islam at the time of the Prophet. She fought for the Prophet in battle. Then my father would ask: 'Who do you choose, Zeinab? Would you like to be like Nassibah and fight for the Prophet, or would you like to be like Huda or Malak Nassef?'

"And I replied, 'I will carry my sword and fight for the Prophet. I am Nassibah, the daughter of K'ab al-Maziniyah.'

"So, my father reared me on the love of Islam, the comprehension of Islam, and the beliefs of Islam, and when he died, my passionate love for my father was channeled into Islam. I began to study it, read it, and research it—and I would ask myself: Do people have a proper and correct understanding of it or not? Do they practice it in the correct way or not? I found out that people do not practice it as it should be practiced, and I decided to endeavor to show it to the people, for Islam is the origin of all things and God's offering."

"Did you join the Muslim Brotherhood when it was first organized in 1927—I mean the organization founded by al-Banna?"

"At first I joined the [feminist] organization of Huda Chaarawi in the 1930s, then I resigned from it. I did not discover in it the way to Islam."

"Because it was a secular way?"

"Yes," she replied. "So, I resigned and established the Center for Muslim Ladies—all of this is chronicled in my book, *Days in My Life* [Ayam fi Hayati]—and the Center remained from 1936 to 1965, when it was banned by decree at the orders of Gamal Abdel Nasser."

"And you were jailed then?"

"I was imprisoned in 1965—for my association with the Muslim Brotherhood. I conceded the supremacy of Hassan al-Banna in 1938 [as the Supreme Leader of the movement] and I had contacts with him from 1938 until his death in 1949. So, I remained the head of the Muslim Sisters Center and an undeclared soldier in the ranks of the Muslim Brotherhood. It was only in the 1965 incident [suppression of the Brotherhood by Nasser] that it became known that Zeinab al-Ghazzali is a member of the Muslim Brotherhood—and the *mukhabarat* [Nasser's secret police] came and took me to jail and Praise be to Allah."

"I do not wish to open a very painful subject, but it seems to me . . ."

"The whole thing is chronicled in *Days in My Life*," she said, dismissing the subject with a faltering voice.

"I know that you mentioned your torture in prison. Can you tell us about it or is it too painful?"

"I have already spoken about it in my book." She was still visibly pained. "You may quote the book. But I will say this: Torture will never make a believer renounce his beliefs. Torture only reinforces belief. Those who suggested torture as a way of making people give up their beliefs were ignorant. They were ignorant because they did not realize that people who have beliefs are ready to sacrifice their lives for these beliefs."

"How were you able to endure the pain of torture?"

"Allah was always within my sight, in my heart, in my breath, and in the very pores of my existence. Allah was not absent, and I was not absent from his presence for a second." She had by this time regained her footing; the fervor returned.

"Your health certainly must have suffered."

"I lost so much weight that I was only fifty-two kilos [about 114 pounds]. But during those years God the Exalted was my consolation."

"How long did you remain in jail?"

"Seven years." She remained controlled, but my question seemed to arouse sadness in her. "I had been sentenced to death, and the sentence was commuted to a lighter one—life with forced labor. I spent seven years in jail, and it was the supplications of Muslims from all over the Islamic world to the late King Faisal of Saudi Arabia that caused him to intervene on my behalf to Nasser. But Nasser lied to him and said, 'Zeinab al-Ghazzali is in her home.' After Nasser's death, King Faisal intervened again with Sadat, who issued a full pardon for me and I was released. . . ."

"Did you actually do forced labor?"

"No, I was put in solitary confinement in a cell two meters by one [about 6½ by 3 feet] at the Woman's Prison in the Barrages.

"The Woman's Prison is more of a hardship than going out for forced labor every day, because there you are living in a sea of crime. I was jailed with Hamida Qutb, who was serving a ten-year sentence and I was serving twenty-five years."

"Were you allowed to read in prison?"

"In the last year, or maybe the last two years—that is the final period—the last two years, or the last one and a half years . . ."

"And in the first four or so years you were living completely alone?"

"Yes. Someone had managed to smuggle in a small radio on

which I heard the news bulletin and some newspapers would be smuggled in for an exorbitant price."

"And food?"

"Food was also smuggled in. The prison food was intolerable."

"To close, what would you like to tell the Western reader?"

"I would like to say: You are a human being and I am a human being and human beings should come to an understanding with one another. Read the Koran, read the book of Mohammed and the sunna of Mohammed, for it is inspired by Allah. Then read the Torah and the Bible truthfully. You will discover that there are many foreign elements that have penetrated the Bible. And with Allah's help you will discover that the Koran is *unchanging truth*—an immutable truth that no one can add to or detract from.

"World Zionism puts pressure on the leaders of the Islamic world to change the Koran. But no one dares to change the book of Allah. Read the Koran, the sunna, and you will find that Islam is the religion of Jesus, Moses, Abraham, Noah, and Adam. Maybe then will you be saved from the seductions of man and find your way to the guidance of God. Maybe then you will call upon your government not to be unjust to the people of the Truth. Read the history of Islam and you will learn that *Jerusalem* belongs to the Muslim world. We do not intend to expel the Jews from Palestine, but we only wish to let the Muslims and also the Christians into Palestine."

"Do you have any objections to the survival of Israel?"

"The Israeli state, Israel? Yes. We are for the establishment of a *multinational* state, a common country for Jews, Muslims, and Christians."

"Christians *and* Muslims?"

"Having Christians, Muslims, and Jews."

"All having the same rights?"

"The same, equal rights. A common country."

"Then the Zionist state is completely unacceptable," I said, and she nodded her head firmly.

AUGUST 11

After my interview with Ghazzali, the epitome of the extreme right, I think it is time to look for the extreme left. Will they speak to me? They have always resented my so-called pro-Americanism.

AUGUST 12

Hussein Abdel Razik

Editor in Chief, Al-Ahali

"From the beginning I was opposed to all of Sadat's policies." This sentence was spoken by Hussein Abdel Razik, the leftist editor in chief of Egypt's only Communist Party paper, which is called *Al-Ahali*. *Al-Ahali* has an interesting history. It was closed down by Sadat in 1978 because of its opposition to the peace with Israel, and it was not allowed to be published again until Mubarak came into power after the death of Sadat in 1981. Actually *Al-Ahali* resumed publication in May 1982. Razik is a thin, small man with a receding hairline. He has a permanent smile on his face. But in a few moments when that smile left his face, what was revealed was a grim, tough, hard exterior: almost a total transformation. A real ideologue, he sat behind a very large desk in his small office in the downtown, overcrowded newspaper office where, outside his office, almost stuck to one another, were desks belonging to writers who contribute to this newspaper—young Communists, real ideologues—like Abdel Razik.

He sat behind his desk, in front of him a very large painting of Nasser, and on it a postcard-size photograph of Lenin. Yet, oddly enough, as he spoke for the hour and a half which he granted me, I noticed that Abdel Razik was not half as anti-American as Mohammed Galal, the editor of the arts weekly, who is not a Communist and is not even considered a leftist. Abdel Razik is a more complicated political animal and a true survivor, as well. He had been unrelentingly anti-Sadat from the very beginning of the rise to power of Anwar al-Sadat as Egypt's president in 1972. I was quite surprised that Abdel Razik even agreed to speak to me. A couple of months before my arrival in Cairo, I read an article, a whole page actually, written by his very doctrinaire journalist wife, also a Communist, panning my book *A Bridge Through Time* (published in the United States) and denouncing me for being an admirer of the "American Dream." So when her husband, Abdel Razik, agreed to be interviewed by me, I was extremely grateful.

As I sat opposite him sipping an excellent unsweetened cup of Turkish coffee (which is the way I drink it), I thanked him for the review of the book. He smiled, almost ironically, at my thanks and said, "I realize, of course, that even a pan is better than no mention at all." And that was thc cnd of that.

Fortunately for me, his wife did not interrupt our conversation. As he talked on, I was aware that I was in the presence of one of those few people in Egypt who are completely fearless. He simply was not scared, even though he was a man who had been jailed several times by both Nasser and Sadat, as he was now in the process of telling me in the interview.

"Why were you opposed to Sadat from the very beginning?" I asked.

"In my opinion," he said, "Sadat represented the right wing of the Nasserist system and this is why in my journalistic writings I was clearly outspoken against Sadat."

"And yet," I said, "it was not known at the beginning that Sadat was 'American.' "

He smiled ironically and said, "I had channels and sources which informed me of Sadat's political inclinations. I was convinced that he was going in a direction which would not lead to the liberation of the occupied Egyptian territories that we had lost in the 1967 war when we were conquered by the Israelis. Maybe," he added, "it is not a coincidence that I was one of the first people to be jailed by Sadat way back in 1972 at the time of the first student riots." Abdel Razik was referring to large student demonstrations against Anwar al-Sadat in 1972 before the October War, when the students on the campuses of Egyptian universities all over the country were protesting the no peace–no war situation with Israel and were actually asking that Sadat go to war. "I was accused," he said, "of being one of the instigators of these events. I was fired from my job during the time of Nasser, but I was jailed during the Sadat regime; I remained in jail a whole month. I was released only by the intervention of a powerful colleague, without having to face charges.

"In 1973," he continued, "I was fired as one of 102 journalists who were members of the Socialist Party in Egypt [the party which was later dismantled by Sadat]. Even though I was originally fired from the organization by Nasser," he said laughingly.

"In other words," I said, "you were fired from a job and then jailed from the job that you were fired from?"

He nodded. "In 1975 I was then moved from one newspaper to another. In other words, I lost my job on one paper, and, of course, all the papers at that time were government controlled and owned, but I was not given a new assignment. In other words, I was shelved. Then I was suddenly jailed again during the Sadat regime in 1977 in the aftermath of the food riots, again with the charge of instigating the riots."

"Did you actually instigate the riots?" I asked, referring to the famous 1977 massive street demonstrations in which Egyptians rioted against Sadat for suggesting that subsidies on staple food products be lifted.

"I wish I could have," he replied, laughing. "In August 1979," he continued, "my wife and I were among seventy other Communists arrested as founding members of the Egyptian Communist Party." The Egyptian Communist Party is an illegal party. It was first established in 1919 and remained legal until 1921, and there were a number of cases against a group or clique of Egyptian Communists who were accused of wanting to reorganize or legalize the Egyptian Communist Party. "I was released after twenty-six days. My wife was released after two months. In March 1981 my wife and I were jailed again with the charge of founding the Egyptian Communist Party once more. I was released after four days, but she remained inside for nine months. In March 1981 I was arrested again at the time of the events of the sectarian strife, and I remained in jail until the assassination of Sadat in October 1981. We were released in December 1981. Since that time we have not been jailed but, of course, we are always under surveillance. There are listening devices in all the offices and homes of the opposition in Egypt. Right now, at this moment, in this office, as this interview is taking place, we are being tapped. In other words, Egyptian Security is aware that you are in this office and they are recording this interview," he said fearlessly.

I coughed nervously, quite taken aback. I was not aware that such surveillance existed in Egypt at this time, since I had been told that during the Mubarak regime all surveillance tactics had been dropped. "Are you sure," I asked, "that we are being listened to?"

"Oh, yes," Abdel Razik said. "We have proof of the existence of listening devices, and we even thought of having a press conference and exposing these devices to the international media. At any rate, the regime at the present time does not resort to framing people in order to jail them as was the practice under the Sadat regime. And," he added, "by the way, the Communist Party trials were heard in May 1986 and those accused of establishing a Communist Party in Egypt were acquitted. So the file of court cases by Sadat against the Communists has been closed."

"Do you feel more secure now under the Mubarak regime?" I asked.

"Well," he said, "you see, the laws which enabled Sadat to do all he did remain. For instance, the emergency laws, the Law of Shame, the laws of the State Security Council, dozens of such laws which enable the regime *at any moment* to arrest any man or woman by law and place them in jail for long periods without charging them with anything specific."

"How is that?" I asked. "What do you mean by that? Do you mean— Aren't they charged with something or other?"

"No," he said, "they are simply considered security risks and jailed."

"Without a hearing?" I asked again.

"Even with a hearing," he added. "Because if the public prosecution releases a prisoner, the following week the same person can be arrested on yet another charge, and the person is released again and can be jailed again because we have martial law in Egypt. We have emergency laws which give the government—the Mubarak regime—the right to jail anyone at any time."

I looked at him, rather startled. I was quite shocked by what he had said.

Sensing this, he said, "The direction of politics these days makes this kind of process more difficult than at the time of Sadat."

"In other words," I said, "people are not jailed so frequently as they were under the time of Sadat?"

"No, I don't think so," he said. "Yet, in spite of the so-called pluralism that now exists, the Mubarak regime believes that power should be monopolized by the ruling National Democratic Party. They are not convinced of the circulation of power—that power has to circulate among many parties, not just one party. And we—the left—are fighting for the circulation of power in the democratic fashion. We would like to see more democracy in Egypt."

"And the government doesn't think this should be so?" I asked.

"No," he said, "the government, even though it declares that it is democratic, really believes that power is a monopoly of the regime, and anyone who is trying to take away this power is conspiring against the present regime, in other words, the Mubarak regime. And I personally believe," he added, "that the regime in power is not democratic."

"Do you still feel threatened?"

"I feel no security whatsoever," he said, "but I have chosen this path."

At that moment the telephone rang, and I turned off the machine. I looked at him in amazement and admiration. This man could be jailed within minutes of the ending of this interview—at any time, at any moment—and he knew it and he didn't seem to mind. After he had completed his telephone call, he looked in my direction for us to continue the interview.

I asked, "Are prison conditions difficult in Egypt?"

"Yes," he replied. "In Egyptian prisons, for instance, there is a practice called solitary confinement where you are put in a small cell all by yourself for two or three days. There is very little food in Egyptian prisons, and what food there is is unfit for human consumption so that your food has to be provided for you by your family. In other words, a detainee in an Egyptian prison must feed himself and those with him. I read once," he added, "that in an Egyptian jail the average prisoner costs the state about three cents a day, so you can imagine the condition of these jails."

"Are you allowed to listen to the radio or read papers in jail?" I asked.

"Sometimes," he replied, "and often this is not allowed. I have not been physically tortured," he said, "but in our presence, in prisons after the assassination of Sadat, we witnessed the torture of Islamic fundamentalists by the state. They were tortured to death. There are also Communists who have been tortured in a terrible way."

Trying to change the subject, I asked now, "What do you think of the image of America in the Arab world? How does it look to you?"

"There has never been any enmity toward the American citizen, to the American person in Egypt. Only toward American policy. But principally two things give the United States a negative image in Egypt. One is its unilateral support for Israel; two, its insistence on enhancing the private sector as opposed to the public sector in economic policies. America's opposition to Egypt's Arab role and its support of liberation movements in the Third World is, of course, a very imperialistic attitude and does not help its image in the area."

"By America's imperialistic role in the area, do you mean its economic or its military role?" I asked.

"America's imperialistic presence is in its military bases," he said. "Also in the fact that the United States supports regimes like the regime of Marcos or the regime of the Shah and other dictatorships against the will of their people."

"What about the rise of Islamic fundamentalism in Egypt? What do you as a leftist think of that?" I asked him now.

He said, "One of the reasons why there is anti-Western feeling today in Egypt, especially among the Islamic fundamentalists, is the presence of an American model or image. The cowboy image—the consumer society—which is also reinforced by the Egyptian media as the ideal model. The cowboy or Western film represents this American model of society. It is a model of affluence and power which we in Egypt cannot attain or even aspire to for the next hundred years and which is not propitious to the economic conditions of Egyptian society."

We were interrupted once more by the phone ringing. He picked it up again. A few seconds later, he smiled an apology and continued. "This model, or image, this cowboy culture is so alien to our own values that it has aroused the anger of the fundamentalists."

"But what you are saying is that the capitalist model is inapplicable to Egypt?" I said, interrupting Abdel Razik.

"Of course," he replied, "only socialism—the total control by the state of economic means of production—can work in a poor, developing country."

"Let's go back to the fundamentalists," I said. "What do you think of the fact that they have so much control in public life today? They control the student unions on campus, the professional syndicates, public opinion, even the economy."

"Of course," he interrupted me. "I am completely opposed to them from A to Z. But I wish to reassure you of the fact that although Egyptian society is religious, it is not fanatic." He emphasized the word "fanatic" very strongly. "After Egypt was defeated by Israel in 1967," he continued, "there was a kind of withdrawal into the past—Islamic fundamentalism is an aspect of this withdrawal—people seeking consolation for their present lives in the certainties of religion. Then Sadat comes along in the seventies and uses Islamic fundamentalism, especially in the universities, to fight and oppose the Communists and the Nasserist left. Sadat gave them money and even weapons."

"Is that so?" I said.

"Sadat always projected himself as the Believer president," he added.

"Do you think the Americans also played a role in encouraging fundamentalism?" I asked.

"There is much that is being said about this—that for the same reasons Sadat also played a role in nurturing religious extremism.

"But I think on the whole the power of Muslim extremism in Egypt is vastly exaggerated, especially in the West, and maybe because of the Iranian revolution. In actual fact, their power is limited—if I may use a Marxist term—to the bourgeoisie. They have no power with the working classes or with the peasants."

AUGUST 13

Fouad Serag al-Din Pasha

Wafd Party leader

Today I learned that there is a $44 billion deficit in Egypt's economy. After many, many phone calls, I finally obtained a promise of a meeting with one of Egypt's most important leaders. It's funny about political leaders—you can spot them a mile away. I had never seen Fouad Serag al-Din Pasha before, but when I was ushered into his office through a large room where he was chairing a meeting, I knew immediately who he was: the anti-establishment figure of the establishment par excellence. An obese man, he was dressed in a beige suit. Smiling happily, he sat at the head of the large rectangular table and looked as if the whole world, and not about two hundred people, were gazing at him in admiration. He had survived Farouk, Nasser, and Sadat's jails and torture, and now, as he was to tell me, he was reorganizing the Wafd, Egypt's longest-standing independent political party, *and* campaigning in the provinces for it. He kept me waiting in an adjoining office for over thirty minutes, but he had given instructions that I have coffee brought to me. The meeting seemed boisterous. Now and then shouting could be heard, but it ended with the sound of laughing and clapping and then the door opened and he entered. He must be seventy, but the man who took his seat confidently before me was energetic, young-spirited, with a handsome, light-skinned face and honey-colored eyes, which spoke of his Turkish origins. As he smiled at me, I presented my Macmillan letter. "I don't have my glasses," he said and took the letter and placed it among some others lying on his desk. Later, when I handed him an English card with my Cairo phone number, he glanced at it and immediately remarked that we were neighbors . . . and that he had been a patient of my father's.

Serag al-Din had been Farouk's Minister of the Interior in the fifties, an Intelligence man, a policeman, I thought to myself. But the man who sat opposite me exuded the kind of breeding and class which went out with the elderly statesmen of the nineteenth century. If I were to describe him for an American audience, I would say try to imagine the body of Winston Churchill and the face of Averell Harriman and the personality of both combined, and you would have Fouad Serag al-Din Pasha.

I have lost my student assistant. I think he has abandoned me because it took so much time to contact people. Telephone numbers have changed in Cairo since the system was computerized. It is summer. They were out of town or they were simply not home. Sometimes it took fifteen or so calls before an appointment was set.

I am still waiting for a press card. But I am not going to let that deter me. I wish, though, that my student had not abandoned me. This is going to be tough.

AUGUST 14

Ahmed Ismail

Journalist, Al-Ahali

I knew Ahmed Ismail, well, in the eighties. When he wasn't in jail, that is. For he was always in and out of jail in the final days of Sadat. Once he even came and worked with me on a documentary I was making. His political sophistication was quite remarkable, in view of the fact that he had never even completed his university education. He told me that he read a lot in jail and listened to the other intellectuals and dissidents who gathered there.

Ahmed is a scrawny young man. The only expressive feature in his face is his large, sarcastic brown eyes. He is always poorly dressed. Sometimes he looked underfed. His body is bent with fatigue. Like an old man. Yet Ahmed was born in 1954.

Ahmed was jailed four times under the Sadat regime. He was beaten and tortured. Cigarettes were burned into his back and on the soles of his feet. In 1977, he was arrested for printing and distributing pamphlets among the workers of a factory near Cairo; he was raped by the prison guards.

Today, bent as he is and clearly tired, he remains unbroken. He works for the Marxist newspaper *Al-Ahali*, of which Abdel Razik is editor, and looks forward to the day when, he hopes, there will be a socialist regime in Egypt. His father, a Muslim fundamentalist, tried unsuccessfully to drum Islamic principles into his son. Ahmed also remembers his own father burning the household Koran lest Nasser's security men discover it at the time of the crackdown on the Brotherhood in 1965.

"If Sadat had not been assassinated, I would not have been released from jail," he told me soberly one afternoon in my office. Ahmed was freed by Mubarak in 1982—among hundreds of political opponents incarcerated by Sadat in September 1981.

Ahmed belongs to a generation of Egyptians in their thirties who either are unemployed or who have emigrated or have jobs abroad. He struggles to make ends meet. Sometimes he does not even have enough money to buy lunch. He is thinking of doing odd jobs in order to supplement his meager income as a journalist for *Al-Ahali*. But he is afraid that such menial work will transform him into a nonthinking person. Then he will have no time to go to lectures or attend the State-subsidized concerts and art exhibitions. Therefore, he opts for hunger; the hunger of body is better than that of the spirit, he says. He does not wish to be like "those Americans" who work sixteen hours a day in order, as he puts it, "to eat."

The young Marxist admits that his political activities were all aimed at re-establishing the Communist Party in Egypt. He is completely opposed to Sadat's policies. "Sadat," he told me emphatically, "worked for the CIA. He also worked for the SS in Nazi Germany, and also for the British. It was the CIA who got rid of him at the end. I am sure of this." When I asked him why he thought the CIA assassinated Sadat, he replied that it was "because he was no longer of any use to them." Ahmed also believed that American AID (Agency for International Development) projects involve espionage. "When they enter a village to begin a project in development, they take pictures of everything," he said indignantly, "and conduct thorough research of the area, the people, the food, and so on. What is that but espionage?"

Ismail claims that only a socialist system with a planned economy can be of any use to Egypt. Socialism failed in Egypt under Nasser because the military regime was unable to implement it. "The great catastrophes in Egypt are caused by the military regime. Do you know that all the governors of the various provinces of Egypt are military men? All the chairmen of the boards in the different companies are military men? Egypt is ruled by despotic, tyrannical, undemocratic military men!"

"So what we need in Egypt is a civilian regime?" I asked.

"Yes, we need a multiparty system and parliamentary democracy."

"And what role is America playing, if any, in all this?"

"The Americans uphold two kinds of regimes: religious regimes and military regimes. They uphold these systems because they prevent communism. They wish to dominate the political system in Egypt because they have military interests here, bases and so on. They call them military 'facilities,' these days, not 'bases.' Practically speaking, the Egyptian public domain belongs to the Americans. Whether we like it or not, Americans now call the shots in Egypt. They rule us. They feed us. They give us 80 percent of our food. How can we deny them military bases?"

"Ahmed, you seem very anti-American. Haven't they done anything good in Egypt?" I asked.

He sat up in his chair and replied quietly. "The Americans have always supported Israel in wars against Egypt. They supported Anwar Sadat and his capitalistic economy, they supported the idea of making us debtors by giving us enormous loans, they polluted the Nile with their sewage systems, and they roam about in our airspace freely; they exploit our military bases, our army—so how can I not be against them? How can I not hate them?"

"Would Russia be better for us?" I asked.

"No, we should not exchange them for the Russians—all I am demanding is that we rely on ourselves. And this can only take place if we have real democracy in Egypt, and it cannot happen in the context of a military system. The Americans are the colonizers today. They are behind religious fundamentalism. Who are the Americans in the Middle East today? They are the Saudis. And Saudi Arabia is the financial backer of the Islamic extremism in Egypt—Jihad, the group responsible for Sadat's murder. The system today is the Americans! They are protecting the fundamentalists."

"How are they protecting them?" I asked.

"They give them *money* and *arms*," he declared.

"But don't you think Khomeini has given the Americans a tough time?" I said.

"Not at all," he asserted. "Khomeini was propped up in order to eliminate the Communist Party in Iran, and this has happened. The only alternative to the Shah's regime was a leftist takeover because the left was very powerful in Iran. The Americans are thus prepared to do *anything* to fight *communism* in the Middle East, anything. They will support any regime opposed to communism in the area. And this is a strange policy, a fascist policy, even an obscure policy. What the hell business of yours is it if a country wishes to become Communist?" he concluded passionately, addressing the hated U.S. in the first person.

"Can we talk a little about religious fundamentalism in Egypt?" I suggested, wishing to get off the sore subject of the United States.

"We've never had religious fanaticism in Egypt before, and we have always coexisted with Egyptian Christian Copts with a policy of containment and appeasement. The Coptic problem is centered on three issues which it is possible to overcome. First, they wish to be represented in government because the state refuses to admit that we have over two million Copts,* whereas the Coptic Church tells us that there are eight million Christians in Egypt. Second, the other issue is that Copts are not allowed to seek high positions in public life. We can never have a Christian president of a university, say, and so on. And why shouldn't we? It's quite silly, really. And third, the Coptic Christians are clamoring for the erection of more churches. So, what I am trying to say is that the Coptic issues are not un-

* Actually, in 1989, the Copts were estimated at twelve million.

solvable. On the whole, religious tolerance has pervaded the Coptic issue in Egypt. So now we must ask ourselves if it has contributed to the flourishing of Islamic societies in Egypt. First, economic conditions are deplorable, so most of the young find solutions in religion. Second, whenever there is a burgeoning of secular life in Egypt, America tries to suffocate it, because secularism paves the way for the propagation of communism, and America is interested in keeping the country backwards. Islamic extremism certainly helps the religious extremists demand of their followers that they retreat from secular society; they also wish to put an end to the arts, to civilization, to culture, theater, sculpture. Do you know that students in the faculty of fine arts are no longer allowed to draw nude figures because they no longer allow nude models to pose? All of this never used to happen in Egypt in the forties, fifties, or even the sixties. In 1938, a series of articles appeared in Cairo with the title, 'Why I Am an Atheist'! Can you believe such a thing?" he asked me incredulously. "People could write things like that! If I wrote such articles today, I would have my throat slit. There was freedom in Egypt in those days. That is why I am saying that I am amazed at the burgeoning of religious life. No one has brought this upon us like the Americans, the Israelis, and the Saudis. It is in *their* interest that such extremism, the religious extremism, dominates the backwardness of society. This religious extremism is a colonial manifestation, which is against civilization, against science, against nationalism. And no one is fighting science, civilization, and nationalism like America, Israel, and Saudi Arabia!"

"Is that then the role that America is playing in the Middle East?" I asked him.

"Yes, all Americans are concerned with is the safeguarding of the area from communism. And in order to do this they have to preserve the status quo with all its backwardness and underdevelopment. It is in the interest of the Americans that the Middle East remains in a constant state of tension, ignorance, and misery, so that it is difficult to build to progress. One of the ways that this is done is the perpetuation of military regimes in the area. Saddam Hussein [President of Iraq] slaughtered twenty thousand Communists in one night! Look what happened to the Communists in the Sudan . . . Look what happened to them in Egypt under Nasser—they were all slaughtered! So you see, America's playing a crucial role in the area: opposing communism by any and all means available to it. By exploiting religion, the economy, corruption, everything, everything," he said with earnest bitterness.

"So you think we are victims of America?" I asked.

"Of course," he replied, "we are the victims of the evil and ugliness of the United States."

Ahmed's views are not representative of the views of grassroots Egyptians. But they are certainly representative of the outspoken Egyptian left and the majority of Egyptian students both on the left and on the right. This is one of the reasons why I chose to listen to him at such length.

AUGUST 16

I was finally given the work permit I needed to get permission to travel and work abroad. My papers were investigated because I had been told that there was a "security" problem in the passport division. How I could be a security risk beats me! As I had sat in the office of Security, an office crowded with sweaty brown faces in white sleeves, a woman came up to me, and looking surprised to see me among the crowd, informed me that they only investigated thieves and prostitutes. So why was I there? Perhaps there was someone political in my family? I informed her that there wasn't. As I looked around, I noticed that there was one person who was having a very hard time. He was middle-aged, obese, and educated looking. He was also an Islamic fundamentalist, which was obvious from his thick, long beard and his manner. In a fit of fury, he declared that he was sick and tired of being persecuted, that he was also tired of being harassed.

The Security official, a swarthy man in gray trousers and a

white, long-sleeved cotton shirt, listened to him in silence. Why had my own papers been held up, I asked him as he handed me my passport. For bureaucratic reasons, he replied shortly.

From now on, I will go about my business quietly and cautiously. Have to be careful what I write.

AUGUST 17

A quarter of a million children will be starving in Ethiopia this year. In Egypt, a million children are born every ten months. What will happen to them, I wonder, feeling quite depressed. Religion is in the air everywhere. The feast of the sacrifice is approaching. Lambs, marked with red dye, are herded to the butcher houses where they will be slaughtered. It all makes me want to get up and leave. But then I think of the empty, sterile Connecticut winter ahead, and I change my mind.

AUGUST 18

Sami al-Atsha, M.D.
Obstetrician

I had a brief meeting with another official from the Ministry of Information. He reproached me for making too much of the population problem. He also hoped that I would not criticize my country in what I wrote abroad. I said I would not. Later I made my way behind a procession of women dressed in black, screaming and weeping as they walked behind a funeral casket. Not far from the procession, a calf, with its legs tied with rope, lay quietly on the sidewalk, waiting to be slaughtered.

My brother's wife had given birth to a son, her third child, in the Coptic hospital on the busy thoroughfare, Ramsis Street. Dr. Sami al-Atsha, who has the reputation of being able to deliver fifty babies a day, stood by as the nurse held up the baby and chatted with me, leisurely, as if time were of no importance to him. "People like to have a lot of children in Egypt because they have so little. They don't care about the population problem. And don't forget, so many men were lost in the 1967 and 1973 wars that they feel that they need to insure themselves against forthcoming wars."

AUGUST 19

An Israeli diplomat has moved onto the same floor as me in the apartment house I live in in Maadi, a fashionable suburb of Cairo. I only noticed him today. Because I was in the States for a year, I assume he must have moved in when I was away. I remember there was much talk in our co-op of allowing Israelis to rent apartments there. Most people were against it. But today, some woman who had welcomed me back said almost in the same breath, "So how is the Israeli on your floor?" I shrugged and said I didn't know there was one. She gave me a disapproving look; the kind of look which says, "Look what we have come to," and stepped angrily off at her floor.

He is a very slender man in his early thirties. He is very white, with curly auburn hair—wears white and could almost be taken for a German or an Austrian. He walks briskly and never smiles. Once we met waiting for the elevator. Inside the elevator, he seemed to fade into the graffiti-scrawled walls. He stepped off first and did not look over his shoulder. His movements, like his appearance, seemed sexless. Did he look like a robot, I wondered. He did not look sideways either, as if he did not wish to see anything. As he stepped onto the street, two security guards wearing black uniforms escorted him to his old-fashioned European car. As I watched him, I knew that there was something I didn't like about him. His haughtiness.

AUGUST 20

Ihsan Abdel Qudous

Novelist and journalist

An average of sixteen chartered flights a day are busy returning Egyptian pilgrims from Mecca. On TV they show *Centennial,* and on the first day of the 'Id—the Feast of Bairam—they showed the final days of the Liberty Weekend celebrations in New York. At the Meridien I had croissants, danish pastry, and a cheese omelette which was cooked before me. I enjoyed it but was feeling so guilty because what I paid for this breakfast amounts to eight hours' earnings for most middle-class Egyptians. I think of the Israeli's security guards filling empty plastic bottles from the faucet in the garage—that is all they will get to drink during their eight-hour vigils, except some tea. I think of the garbage collector who climbs fourteen stories in our luxury high-rise to collect the garbage—and I can barely get through my breakfast.

This morning I interviewed Ihsan Abdel Qudous, a confidant of Sadat's, a novelist and famous journalist and writer. It is the morning of the 'Id. In the evening I saw a boisterous group of young Israelis who had obviously been partying at my Israeli neighbor's, talking and gesticulating loudly at the elevator. I marvel at their audacity.

Ihsan, who has written three hundred short stories and thirty novels and has been jailed four times, has changed. He used to be a bon vivant, a writer feared by the establishment. Nasser tried to have him killed. Now he is thin, old, and quiet. While his wife was saying prayers over the slaughtering of a calf in the country home garage, he and I sat in a garden, overgrown with mango trees, talking of the U.S. role in the Middle East. His son Mohammed is a fundamentalist, even a leader of the Jama'at al-Islamiya, but we did not talk about him. I sensed that Ihsan did not want to. At the end of the three-hour interview, he saw me to my car and, hugging Mohammed's lanky, seven-year-old son, he said, "My sons bear no resemblance to me. They have drawn apart from me. But my grandchildren are my hope." His other son, Ahmed, has turned religious and makes his wife wear the veil.

During our interview, Ihsan had talked mostly about the Arab-Israeli conflict. To him, U.S. had the power to settle it. And nothing could be done, he had told me, without finding a solution to the Palestinian problem. He had emphasized this several times during our long talk.

AUGUST 21

Fouad Serag al-Din Pasha

Wafd Party leader

He belonged to one of Egypt's richest landowning families, if not the richest, but his office in the Wafd headquarters, though spotlessly clean and furnished with expensive, modern, green-upholstered furniture, was relatively simple. What distinguished it was the large boxed Koran lying squarely in the middle of his desk and a small prayer mat which lay folded in two and was placed at the side of his chair. Otherwise the room was bare. "Ask me any question," Fouad Serag al-Din Pasha said at the beginning of the interview, but when I asked him why the number one opposition party of Egypt had decided to join ranks with the Islamic fundamentalists, he almost lost his cool: "Not everyone who prays is an Islamic fundamentalist," he said, also avoiding my question. Like them, he was also anti–Camp David. Though at heart he was a Western-style parliamentarian, it was obvious to him that the Islamic fundamentalists were essential to the survival of his party. But he was not about to admit that.

"Why were you jailed on September 5, 1981, with the other

members of the opposition to the Sadat regime?" I asked as we settled down.

"This is perhaps the fifth time I have been jailed in my political career. Twice before the revolution, at the time of King Farouk, and three times after the revolution. Would you believe me if I told you that, of these, four times I didn't know why I was being jailed and why I was released? But the last time, in September 1981, I discovered *after* I was released why I had been jailed. There was no direct reason—because the Wafd had no political or party action or even a newspaper. We were pledged to silence and peacefulness."

The Wafd, which was founded in 1924, is Egypt's oldest nationalist party. It was originally established to counteract the British occupation. Its founder, Saad Zaghlul, became prime minister that year. He was the first peasant grass-roots Egyptian to occupy that position. Therefore, the Wafd's grass-roots appeal was not to be underestimated.

After the revolution took place in 1951, Nasser banned all political parties including the Wafd. When Sadat came into power in 1970, a more liberal atmosphere began to exist in political life. Political platforms (*manabor*) had been formed as a first step toward creating political parties, which soon came into existence. The new Wafd party under Fouad Serag al-Din was reorganized. But, when it began to criticize Sadat's policies, it was proscribed. Serag al-Din was jailed in September 1981 by Sadat. When Mubarak took power, he was released. He reorganized his party. This is what he was referring to now.

"You mean your party had been banned immediately after the revolution?"

"The incarceration was a surprise. There were people who had been instigating sectarian strife and others who had attacked Sadat personally in their articles, but I did not belong to either group. So, I told myself, this is another time like the preceding ones. I am jailed and I don't know why. And I am released and I don't know why. But, when I was released from prison, I heard a recording at home of a speech given by Sadat on September 15, in which he attacked me violently, saying, 'I will teach him how to talk to his leaders.' "

"Which means?" I asked.

"It means that on May 21, 1981, before September when I was jailed, I had sent him a well-known letter in my own hand and I went to the republican palace and handed the letter to the chamberlain and asked him to deliver it to President Sadat, and it was a tough letter but it was properly phrased—but tough, edgy."

"And what was in the letter?"

"In the letter I tell him, 'You have persisted in attacking the Wafd and its leaders in the past and the present, and you use in your attacks improper words and other expressions unknown in the political vocabulary of Egypt. And you who speak of principles and morals, is it principled to tie up the arms of your opposition and then beat it? If you are really democratic and you have moral courage, then publish this letter.' It was a tough letter which referred to Sadat as a liar, a coward, insolent and disgusting. But it contained none of these expressions. He, Sadat, was furious when he read it and I waited for days, but the letter never got published. We did not have a newspaper so I gave it to another opposition paper to publish and it was published and when he learned (probably before it went to press) that the letter was to be published, he let one of his papers publish it, and it appeared in *Al-Akhbar*, which accompanied it with an attack on me. He had kept it all inside him from May until September and then with the wave of arrests, he told himself, 'Now I will be revenged.' "

"That means that Sadat disliked criticism?"

"Absolutely, he couldn't stand opposition or criticism and in his final period, he went through some kind of apotheosis. . . ."

"In 1978 your party was organized and then it was frozen? Why?"

"Yes." He was silent in response to my second question.

"But what do you think of Sadat—if you would like to evaluate him for us?"

"In very simple terms, his terms in power can be divided into two: the first from 1970 to 1976 was a good period. But after January 1977, he changed completely—like one who loses his equilibrium and his feelings, and he became impatient with democracy, freedom, and the opinions of others . . . and this state increased with time until it climaxed in the September events."

"Was the Wafd opposed to Camp David?" I asked.

"We were not there as a party at the time of Camp David. We reorganized ourselves on November 14, 1978."

"But your deputies in parliament asked for the cancellation of the peace or of Camp David."

"We had fifteen deputies in the parliament who had independent political activities, but they were not Wafdists—they could not talk in the name of the Wafd Party. They did have a position vis à vis Camp David which was also the position of the dissolved party, and it consisted of ten remarks on the Camp David agreement. This was presented to the parliament and distributed among all the members—our remarks were even sent to the president at Camp David. Meanwhile, our party was organized, and when the peace treaty was drawn up, we had now an official vote, and we had reservations about the peace treaty—but our reservations were ignored so we did not vote on the peace treaty."

"You didn't vote because of the reservations you had on the peace treaty?"

"Nobody hates peace—but [we want] a just peace, a fair peace, an equivocal peace, not peace from one side."

"What are your main reservations on the peace treaty?"

"Sadat said, 'I have returned Egyptian sovereignty on Sinai.' But Sinai was returned to us burdened with cumbersome rights: for instance, the limitation of an Egyptian military presence in Sinai. Second, a part of Sinai is demilitarized and a third is occupied by a multinational force. And that is the most dangerous thing—because it is an occupation. Until Israel agrees to evacuate. Can we then say that sovereignty was returned to Sinai? The answer is no. There is an airport in al-Arish which is only three minutes from Israel by air—this is against us. We should not accept this airport but we are obliged to keep it because of a clause in the peace treaty. Israel will use it as a civil airport, but when necessary she can use it militarily. We are also obliged to sell Israel petrol. All these remarks were not communicated to the parliament."

"Do you think Egypt is better off politically without Sadat?"

"Politically speaking? What do you mean? Internally and externally? Internally if he had lived and continued with his policies since 1977, he would have created a lot of political hardships for the country."

"Do you mean being isolated from the Arabs?"

"No, internally he would have created instability and repression and jailings and so on. Externally, before he died he was the reason for the disruption of the Arab League and Arab unity with his visit to Israel . . . and I don't understand why he did not confer with the other Arab leaders before his visit."

"What do you think was the real role of America in the time of Sadat?"

"America. The media in America are greatly responsible for the dangerous developments which happened to Sadat because they lionized him, and the media are, of course, under Jewish influence."

"What is your opinion of the role that the U.S. is playing in the Middle East conflict?"

"A sorry role, really. If it were a healthy, straightforward role then would it prefer the friendship of Israel—three million—to the friendship of 100 million Arabs? Of course, in my opinion, this policy is wrong. It puts Israel on the same scale as the Arabs even when it comes to financial assistance; it supports Israel wholeheartedly. And this support of Israel alienates [America] from the Arabs."

"Is it possible for America to improve its relations with Middle Eastern countries?"

"Only if it takes a just position toward the Palestinian question—that is the only solution."

"In America, they are very concerned with the flourishing of Islamic fundamentalism, and it is said that Egypt will be the second Islamic country after Iran, that it will be a religious country."

"No, I don't think so. There is a big difference between the militants and the Brotherhood. The Jamat think that the Brotherhood is conservative, and they consider them impious. . . . But there is a difference between the Ikhwan [the Brotherhood] now and the Ikhwan forty years ago. The leadership of the Muslim Brotherhood is moderate, and there is no danger from them at this time. But the Jama'at al-Islamiya are people who are rash."

"It is said that the Jama'at al-Islamiya might win the elections in all spheres—in addition to the parliamentary elections in 1984. In this way they would be dominating all spheres or domains of society," I commented.

"No, no, not to this degree; in any elections—free elections—the Wafd, even without too much freedom, would win it with an overwhelming majority."

"So you think the Islamic groups will not win?"

"No, no. Don't think that whoever prays is a Muslim fundamentalist. For instance, at the prayer of the Feast of Sacrifice in Alexandria there were one hundred thousand people in the Stadium. Of these two or three thousand were extremists, but the majority were ordinary people. It is true that there is an extremist trend among the youth . . . and the reason for this is the past forty years. And I even told Osama al-Baz, 'You are responsible for the activity of the Islamic groups in the university because you forbade the political opposition parties to have any activity on campus.' This used to happen in the past. The opposition was represented in the university in the form of committees, and it was this kind of activity that acted as a check to the Communists and the religious extremists. The regime is more scared of the Wafd than it is of religious extremists."

"Why?"

"Because the Wafd is the imminent danger at this point. It can overturn the regime, but the radical groups will be dangerous only after ten or twelve years. The present danger is the Wafd. So the government wants to hang onto power, and the country can go to hell in ten years' time. Do you know the story 'The King dies, the donkey dies, or I die'?" he asked suddenly.

"A crazy sultan wanted to teach his donkey how to read and write. Nobody offered to take this job, but Goha [a comic character] presented himself as a candidate for the job, and he told the Sultan that he will teach the donkey. 'If you succeed in teaching the donkey, I will give you a thousand dinars, and if you fail, I will chop off your head.' Goha agreed and asked to take the donkey home in order to teach it there, as well as his expenses, plus a ten-year delay. The Sultan agreed and gave Goha the donkey and a couple of thousand dinars, and people disapproved, saying, 'How could you do this? How can you teach a donkey?' And Goha said, 'You don't understand. In ten years either the Sultan or the donkey or I will be dead.' "

Postscript: Serag al-Din's party lost in the 1988 parliamentary elections.

AUGUST 22

I indulged myself by spending the afternoon at the Meridien pool where I discovered that happiness in Egypt lies in basking in its glorious sunshine and swimming in the turquoise water of its luxury hotels. It's as simple as that. Most important, at the Meridien, the noisy city is kept at bay. And the vast, wide Nile keeps both the noise and the poverty concealed. Even for a day—it was bliss.

AUGUST 23
Evening

"Laila, I have been hearing that you are talking to the opposition for your book," said the voice on the phone. "You should talk to the regime. All that the opposition will tell you is that we have an unstable regime. That is not true. . . ."

"I am willing to talk to whoever will allow me to interview them," I replied. "I have no preconceptions. This is an objective book, believe it or not."

Nonetheless, I was startled. I immediately made a new list with prominent establishment figures.

AUGUST 24

Dr. Butrus Butrus Ghalli
Minister of State for Foreign Affairs

"I thought you were coming to have a paper stamped," said Dr. Butrus Butrus Ghalli, Minister of State for Foreign Affairs, kissing my hand in his high-ceilinged office in the baroque villa off Tahrir Square which houses the Ministry of Foreign Affairs.

"I am no longer at the mercy of my fellow countrymen," I said, displaying my Macmillan letter.

He glanced at it. "You must meet the PLO," he said.

"Do they have a number two man here?" I asked. He shook his head.

"I want to meet Arafat," I said affirmatively.

"Come to Zimbabwe," he said earnestly. "He will be there." I hesitated for a minute. I didn't want to go to Zimbabwe, even to meet Arafat. "That's the only way to do it," he said.

"Maybe I can go to Tunisia," I said.

"Are you planning to go to Israel?" he asked out of the blue.

I nodded. "Then don't surprise the Egyptians with that—let them know you are going."

"I'll be going from New York," I said.

"Ah," he said, relieved. "Then there's no problem," he said, kissing my hand again as he escorted me to the door. He had given me ten minutes. After all, he was a Minister.

Later, I went to the Press Center to get my much-needed press card. The official I had asked to see kept me waiting for forty minutes. I had come without an appointment. The place was full of men and quite a few pregnant women, employees. Finally, a kind of assistant came in and asked me quite a lot of questions: Did I like America? Surely over there people were not as warm as they were in Egypt? I nodded. Was I planning to see political people? Was the book political? I said it was all-embracing and that I wanted to see Mubarak. They could make the contacts from the office, he said. That would be rather ludicrous, I said, since I knew most of these people. He looked disappointed. Then the other man, the boss, came in. Did I get my work permit? Yes, I replied. Why did I have two names? "I use a pen name sometimes," I said, trying to avoid any mention of my book—the previous one!

"We will need a curriculum vitae and your permit before we issue a card," he said. He knew I had a Ph.D. in theater, that I was a Christian and that my father was a famous doctor. All these things seemed to reassure him.

They don't take me seriously, I thought to myself, because I am a woman. I remember thinking that when I was waiting for the okay in the Security Section of the permit office, a woman came in and asked me: "Are there any political people in your family?" She was seeking an explanation for the fact that my papers had been held up. It never could have occurred to her that I was the political one.

After I left the Press Center—with some relief—I went in search of my waiting taxi. Not far from where the taxi stood, a group of people were lined up waving some sort of paper. I was hot and I wondered why they were all standing there. I asked the taxi driver.

"Soap," he replied monosyllabically.

"Soap?" I asked, not understanding what he meant.

"They are lined up to buy the subsidized soap, of which there is a shortage."

"A shortage of soap . . . but the stores are full of it."

He looked at me ironically in the mirror. "Yes, the soap for sixty-four piasters. But who can buy that . . .? That's gone after one bath. We're talking about subsidized soap for six or seven piasters . . . that's all they can afford, and that's short."

Mustapha Kamal Murad

Independent Liberal Party leader

My next meeting was to be at the headquarters of one of the official opposition parties, the Independent Liberal Party, founded in 1978 by Mustapha Kamal Murad, himself one of the Free Officers to take power in 1952, a friend of Sadat, whom he accompanied to Jerusalem. He was supposed to be a friend of Mubarak's. I was told that his party too had been taken over by the Islamic fundamentalists, and so I was not surprised to see that he had grown a beard. I was ushered into his office right away, and we started the interview almost immediately. He glanced at the Macmillan letter and then asked me if I preferred that he speak in English. I nodded. He then gave me a two-hour, brilliant interview, rather a lecture in which he answered all my questions without my having to ask them. He even referred to the beard: It had just grown, he said, and he also mentioned that he did not drink. This was obviously in reference to the fact that we used to meet at the parties of a German Cultural Counsellor where we all did a lot of drinking. In his sixties, he now looks much more slender and ascetic—but tired. Two or so hours into the interview, the door opened and three bearded men and a sheikh walked in. I remembered that they had been in the antechamber when I had arrived. He had kept them waiting all this time. I felt extremely flattered—but then I remembered that it was America he had been speaking to, and he didn't like to keep it waiting. "Here are some of the boys, the Islamicists, you are so afraid of," he said laughingly, as he introduced them to me. They nodded in my direction respectfully. "You see they are nice people," he said. "Some of them used to be extremists, like my friend here [pointing to a man in his thirties], but now they are all my friends and like me they are fighting for democracy."

One of the bearded gentlemen left, and three of the party organizers remained. The conversation which ensued surprised me: it seems that the party couldn't find a place to convene their next rally in. The government had forbidden them to rent school auditoriums or to hold their meeting in most of the public places available to them. "You will have to talk to the prime minister," said one of them to Murad.

"Yes, I suppose I will have to," murmured Murad with fatigue.

"But I thought there was democracy," I said in genuine astonishment.

"No, there are only the contours of democracy, the appearance, the form, but not the content. You know that the government is spreading pamphlets against me among the fundamentalists saying that I am a secularist and that I drink—they are trying to discredit me," he added. "But we will not stand for oppression anymore. Sadat did not understand democracy either."

"How?" I asked.

"After his trip to Jerusalem, Sadat allowed the opposition forms to exist only so as to show that in Egypt, like Israel, we have democracy. But it was a command performance. He asked me one day, 'How long would it take to form political parties?' 'Five years,' I told him, 'at least.' 'But if we were to do it quickly,' he persisted. 'Three,' I told him. 'But if we were to do it very fast express,' he persisted. 'A year, with difficulty,' I replied. You know what he did? Two days later, he said that there would be political opposition and political parties in Egypt! Sadat too did not understand democracy. When he jailed all these people in September, I asked to see him. But he wouldn't see me. He knew what I was going to tell him. He didn't like opposition.

"Look at this young man, here," he said, pointing to one of his bearded assistants. "He was graduated twelve years ago from college and he earns eighty-five pounds [about $30] a month from the government. How can he live on that? We must be able to discuss all our problems openly—that's democracy. They have democracy in Israel," he added. "I admire that in their system. I saw an Arab member of the Knesset once get up and in Arabic give the entire Knesset a piece of his mind. He didn't spare anybody, not even Begin. People have had it. Something's going to give this year. We've reached a plateau. And the trouble with Mubarak is that he doesn't know which way to go—right or left. One only goes one way—either a free economy or a socialist economy. There's no in-between."

The man spoke so bravely that I had to mention it then. "Why should I be afraid?" he said. Of course, he had never been jailed, and I realized that I was in the presence of one of the political leaders of the country whose spirit had not been broken.

AUGUST 25

Mohammed Galal

Novelist, journalist, and editor of Radio and T.V. News Magazine

"The Americans have invented a new style or form of imperialism in the Middle East. They did not invade the area militarily as the British did, but they began their imperialistic thrust with culture, with the American movie. The American film is the foremost weapon of American imperialism in the Middle East." Thus spoke Mohammed Galal, editor in chief of a leading arts magazine in Cairo, author of sixteen novels, and a well-known, respected journalist. Galal is a dark-skinned man. In America he would be considered a black man. He has bushy white eyebrows to match his thick lamblike crop of hair. His lips are thick and his features almost negroid. Yet he is quintessentially an Egyptian in that his appearance is like so many of the Egyptian fellahs—peasants—who live in the rural south of Egypt. We sat in my home, where Galal often visited me. In the past, we often had conversations of this sort. I have known him for twelve years. Occasionally, he has written about my theatrical productions in Cairo or listened to my laments about this or that happening in the media world. He spoke to me now animatedly, gesturing with his hands, moving his feet about, raising his voice loudly, banging with his hand on the table, and all the while munching chocolates and drinking the soft drink I had offered him during the interview. We spoke for almost three hours. He seemed to pour out his soul to me, knowing of course, that what I was about to write would be printed in the Western or American press. His eloquence, therefore, is matched only by his eloquence as a novelist in the Arab world. His need to communicate was almost overwhelming. I have found this in many of the other interviewees whom I have spoken with subsequently in Cairo over the past months. People have a need to communicate to the West. They want to be heard. And yet, as I write these words, I wonder—do the Americans want to know what the Arabs think?

I was reminded of a real estate agent who came over to look at my apartment, which I was anxious to rent while I traveled in the Middle East. She had looked around at the objects which clutter my little place and commented, "Of course, if you want to rent this place, you'll have to remove the orientals." By "orientals" she meant handwoven Persian carpets from Kashan, some original oil paintings by Egyptian artists, mother-of-pearl hand-made boxes, engraved brass trays, and little rugs woven by Egyptian children in small villages: an assortment of my culture. It was this culture that she was asking me to remove before my apartment would become acceptable to an American renter. But it was with these very objects that I was trying to protect myself from the plastic of American life, indeed from the very culture that Galal was attacking. But she was quite right. American culture has invaded the Middle East in a way that the American armies have not, and, as he spoke, Galal was making a point that it was through this cultural invasion that Americans had won the hearts of the ordinary Egyptian. The reinforcement of this culture was by TV, and the coup de grace was satellite: Satellite made its invasion into the smallest Egyptian village and the poorest Egyptian hut, where sometimes there is no furniture, and where the fellah and the cows and the geese and the television are the only occupants.

Galal's eyes widened as he said, "The poor are dazzled by these American films, and they begin to be angered against their own lives, their homes, their streets, their appearances, their own minds, their own cultures, and they even begin to rebel within themselves against Egyptian culture because of what they see in the American films and the American cinema."

"But is this inward rebellion a bad thing necessarily?" I asked him. "I mean what we're seeing in the American films is a better, more affluent society, a wealthy society, a healthy society."

"Of course," he replied indignantly, "but you are not supposed to become an American. This is a subject in all of my novels," he continued. "In one of my novels, which I call *A Sea of Love*," he said, "I deal with this interaction between Middle Easterners and American culture and how American culture, in a way, destroys the Arab mind and the Arab mentality. Although, of course, we have to deal with it," he added. "In another of my novels," he added, "my hero goes to Amsterdam in order to study botany. He falls in love with a Dutch girl, but he remains loyal to his fiancée at home and returns to Cairo and marries the girl that his family has chosen for him. And then he starts to work in the desert to make it bloom with the techniques he learned from the West. This is the way the West can be useful to us," he said.

"Do you find me objectionable, Galal," I asked, "because I am Westernized?"

He looked at me ironically but with much affection. "Laila," he said, "each time you go to America you can sit there with Reagan and put one leg over another and tell him that you are not scared of him because you have roots, because you are an intellectual. But when the Egyptian man in the street watches *Dallas* he sells himself, he sells his principles. He wants to become a millionaire overnight. People's values are turned upside down. People's identification with their culture is destroyed because of these *Dallas* films that we watch on television. And," he added, "I believe all of this is a Zionist plot!"

"How is that a Zionist plot?" I asked, trying to conceal my humor.

"The Zionists alienated us from our country by turning our society into a consumer society," he said. "They made the Egyptian man nonproductive. They made him into a consumer, and the transformation of the Egyptian people from a productive agricultural society to a consumer society, to a society whose images and whose symbols are dictated by American films—having a car, having a video, owning an apartment, having flashy clothes—was instigated by the Zionists!"

Helping himself to a Turkish delight (Mohammed Galal is a man who loves food) and speaking with the humor which is characteristic of so many Egyptians when they talk about politics, he went on to say that Americans had corrupted Egyptians with their culture.

"Let's return to the forced attitudes of the man in the street," I said, interrupting him. "What exactly are they—materialism, the love of money? Or is it modernization that you are against?"

"No, no," he interjected, "I have definite views on this matter. In my opinion, in the rural world the poor are as much entitled to Western civilization, have a right to it, as the West does."

"Why?" I asked.

"Because human civilization began with ancient Egyptian civilization. Then you had the Greeks, the Romans, and then there occurred the gap to the Middle Ages, then came the Renaissance, and from these Western civilizations flourished our modern technological civilizations. So we have as much of a right to it, we are as entitled to it, as the West is."

"But then don't you think," I asked, "that modern technology has been detrimental, that American influence has hurt the Arab culture? I mean isn't that what you're trying to say?" I asked.

He stopped for a moment and said, "Yes and no. It was only after the victory of the October 6 War that the Arabs really started to absorb the good things of Western civilization because they were technologically victorious. Do you remember once that a Phantom managed to destroy all of the glass in the city of Cairo during an air raid in 1967? Well, that was the time of defeat. But in 1973 it is a young Egyptian soldier (he is also in one of my novels)," he added, "a super soldier who carried an SA-6, an antiaircraft missile, on his shoulder and prevented that same Phantom, the Phantom of the earlier years, that ghost, from ever entering Egypt again. Now, *that* was victory because the SA-6 had put an end to American terrorism in the hands of the Israelis," he said, banging on the table. "The Phantom is a symbol of the age of technology, but instead of using this newly acquired weapon," he continued, "instead of using the symbol of the Phantom for production, something else happened in Egyptian society—something satanic. Suddenly Egyptians were transformed into *consumers* by Sadat's liberalization of the economy. Capitalism! In Egypt capitalism meant that everyone had his hand in everyone else's pocket! The symbol of success," continued Galal, speaking with a great deal of enthusiasm and sincerity, "became not the soldier carrying the SA-6 but the beggar who suddenly becomes a millionaire by illegal profiteering. That was the tragedy."

"In your opinion, then, this was some kind of Zionist conspiracy?" I asked.

He looked at me, smiling. "In my opinion, this was a conspiracy to strangulate the spirit of the October War. But then I ask you," he said, "who lets this Satan loose?"

"Who?" I asked Galal.

"The capitalist system," he replied indignantly. "Osman Ahmed, Sadat, the entrepreneurs, and consumerism gave rise to inflation."

"But the rise from rags to riches," I said, "is the American dream."

"Oh," he said, flourishing his hand in the air, "over there they have traditions, they have a system, they are entitled to their dreams. Even the Mafia has laws in America, but in Egypt we had a kind of Tartar invasion of consumerism."

He stopped to take his breath. "Then Sadat did something terrible to Egyptian society."

"Sadat?"

"He had a golden opportunity to save the Egyptian revolution which was aborted by the defeat of our armies on June 5 at the hands of the Israelis, and Sadat just didn't cut it."

"And now?" I asked.

He shrugged. "The Egyptian people in the hands of Mubarak have disintegrated. They are in tatters. Everyone is trying to steal from one another."

I interrupted him at this point by saying, "So you think America played a very negative role in that it encouraged capitalism and the consumer society?"

Galal looked at me and said earnestly, "I am not blaming America, at least that's not what I am trying to say, but I cannot conceal the role of world Zionism in our destruction as a nation. World Zionism wishes to have power over this area and become the policeman of the West in the Middle East. And in order to do this, it has removed us militarily from the battle. Now that Egypt is no longer militarily involved as an opponent to the Israelis, the Israelis can control the area. It's as simple as that. Because, of course, Egypt was the strongest military force, as you know, to fight the Israelis up until the peace treaty. And now Egypt is no longer fighting for Arab rights in the area." He paused here.

"And this, you think," I said, "is the grand conspiracy against Egypt?"

"Yes," he said, "and the Americans are a pawn in Zionists' hands."

"How?" I asked.

"The spirit," he replied, "of the victory of the October War did not penetrate the village or the countryside as it was meant to do, but quite the contrary, it was corrupted by this consumerism, which began to regulate every aspect of life here. And consumerism, of course, was preceded by a wave of American propaganda and of American culture. You've heard the expression 'the Coca-Cola-ization of society,' which is that rags-to-riches dream you spoke of. The dreams of the Americans became the dreams of Egyptians. But Egyptians don't have the means to realize such dreams. The dreams, for instance, of social mobility only served to agitate, to destroy the social fabric of Egypt," he said. "And, of course, the inflation in oil prices helped this along. And that was part of Zionist tactics since this could only be a phase. The inflation of oil prices was bound to change. And people actually started to leave their land. The agricultural land which we have been growing our food on. They began to leave this land and to go and get jobs in other Arab countries which were paying them in foreign cash." He paused here. He could sense that I disapproved of his opinions. He knew quite well that I saw nothing wrong with Egyptians going to work in countries where they could earn better salaries than they were getting in their own.

"What's wrong with that?" I asked.

"I am against sending migrant workers outside Egypt," he said. "What we should have done is export the products of the Egyptian worker—not the Egyptian worker himself. The whole idea of the Egyptian revolution was to industrialize society, to improve the means of production, including the means of agricultural production. And all of this was destroyed by this American myth, this American dream of consumerism which Sadat had to usher in. There's something else too," he said, almost without taking a breath. "The Egyptian revolution was supposed to give our people a sense of identification with the land. And that was destroyed too. We were supposed to be proud of our ethnicity as Egyptians, not to emulate, not to copy the Westerners, not to be like the foreigners. But now our dream became to look like Americans, to act like Americans, and even to speak like Americans. Look what's happening in our soap operas," he said indignantly.

"And all of this," I asked, "is a Zionist plot?"

"Laila, don't be whimsical," he said. "Don't be ironical. You know exactly what I'm speaking about. The Zionists, with the Americans, distracted the Egyptian worker, the Egyptian peasant, from his productive duty to his country. It's as simple as that. People have simply stopped working in Egypt. All they want to do is watch television." I laughed at this remark, quite agreeing with him. It is a fact that in Egypt, even Egyptian soap operas are just poor imitations of American soap operas and there are not so many soap operas which deal with social development themes, although they do exist. The American model, of course, is the overriding one.

"Galal," I said, "you look tired, but I want to ask you about this business of normalization of relations with Israel which everybody's talking about in Cairo. Now I know you are against it," I added quickly.

He smiled, almost giggling. "Well, what do you want to know about normalization?" he said.

"Do you think we will have normalization with Israel?" I asked.

"Look," he said, "the Egyptian people do not want to open their homes to the Israelis. You cannot impose peace. The Israelis do not want peace. They do not respect peace. But we Muslims, we respect peace. Even the way we greet each other—we say *'al-salamu alaykum*—peace be with you," he continued.

"So," I said, "you don't think there will be normalization?"

"No," he said, "there will be no normalization. Of course, there is normalization between governments. The governments say that they have normal relations with one another, the government of Israel with the government of Egypt. But the Egyptian people will not open their homes to the Israelis as long as the Israelis continue to kill Palestinians and other Arabs in this area."

The events of the Palestinian uprising in the occupied territories since December 10, 1988, have borne Galal out.

AUGUST 28

Tawfiq al-Hakim

Novelist and playwright

"The trouble with America is that it controls the world with money and a pistol. I have money and I have force, and I can buy you out, it tells us—and this is how it operates as an imperialist power in the Middle East. Tell the Americans, the cowboy style won't work. It has to negotiate with the Soviet Union. When these two superpowers get together and decide to coexist peacefully, the problems in the Middle East will be solved. I feel despair about the internal affairs of Egypt. Just despair. I am a believer, but I use my brain—but it's happening around me," said Tawfiq al-Hakim, at eighty-seven Egypt's oldest novelist, essayist, and playwright. He received me on the balcony of his home overlooking the Nile. His eyes twinkled with gaiety, and he laughed and giggled even though we spoke of serious matters.

Hakim was casually dressed in pajamas and a dressing gown. He held a famous cane and sported an equally famous beret on his head. Hakim prides himself on his Western "hellenic" background. He has no hang-ups about being influenced by his readings in European and British literature. Nonetheless, he blamed the West, the power game, for all the troubles in the Arab world. "We are just their pawns in this chess game," he told me philosophically.

This was one of the final interviews Hakim was to give. He died on July 26, 1987, at the age of eighty-eight. In an obituary in the London *Times,* he was described as the "first really distinguished modernist in Egyptian and Arabic literature."

AUGUST 29

As I was riding the elevator up after walking my dog, I found an elderly veiled woman with me in the elevator. "Keep the dog away from me," she said quite pleasantly, "I pray."*

In the afternoon I met a Lebanese woman at a tea at my sister-in-law's. She said that during the entire civil war in Lebanon, she and her family lived in Beirut. "We got used to the bombing," she said. She was Christian, tanned, thirtyish, and wearing an imported silk print dress. "You can buy designer clothes in East Beirut to this day, and we have everything there. We don't want to leave there—we have business concerns in Beirut. When a site is bombed, people just rebuild it. If it's bombed again, they rebuild it again," she said, smiling calmly. She said that Christians and Muslims live separately now, but that she was not a fanatic like the Maronites, and she would prefer it if they all lived together again. . . .

It was all said with genteel nonchalance. Cakes and sweetmeats were served and there were lots of other women relatives dressed in boutique clothes. It made me very uncomfortable, perhaps because they stared at my jeans. I think I will avoid Syrian tea parties in the future!

"What do you think of Fouad Serag al-Din?" I asked my Marxist friend Ahmed later that evening.

"He was with me in prison," he replied, and told me that,

* To a good Muslim, pigs and dogs are impure and contaminating.

while there, Serag al-Din had refused to talk with Sadat. A prison envoy was sent to negotiate with the jailed opposition. "If you want to negotiate," Serag al-Din had said, "then you must set us free—then we will talk."

AUGUST 30

Another day at the pool after an aborted meeting at *Al-Musawar.* To get to Dar al-Hilal, in downtown Cairo, I had to walk through a disemboweled street where the sewage system was being repaired. The smell was unbearable. I felt sorry for the laborers. The water at the Meridien had been cut off because a pipe in the street nearby was being repaired. Fortunately it was repaired in time for me to have a shower. The August heat is suffocating.

AUGUST 31

Ibrahim Sa'ada

Editor in Chief, Akhbar al-Yom

Ibrahim Sa'ada is a friend, and he couldn't be more establishment. Rumored to be one of the journalists closest to the president, he now occupies a powerful position in the media. I had first met him in 1979 when he reported my trip to Iran in March of that year. I had joined a feminist delegation out of Paris to support the Iranian women who, in a demonstration on March 9, had protested Khomeini's making obligatory the wearing of the *chador.*

The story was given a full page in a very sympathetic way, tracing my sojourn there on a day-to-day basis.

It was not a surprise, therefore, to find that Sa'ada was vocal in his opposition to the growth of Islamic fundamentalism. At least that's what he told me when I went to visit him.

Sa'ada sat in a large office on one of the top floors of *Akhbar al-Yom's* high-rise. I watched him light cigarette after cigarette. He spoke quietly. The soft, almost murmured tones of this fortyish journalist in dress shirt and silk tie, with a debonair face and large brown eyes, did not conceal his anger. "How are you doing?" he asked.

"I live in America now," I replied. "What's the literary market like?"

"Religious books command the highest distribution of any publication in Egypt today. The highest royalties are given to the religious writers. The writer who gets the best fan letters from his readers is the religious writer."

"Do you think there is a danger in this?"

"Yes, there is a danger. I can feel it day by day. Kissing is not allowed to be shown on TV films anymore. Or even belly dancing! Beer or any other alcoholic beverage is no longer being served in private and country or social clubs. Television censorship is controlled by a band of veiled women."

"But as a leading media figure, why are you not fighting this?"

"We have protested, but it is useless. The Egyptian parliament, the National Assembly, is demanding such things. MPs comply. You see, the popular currency today is religion—Islam. The parliament is demanding the application of sharia law in Egypt."

"Do you think it will be applied?"

"No."

"You mean not during this regime?" I ventured.

"Maybe, if Mubarak were overthrown, then maybe the fundamentalists will get their day. Actually, very probably they will.

"Do you know that all the major cabarets and nightclubs that used to exist by the Pyramids Road [a red-light district] have all been burned by Islamic extremists? Of course the authorities assure you that they will all be rebuilt again because they are so important to Arab tourism—but nothing of the sort is taking place. A couple of weeks ago several video shops were also burned down. A grocery store in Zamalek called Thomas (for its Greek owner) which has sold liquor for years has also been burned down by them. They are also burning schools and anything which will help them create anarchy and chaos."

"Doesn't the government realize the danger in this?"

"Of course it does. But many of these terrorists remain loose because it is not easy to pin these crimes on them. They don't confess easily. The government is arresting vast numbers of them, and they are being confronted. You see, diplomatic tactics have failed."

"So their intention is to overthrow the regime by creating chaos?"

"Yes," he said quietly.

"I heard that you wrote a couple of very outspoken anti-fundamentalist articles in *Akhbar al-Yom* in July 1985, such as 'A Quiet Exchange with an Extremist.' Did these get you into trouble?"

"You should see the letters I received from my readers. They call me an atheist, among other things."

"Are you afraid for your life?"

"I have a bodyguard twenty-four hours a day. But I think it is useless. After all, Sadat himself was killed in the midst of his bodyguards. And anyway I don't like the form of protection. Initially, I had turned down the government's suggestion of a bodyguard, but I gave in. In reality, I was afraid to refuse it because I didn't want to upset the Security authorities."

"How is that?"

"You see, the essential function of a bodyguard is spying. This is their way of keeping tabs on you. They are entitled to do this. After all, I am in a leadership position. They are entitled to know everything they want to know about my relationships, etc. After all, I even attacked the internal security system in one of my articles. ['The Apparatus of State Security! Where To?' *Akhbar al-Yom*, March 15, 1986.] The article made a big splash, and I almost got fired."

"What do you think of the role of the United States in the

Middle East?" I asked him now. To this he did not reply. "Is it backing Islamic fundamentalism?" I urged. He remained silent and eyed me skeptically. "I want you to speak frankly, please," I persisted. "If you wish, criticize America as much as you want." He remained silent, shuffling his overflowing ash-tray with yet another Kent cigarette.

"I think it was very brave of you to attack the security system in Egypt," I said, trying to break an embarrassing silence.

Now he spoke again, saying, "It is the most dangerous and crucial institution in the country."

"Why?" I persisted.

"Because it dominates the country. They take their job very seriously over there. Especially after that incident when those Israelis were killed.

"Last year, at the Cairo Book Fair, [the Israelis] had a stall. Their minister of tourism was supposed to make an appearance at it. But at the last minute he didn't manage to make it. Those in charge of the stall—there were three of them—locked up and left the fairgrounds. They were machine-gunned down as they stepped onto the street. They all died, a woman and two men. They still haven't caught the killers. This incident, to the Security police, indicates there is an armed underground organization."

"Let's go back to the American role—do you think they may be promoting instability in the area?"

"I don't understand this obsession of yours. If a fundamentalist regime takes over, it is bound to declare war on America. So what would America's interest be in promoting all this?"

"To oppose communism," I replied.

"Communism cannot take over in Egypt. It will never work. I am a Muslim. I am not fanatically religious or extreme in my views. I am not against other religions; on the contrary, I am married to a Frenchwoman, and I drink, but the moment I feel that someone doesn't believe in God, I instinctively reject them. So, you can imagine how the extremists must feel! Do you know why there will never be a Communist takeover? Because only the army can stage a takeover. And in the army there are fundamentalist elements, as, for instance, the ones who assassinated Sadat. Egyptians are believers. The Communists are very scared of the fundamentalists because they know that if the latter take power, they, the Communists, will be the first to be butchered. In my opinion, America must be quite upset about the rise of fundamentalism in Egypt. Moreover, the fundamentalists oppose Israel. It's the first taboo on their list. They assassinated Sadat because he made peace with Israel; that is why they can never be on America's side."

"But everyone seems to be anti-American," I ventured.

He lit another cigarette and said, "I don't feel that to be the case. Only the leftists are anti-American, in my opinion."

"What do you think the U.S. can do in order to improve its role in the Middle East?"

"Of course, America's lack of recognition of the PLO is a problem. The Americans too are refusing to recognize Yassir Arafat. The Palestinians have chosen him to speak on their behalf, so it really shouldn't be America's business who the Palestinians choose as their leader. They cannot endorse the Palestinian leader the Israelis select for them!

"This is the main position of Egypt's rejection of the U.S. role in the Middle East. The U.S. loses the support of Egypt a little with each day because of its unreserved relationship to Israel. Thus it has become more and more difficult for Egypt to defend its peace with Israel."

SEPTEMBER 1986

SEPTEMBER 1

Laila Takla

Member of parliament

"I like this man Mubarak because I think he's good for Egypt," said this prominent Egyptian woman and member of parliament. In her fifties, the articulate Laila Takla, a Ph.D. in political science from New York University, is an attractive woman. When she was appointed by Sadat to his National Assembly, she moved in the orbits of the power lobbies of Europe and America. She was just back from the U.S. where she lobbied for Mubarak with members of the U.S. Congress. We sat in her shaded, well-cultivated, lush green garden in the fashionable suburb of Dokki. She wore a short white dress with black polka dots and chuckled as she spoke over homemade cake and percolated coffee. Our families have known each other for years.

"But everyone, as I can see, seems so depressed and despairing," I ventured with some hesitation. As I looked around me, several Security men were guarding her whitewashed villa, for Laila Takla is married to the Deputy Minister of the Interior. In other words, the police. Since she is an old friend of the family, I felt no fear in speaking frankly in her presence.

"It's the pangs of growing up," she said in reply to my comment. "Because for the first time we know how bad the situation is. The Sadat period, you know, Laila," she said, "was like being married to Miss Universe—it's beautiful at the beginning, but after a while you get tired. It's all nice, but it's too much! A man tells himself: 'I want a nice housewife who takes care of my internal affairs . . .' "

"But there was an optimism at the time of Sadat—maybe it was euphoric," I said. "It was euphoric, there were always festivities—build a statue for Simón Bólivar, galas, festivities . . . and people were kept busy with these things. But Mubarak is concerned with *internal* affairs. With production. He wants Egyptians to wake up and to stand up on their own feet. And people don't like that. They don't want to face facts. At the time of Sadat, women had their jewelry out, and we had queen this and queen that visiting us! It was beautiful. But the show is over. Let's get back to work. Mubarak can be very popular tomorrow, in America, if he keeps friendly with the Israelis—hugging and kissing. He is going to be popular in America. But why do we always have to have good relations with America via Tel Aviv? The only way Mubarak can be popular in America is to throw himself in Israel's arms. Besides, Mubarak is not glamorous, but who wants a movie star like Reagan?" There was a pause. Seeing her enthusiasm for Mubarak, I mentioned hesitantly that the turnout for Mubarak's *Shura* (upper house of parliament) election had been extremely poor. So where was this popular support for him? She admitted that there were serious flaws in the electoral process, but she asserted that Mubarak had "integrity." "He is telling people the truth and stimulating their participation. He's a low-key man, he leads a low-key life. Very decent."

"Do you think Mubarak has reversed Sadat's policies in any way?" I asked her quietly.

"No," she replied quickly. "I think he has corrected Sadat's mistakes."

"You mean, Sadat's style?" I interjected.

"More than style," she said. "He has corrected Sadat's liberal economic policies of *infitah*.* Don't you think we can

* The open-door economic policies introduced by Sadat to liberalize the Egyptian economy and to encourage the private sector.

live without the gruyère and the brie, those smelly French cheeses? Mubarak has put a limit on foreign imports because we need the foreign currency. Why should it be an issue that he has stopped the import of French cheeses?"

"But it's not only cheese. It's essential things, like medication, spare parts for gadgets, and cars . . ." I said.

"That's not true," she said, interrupting me. "We have foreign companies operating here, but they use Egyptian labor."

"So you think Mubarak is tackling the economic problems that Sadat has left?"

"Yes. I think this is the first time that we have a president who is telling us, 'Your debts amount to so and so.' This is why Egyptians are a little bit depressed—because we *know* how bad the situation is. For the first time we realize we have economic problems, and there is an honest man, a 100 percent honest man, who is telling us the truth on two important issues, food subsidies and the foreign debt. Food subsidies are the doing of the Nasser socialist era, and the foreign debt, especially to the United States, is the doing of Sadat. Let's talk about the debt briefly: Every single year we have to pay to the United States about $700 million, which is only the *interest* on the debt, on the money that Sadat borrowed from the United States as one of the factors of the Camp David agreements. Now Carter was an interesting but simplistic-thinking man. He thought, or so they say, that if he raises the price of arms, people will not buy them and there will be peace. So the prices *were* very high—but people did continue to buy them. So Sadat made an agreement with him by which we buy arms, lots of arms, of course. So we sign a peace treaty and we buy arms for a billion. How come?

"The result today is that Egypt has to pay about $700 million in interest alone. The problem there is that we are paying the United States an interest rate of 14 percent or 16 percent or thereabouts. We are allowed only *a one-year delay* in paying this interest. If we do delay, then we evoke something called the Brook amendment, which says: If you don't pay the interest rate on time, you are disqualified from getting any

American aid. So, of course, this past year everyone in government was running around collecting dollars in order to pay the debt. We are trying hard not to evoke the Brook amendment. And all of this to pay the interest rate on the debts which Sadat incurred by borrowing money from the United States in order to buy arms."

"But isn't Mubarak continuing to buy arms?" I asked, interrupting her.

"Okay, but this is a different story. During Sadat's lifetime it was a *loan*, but now we get it for free, like a grant. I think Sadat had protested, and they agreed before he died to give us military aid on which we pay a very high interest rate of 17 percent while the market rate is 7 or 8 percent. So the United States is making money off Egypt! Sadat thought he could get the Americans to lift the interest payment. He was very full of himself. But, of course, the Americans didn't. So Mubarak is stuck with the fact that we have to pay the United States $700 million yearly in interest alone. Now Mubarak is trying to negotiate with the Americans to reduce the interest rate. I told the Americans when I visited Congress recently, If you are serious, you should write off the debt. Americans cannot make a Sadat out of Mubarak, and it is not to their advantage to have a president in Egypt who runs after Begin. Mubarak also believes in production. We should work, start exporting goods, and not borrow any more.

"So, the foreign debt is one of the economic problems facing Mubarak and it is in the hands of America either to write off the debt or to reduce the interest rate. Meanwhile the Israeli lobby is at work in the United States. They are upset that we withdrew our ambassador from Israel. The first question I was asked by some senators when I was there was, 'When are you going to return your ambassador to Israel?' So I told them, 'Can you please think of the United States for a while.'

"However, in all fairness, in all fairness to the United States, they are now giving us military aid. We don't have to repay anything."

"You mean we get all these arms free?" I asked.

"Free. But they have to be from American companies.

"The second issue is subsidies. Subsidies are a big fat mess. This is the first time that Egyptians know what subsidies are. Some people did not know what it meant. I even had to go on television to explain what a subsidy is: The product which costs the government twenty piasters [less than $.08] is being sold to us for five piasters!"

Laila Takla could have gone on for hours talking about the benefits of Mubarak's regime. I thought it was time to change the subject. Since her husband must have played a role in the rounding up of Muslim extremists, I began to question her on that subject.

"There are a lot of women covering their hair," she said, "but it doesn't mean toppling the regime by force."

"But what exactly is the policy of Mubarak toward the Islamic fundamentalists?" I asked her.

"They are stopping them," she replied quickly. "We don't want a religious state. As a matter of fact, we want a secular state."

"But is fundamentalism strong?" I persisted.

"Yes, they are strong. But fundamentalism is all over the world, in Israel, in the U.S. It's a bit stronger here. Now the Irani revolution started—the big powers are helping both Iran and Iraq, so they are responsible for that also—so those people here are strong, they exist, they are a power to be reckoned with, but it is not like they are around the corner. When Sadat was assassinated in Cairo, 120 soldiers, officers and civilians were killed in [the southern provincial town of] Assuit. Many of the fundamentalists were arrested, but they released a lot of them and kept a few whom they had seen shooting and looting. You must remember, at the time we didn't know if it was a revolution or a coup—and security had to get to the bottom of it, so those fundamentalists were beaten up. They were obviously guilty. I condemn torture, but the alternative was going to be lack of human rights for the rest of Egypt."

"Did the torture help the police find out what was happening?"

"I don't know, but I think they found out a lot. My husband never discusses these things with me. But gradually we started knowing they had a communiqué ready, that they were planning to take over the television."

Suddenly the interview took a different tone as she remarked, "Do you know who is the best friend of the Islamic fundamentalists?"

"Who?"

"The United States."

"How?" I asked.

"Some Arab countries, Libya, and Reagan (and his company)—they are the ones who are feeding them. One is feeding them with money, the other with reasons. Who says that Americans want Egypt to be strong or stable? They don't want things to collapse, but they always want to have the upper hand! Okay, there's some kind of a threat, whether it's right or left. This is politics. This is what the British did! Divide and rule."

"But is it in America's interest to destabilize Egypt?"

"No, I don't think so. Regardless what else happens, the rest of the Arab world is tied to Egypt with invisible threads. What happens in Egypt happens in other Arab countries. The influence of Egypt in the area is great. Nonetheless, the Americans don't want a very strong Egypt—a stable Egypt with a continuous threat of instability. Because, in the final analysis, poverty and lack of stability would be the perfect atmosphere conducive to the growth of communism. So, the biggest support of the fundamentalists comes from two sources, Libya and the U.S."

"Like what for example?"

"For example the *Achille Lauro*, when they hijacked an Egyptian plane—this just fuels fundamentalist feeling. A leftist told me once, 'I don't like Mubarak, I don't like his wife or his political style—they are not giving me the provocations, the tools, I need to work with. Jihan Sadat was always doing things I could use to stir up people against the regime. But this Mubarak is too low key—he doesn't go around kissing the Israelis or the Americans.' This is why I like Mubarak. The fact that he doesn't have this shiny charisma is his saving grace. Both Nasser and Sadat had charisma, but where did it take us? When he went to Jerusalem, everybody thought that dollars and American chicken are going to be growing on trees."

"But it didn't happen?"

"It's all economics. It's thanks to Mubarak that for the first time we know the magnitude of our problems."

"Laila," I said, "it's time I leave."

"We will talk again," she said brightly. Then she escorted me through the garden to her waiting car outside. Her chauffeur, a young policeman dressed in khaki, opened the door for me. I waved goodbye as he started the car to drive me home.

SEPTEMBER 2

Al-Sayed Yassin

Director of the Center for Political and Strategic Studies at al-Ahram

I had an interview with Al-Sayed Yassin, an academic in his fifties. He is the director of a think tank at al-Ahram called the Center for Political and Strategic Studies. When the recorder was off, he told me an interesting fact: Egyptian syndicates and professionals have taken a joint decision *not* to normalize relations with Israel until the Palestinian problem is solved. He hates the Zionist state with a passion, but most of all he hates America's unequivocal backing of it. Later, we went to lunch with a young Marxist intellectual who said all the things that Yassin, I think, was reluctant to say: that Islamic fundamentalism was a grass-roots movement with enormous popular support, that the Islamic groups offered all kinds of public services, which even Yassin admitted taking advantage of, such as cheaper health services offered in Islamic centers, which are usually adjacent to a mosque. Yassin said I should go to Syria, but warned me not to ask any questions about the regime of Hafez al-Assad. Apparently anyone who speaks against the regime, or even questions it, is immediately executed. I asked Yassin after lunch if he didn't think that all our military and police systems were not partially responsible for our weakness vis-à-vis Israel. "Of course," he replied quickly.

Tomorrow I have a meeting with Naguib Mahfouz.

SEPTEMBER 3

Naguib Mahfouz

Novelist, Nobel Prize for Literature, 1988

Naguib Mahfouz (b. 1911) is a household name in all Arab countries. Here, his name commands respect, even veneration. Every man, woman, or child who reads or sees movies has been exposed to his politically and socially committed ideas. Nasser and Sadat courted him for their regimes. And every week he is given two full pages in *Al-Ahram* (the major government-controlled paper) to dispose of as he wishes.

To the Arab reader, whatever Mahfouz writes is not only great literature but the truth. Naguib is the first writer in Arabic to be awarded the Nobel Prize for Literature (1988).

It was, therefore, quite difficult to arrange a meeting with this formidable man. Several phone calls were made. Finally, he gave me an appointment.

The rendezvous was at Casino Cleopatra along the banks of the Nile in Zamalek; a dark, open-aired sort of terrace restaurant which is usually considered a place of assignation. It was a hot, humid August night and there was a cool breeze in the restaurant situated at the edge of the Nile; a kaleidoscope of glistening lights and sounds came from across the water. This was Naguib Mahfouz's haunt. This was where he spent his evenings, sitting alone at a table, sipping an unsweetened cup of Turkish coffee.

He is not a young man, but he is still very much at the center of the intellectual mainstream of Egypt. Mahfouz began to write historical novels in the thirties, and then in 1945 he wrote the first in a series of novels in which he recorded contemporary Egyptian life with great realism and skilled characterization. In 1956 and 1957 he published a trilogy in twelve hundred pages about an Egyptian middle-class family during the two wars, and recently he has published a short novel on the assassination of Sadat—for which, when I met him, he was trying to find a film producer.

When I approached his table, I introduced myself, and he got up immediately and shook my hand warmly. "What will you have to drink?" he said. I also asked for a cup of unsweetened Turkish coffee. At first we talked a little about the oppressive heat, and he began to tell me about places that were cool and where one could get away from the heat in the evenings. As he talked, I felt very humble to be in the presence of this great novelist. He is a thin man and wears dark sunglasses, even at night. His head is bald, and he was wearing an inexpensive cotton suit with no tie. Both Nasser and Sadat pandered to him to win him over to their policies—for what Mahfouz writes in his columns and novels is taken seriously. But after talking with him, I sensed a deep disillusion with the rulers of Egypt in the past thirty years, even though he was not about to express that in so many words. We talked about American cultural influence and the Islamic movements. Mahfouz reacted as a humanist; he is open to other cultures—in fact he believes in such interaction. But the Muslim fundamentalists scare him, even though he would not admit it. They are the "ghost" which the "intellectual or the writer sees perennially before him as he tries to express himself," he said quietly.

A slight breeze came from the river. We sat quietly a few minutes, sipping our coffee. "Do you mind if I use a tape recorder?" I asked.

"No," he replied.

"Tell me about the religious movements."

"The religious movement is old in Egypt—so that you can say that the modern revival began as a religious revival, as in the case of the Imam Mohammed Abdou [a religious reformer who died in 1905]. And in a similar fashion, the old movement of the Muslim Brotherhood of 1927 had as its main objective the education of the ideal Muslim youth within the context of the Islamic religion. What was the inevitable result of this? Since religion is belief *and* religious law, this idealist movement began to demand the application of sharia and thereby clashed with the state. That's what happened."

"But they [the Islamic movements] seem to be flourishing these days. What happened?" I asked.

He was silent for a few moments, then speaking cautiously, he said: "The Muslim [Brotherhood] had a real understanding of Islam and forgiveness, and modernism—they understood the spirit of their age—they were not closed and that is why many enlightened people joined them. And when there was war between the Brotherhood and the authorities, they were tortured in prison and the reaction to this torture was extremism. And there emerged certain militant extremist tendencies which proclaimed that all of society was impious, infidels. Of course, what made matters worse was the 1967 defeat and the economic situation. They are all depressed young people and they have been exposed to many slogans—democracy, socialism, and this and that, until there is nothing left for them to try but fundamentalism."

"And that filled the vacuum?" I asked. "Extremism is a result of negative pressure from society. Whenever you have bad conditions in society, you will have extremist trends. Like Russia before the revolution. There was chaos there because of the social ills. Maybe there is a need to change the regime? Maybe people are tired of thirty years of the Egyptian revolution?" I volunteered.

"It is true, at present there is a lot of freedom. If there were no freedom, we wouldn't hear the voices of the extremists, in spite of the fact that they are not recognized. But the economic situation is suffocating. The young Egyptians are depressed, the future before them is dismal. In our days, life was hard, but there was hope. Why? Because there were people who could get jobs if they had a university education."

"Are you not anxious, then? I mean if they apply sharia and take power? And then we would become like Iran? Would this make Naguib Mahfouz anxious?" I said leaning forward, speaking in hushed tones.

"Anything unknown would make me anxious. How?

"If they had translated their aims into modern language and declared: This is our constitution, our regime will be thus, human rights in our system will be thus, the treatment of minorities will be thus, our position with respect to science is thus, and with respect to the arts thus and with respect to ideas thus, and our position with respect to economics is this—then I would tell you, only *after* they take power, what I would be. But I don't know anything. If you hear them say: Our constitution is the Koran, okay, the Koran was the constitution of Omar Ibn al-Khattab [the second caliph of Islam] and it was also the constitution of Sultan Abdel Hamid [Turkish caliph of the later nineteenth century]. Not so?

"We had bad Islamic periods where the Koran was the constitution. We had, for instance, in Egypt the 1923 constitution, under which we witnessed good political eras and others which were of the worst kind. Therefore, when you ask me how I will be when these [extremists] take over, I can only answer, I will be faced with the unknown and therefore I don't know. Whether they will improve or make things worse, I can't tell. You are asking me if it will be like Iran—I don't know. Because all I hear about Iran is from people who don't like it. And I have become accustomed not to make a judgment until I hear both sides. I do not know what's happening in Iran and what kind of rule they have, what economic policies they have, what kind of political system they have, and I can't judge from here."

"If there is an application of the sharia, will we be governed by an imam, do you think? Not by a secular president?" I asked.

"It is not a question of secular or an imam. The important thing is how will I be governed."

"Nonetheless, when the man of religion rules, it is quite different from the man of politics. Not so?" I asked.

"Yes. But I have never tried the rule of religion."

"Maybe he will be an improvement, I mean the imam?"

"My position vis-à-vis these tendencies is the same as the position I have vis-à-vis the unknown, which one cannot be reassured of or confident about. By the same token, this lack of confidence on my part is not factual. I hear nothing but slogans and criticisms of everything. And the worst part of it is that their opponents have brought the country down to the worst level. If secularism had given us good things, it would be fine, but I can find nothing to say in reply [to the Islamists]."

"They say the United States is the cause of all this. That it is encouraging extremism—if you consider extremism a reactionary thing—America, of course, wishes to fight communism with any means so it encourages those Islamic movements. Sadat opened the door for them and that, at least, is what is being said abroad. So what is your opinion on the role the U.S. is playing? Is it a positive one or not?"

"What can one, ideally speaking, demand of a superpower like the U.S.? The answer is that its responsibility with the world should be commensurate with its size. That, you will tell me, is an ideal position. Maybe. Let's leave it. Because idealism is rarely realized. Let's be realistic. A great country like the U.S., why should it concern itself with the Middle East? No doubt there are interests? Maybe I don't know these interests. But I know that a country like the U.S. doesn't concern itself with a country such as the one I am living in unless it has a specific interest: political, economic, and the two together; and surely it must have certain demands. Fine. It's wise if it reconciles between its own interests and the interests of the others. What do we need America for? For our development, technologically? For our debts? In return for this, we have to do certain things. And we should understand that. But the man in the street must not feel that he has given up his freedom for his bread."

"I feel that the man in the street is not too crazy about America. What do you think?" I asked.

"The man in the street suffers. And since he suffers, he will not like anything. Not Egypt and not America. Only those who are not suffering like America."

"The Egyptian left says that the U.S. plays a negative role: It gives us aspirations and models which cannot be realized, the stereotypes we see in films, the consumer society, etc. In other words it creates an image of a lifestyle which can never be realized in a poor third-world country."

"Yes, but it does not do so *on purpose*. Their films reflect *their* lifestyles. We think it's a conspiracy, but there is no conspiracy."

"So, you don't think it's propaganda."

"Of course not. They are a consumer society and they buy everything on installments and they are always in debt to their companies, but I can help them if they help us improve our situation. They want to oppose communism for instance. In Egypt that can only happen if we improve our situation and not by encouraging those trends."

"But don't you have any reservations about the role that the U.S. is playing?"

"I don't like Libya or Qaddafi. But I didn't like his being bombed. As for the rights of the Palestinians, look at how America is *prejudiced* toward Israel. She, the U.S., speaks about peace, but she does not look at it from both sides with equilibrium. The Palestinians are the victims."

"What do you think of the peace with Israel and the normalization of relations?"

"I am for the peace which Sadat brought about. Because the war had brought us death and impotence. And only several years *after* the peace have we started to establish our basic infrastructure, as if we were a country which was just about to begin. We have seen four horrible wars."

"That's right, I have seen four wars."

"Do you know of any country which has been through this? Four wars spaced out with four- or five-year intervals until we were *liquidated*. We lost one hundred thousand million pounds and then we complain that we are in debt? How can we not ask for peace after that? The Arabs treated us very badly. How can we be where we are today and they are so wealthy? I think, therefore, we are indebted to Sadat for the peace and for the liberation of the land, and the fact that at least now we are preoccupied with our *own* problems.

"Why is it that there are intellectuals like Yussef Idris who say, 'This is treason,' and, 'How can we have a demilitarized Sinai?' and so on. There are people who think the peace is a good thing."

"But it is a minority, not so?" I asked.

"A minority. I think it is a minority. We have a cause that we tried to resolve with war and couldn't. Then we have to do it with peace, and let's end it. The very fact that we got involved in the first place was wrong. The Palestinians are the victims of the Arabs before they became the victims of the Israelis. If they [the Arabs] had not interfered in the Palestinian problem today, these same Palestinians would be in their homes."

"How is that?"

"Look at it from the beginning: Didn't the League of Nations give Britain a mandate over Palestine? And didn't it encourage immigration to Palestine? And it had to accommodate the immigrants with the original owners of the country. At any rate, the Palestinians would have remained in Palestine because the British couldn't tell them to leave, because they allowed immigrants to come in—no? It would have been solved even in the worst of cases, even if the country had been divided into two, but its owners would have been part of it."

"This was the lost opportunity. You are right."

"But the Arab countries said: Give them homes in the Arab countries, and then they themselves began to kill them. So that if you figure out the number of Palestinians killed by Arabs, you will find out that it exceeds those killed by Israelis.

"To this very day, the Arabs are the reason for the lack of resolution—it is a matter between the Jews and the Palestinians and they should sit down and solve it. After the Peres summit I think they have found a formula. Look at Qaddafi—instead of waging war on America, why doesn't he fight Israel?"

"What about terrorism?" I asked.

"Terrorism is not just Arab. There is terrorism in Germany, Japan, and Spain. It is the way that today's youth rejects the world around it. Terrorism in the Middle East is caused by the Palestinians, people who have been expelled from their countries; they have become terrorists. It is the only tool in their hands. They see the world opposing them, so they hit back at anything. To resolve Arab terrorism is to resolve the Palestinian problem."

"You mean if they had a state there would no longer be any terrorism?"

"If they had a state, or even a bi-national state with Jordan, then the terrorism would disappear."

"What about the extremists—do you think they would accept the solution of a Palestinian state in the West Bank?"

"When the Palestinians themselves accept a solution, then all other tongues will be silenced."

"Do you have any hopes that Israel will accept the establishment of a Palestinian state in the West Bank?"

"Yes. I am not optimistic, but after thirty years of blood and wars it seems to me that the Palestinians themselves want to resolve it, and that's what's important."

"I am more pessimistic than you are," I replied. "The Israelis will never accept a Palestinian state because they do not want a Palestinian military army next door to them. . . ."

"And the Arabs, too, don't want this kind of a state. Why? Maybe it would be a Communist state. But maybe the confederacy with Jordan will work."

"Let's talk a little about American culture in the Arab world. What do you think of the influence of the American example? You write in your novels about the originality of Egyptian mores and traditions, and how we must *not* forsake them."

"Are you indicating, maybe, the cultural invasion of the

U.S.? First of all I don't like that concept. The two words 'invasion' and 'culture' should never go together because the word 'invasion' is associated in my mind with militarism and colonialism and the word 'culture' is the arts, literature, behavior, and attitude in life. We are in the age of communication and information—the whole world knows each other—I prefer to call all this *interaction* and *not* invasion. And we can always learn from it. We have always been open to this so-called cultural invasion and we were never scared of it."

"So you are not rejecting Western culture, you are not opposed to it?"

"I am an admirer of Western culture. I can learn a lot from it as I do from science and technology. What I hate is negativism. I always want my mind to be active, to be able to differentiate what is beautiful from what is ugly. What I call invasion is not cultural invasion but *internal* invasion. When I accept everything without questioning whether it is useful or not. If you train your young to be intellectually independent, to be thinkers and to have vision, then you can throw them into any culture."

"But that is secular thinking."

"All cultures are humanistic. Humanistic culture illuminates everywhere. Some cultures can be suitable to all places while others can only be suitable to the place whence they emanate.

"Their culture, the others [the Americans], is what they bring up their children on, so it's not poison, right? So that when they export their cultures, they export the best they have—not so? If you submit to it negatively then it's your fault, not the culture's fault. That's why I don't like this term *cultural invasion*."

"Do you say those things in your novels?"

"I think it is reflected in my stories and articles and all that I say because I firmly believe in it."

"And you have never been attacked by the extremist elements that now exist in our society?"

"The extremist elements are closed minds and one-dimensional—they are ideologues."

"You are considered today the greatest novelist in the Arab world. What would you like to say to the U.S.? Do you have a message?"

"America is a superpower and should put itself in the service of the principles in the United Nations Universal Declaration of Human Rights. It should put its power in the *service* of those principles and not in humiliating people."

"Do you feel that the U.S. is humiliating us now? Is not giving us enough money? Or enough aid?"

"No. I didn't like that the U.S. bombed Libya or Lebanon—this is not the U.S. I admire. I do not deny that it helps us substantially and that it lends us things, but we are going through a severe crisis; we are not escaping our debts, and we need a little bit more flexibility, more facilities in the repayments. And I think it is in the interest of the U.S. that I rise—not that I kneel."

"The U.S. says that in order to postpone the repayments of the debts, you have to improve certain elements in your economic life—for instance the food subsidies."

"You mean we must take certain measures?"

"Birth control, the population explosion."

"We are trying to do these things but we are also trying to avoid an explosion."

"But what do you think of the population explosion? Is there such a problem?"

"Of course. But birth control has to be practiced through education and culture."

"What about the changing of women's role in society? Women are fifty percent of the population in Egypt."

"Birth control, as it is called, we have practiced for tens of years at certain educated levels of society—so it's a matter of spreading education and culture."

"What about the religious movements in the country who say that we must increase?"

"I know. This is the opinion of all the men of religion."

"What about the poor?"

"The poor? Who are the poor today? They are the government bureaucrats."

"What about the peasants?"

"The working classes are doing fine these days. Their emigration in the days of Sadat to the Arab countries improved their lot, but the ones whose level of living declined are the urban proletariat—those with fixed incomes or salaries."

"So you are not against the open-door economic policy?"

"No. Only against the way it happened. It was a consumeristic infitah. That was destructive."

"Then you approve of the austerity that's happening now? The restrictions on imports, etc."

"Of course, of course."

"You approve of all those things that are happening in Egypt now?"

"Many things are happening."

"Economically, politically?"

"No doubt. Since Hosni Mubarak has come into power, the country has new policies, but the fault lies with the executive powers that are slightly incapacitated by the economic and moral erosion."

"Then you think that things can go on in this way?"

"It all depends on the patience and endurance of Egyptians because everything is taking so long to get accomplished."

"But who is to blame?"

"All those wars. And Mubarak inherited all those things."

"If you were to go to the election polls, which party would you want in power? This is an abstract question."

"We have two parties, the NDP and the Wafd. But I think they are one party with two wings—one is more inclined to democracy, the other to socialism—and that is the Wafd. If we leave the parties to form freely—I have demanded this more than once—then these two will become one."

"What about the Islamic party?"

"They are obscure—unclear program."

"And emotional?"

"Very emotional. And they've made a lot of enemies—the Christians, the Jews, and the Muslims. Honestly, the Muslims. Who is with them? They are by themselves. They want to fight the whole world."

"Then you would vote for democracy and freedom?"

"Social democracy."

"What was the latest novel you wrote?"

"*The Day the Leader Was Assassinated.* About Sadat. I've also written *Causeries in the Morning and Evening*. It's about a family living at the end of the nineteenth century and the beginning of the twentieth century. Three generations of the family."

"But the novel about the assassination. What's the point of view there?"

"It's basically about the difficulties facing today's youth, the infitah, and it ends with the death of someone who could be Sadat."

"Do you think Egyptian society is going forward—toward modernization?"

"There is development, but as I told you before, those executive powers are handicapped. The forces that are pulling us back are strong."

"What do you think of the veiled woman?"

"She is being pulled back and she thinks she is going forward."

"You mean this is an example of totalitarian thinking?"

"No. There is a new kind of censorship these days—not government. It is a ghost, *their* ghost. It will attack verbally and in writing, and it may even sit in judgment."

As I parted from Naguib Mahfouz after this two-and-a-half-hour interview, I couldn't help wondering why he was so guarded when speaking about the militant Islamic movements.

It was still early, only 9 P.M., as I made my way to Heliopolis to visit some Syrian friends. Over drinks, a young businessman from Aleppo scrutinized me over his arak and then blurted out, "Anyone who is now gathering information about Egypt must be suspect as a CIA agent."

SEPTEMBER 4

Dr. Fouad Zakaria

Chairman, Department of Philosophy, Kuwait University

"You must include Fouad Zakaria in your book," said my friend Ahmed one day.

"Why?" I asked.

"Because he is the most famous anti-American intellectual in the Arab world."

"Can you set it up?" I asked.

"Sure," he replied. A couple of days later a meeting was set up.

Fouad Zakaria is an expatriate intellectual who now heads the department of philosophy at Kuwait University. He is certainly not an establishment figure. He left Egypt shortly after the October War because his leftist magazine, *Al-Fikr al-'Arabi*, was closed down by Sadat in 1971 when the latter clamped down on most leftists in Egyptian universities. His book *The American Model* (*Al-Namouzag al-Amriki wa'l Fikr al-'Arabi*), published about five years ago, is a kind of indictment of the United States in which he claims that the American model expounded by Sadat as a model for Egypt is singularly unsuited for the Arab world. "The conditions in which America was established do not exist anywhere in the world today," he told me as we sat on his terrace in Medinat Nasr, Nasser City, a sprawling desert suburb of Cairo near the airport, where he owns a villa. A short man, with a kind of Mickey Rooney face, he eyed me with some suspicion, even though his daughter, who had let me in, reminded me of a lecture on Ibsen which I had given about five years ago which she had attended.

Zakaria attacked Islamic fundamentalism, but he disavowed all those leftists who had turned Islamists. I wondered if he realized that I was a Christian. He seemed so fearless in his criticism of the right wing in Egypt. "Ask them where in Islam it tells how to deal with the World Bank," he asked earnestly. He was a man who smiled little, even though he had this rather comic little physique. "They want to take us back fourteen centuries—Islamic fundamentalism is just an escape—and if the government wanted to, it could suppress it. But they don't want to. Wouldn't it be better if we spent more time collecting the garbage in our streets?" he concluded, pointing to the street beneath us.

SEPTEMBER 5

Makram Mohammed Ahmad

Editor in Chief, Al-Musawar

Islamic fundamentalists tried to assassinate Makram Mohammed Ahmad, editor in chief of the weekly *Al-Musawar,* in 1987. He is the only journalist to visit Jerusalem *on his own initiative* after the Camp David accords. Makram Mohammed Ahmad gave me an appointment at his office in Dar al-Hilal but was unable to see me because he had a meeting of an impromptu sort with the Minister of Foreign Affairs. I left my number, and he was quick to call me back and by way of apology said that he would meet me in my office. I was quite taken aback, for his is one of the key figures in the Egyptian media today, heading a widely read government-sponsored weekly magazine. He was hired by President Mubarak.

Dressed in an immaculate white cotton suit and holding a

cigar, he came, a few minutes late, to my office in Garden City. I asked what he would like to drink, and he said he didn't mind coffee, "if the quality of it is good" . . . Makram is dynamic, *the* journalist par excellence. He had the guts to go to the Egyptian front as the Yemen correspondent of *Al-Ahram* in 1964 and to write critically of that military adventure. "The Egyptian soldiers fighting that war didn't know who was the foe or who was the friend," he said. "The whole structure, the system collapsed after that," he told me. In between the lines he was trying to tell me the whole July revolution—as we came to refer to it—came to lose its credibility, but then he added that in 1973, the soldiers, the armed forces, *knew their tasks*, which they didn't in 1967. The problem with Sadat was not his peace initiative—Makram supported that even to this minute and strongly believes in a dialogue with Israel. Having been to Israel, he is not even scared of it. "It is a small nation." he said. "How can we think it can swallow us up? The problem with Sadat was that he lost the confidence of the elite and dismissed them or jailed them when they opposed him. He was, contrary to what the West thinks, an autocratic man who did not like dialogues. True, there were those who were predisposed to oppose him, but in the final analysis he demeaned them by choosing as their bosses corrupt and inept men—in order to humiliate his opponents." Nonetheless, he, Makram, was extremely critical of such leftist intellectuals as Mohammed Sid Ahmad, who dialogued with Israelis in the U.S., but when the same Israelis appeared in Cairo, refused to see them, let alone talk to them.

Rumor has it that Makram was made editor in chief of *Al-Musawar* because he went to Jerusalem. But after meeting him I can only think that if there were more Egyptians with his daring, we might be a different nation. "I believe in dialogue," he said, "as an alternative to war. We have been through four wars; why not try peace?"

The Islamic extremists tried to assassinate him because of a series of articles he wrote against them in *Al-Musawar* in 1987.

SEPTEMBER 6

The English and local news on Egyptian television is nearly all international. For instance, today we learn that some Portuguese captain in Lisbon had his leg blown off or that Mrs. Thatcher visited the Grand Hotel in Brighton, complete with clip—but hardly any local news of accidents, incidents, crimes or anything of the sort. A little earlier we watched an American TV serial about some man who spoke to a computerized car called "Kit." The program was interrupted for the evening prayer.

Earlier on I talked to a veiled woman in the health club. She had decided to wear the veil three years ago because, she said, it was her religious duty to do so. "Now I can accept everything with serenity. I don't even watch television but I read theological books." I asked her if the veil was practical. "At first, my hair was always sweating and I felt hot, but later, I stopped feeling the heat," she said, "because I felt good about myself." Later, when she dressed, she wore a long skirt and long sleeves, and nothing but her face and her palms showed.

As I left the health club, I stopped by a greenhouse on the sidewalk, run by a peasant woman. I bought a rubber plant for five pounds. As the woman showed me four potted plants, I noticed that she lived in one room, which contained nothing but a bed and television. Two of her children were watching TV while something was cooking on a gas stove. I wondered what her children, ragged as they were, and wretchedly poor, thought of the computerized car "Kit." I live on the twelfth floor of a high-rise in Maadi, not too far away from the woman with the potted plants. From up here you can only see the Nile and an occasional motorboat racing by.

They are still showing *Centennial* on TV. Earlier they showed us clips of Nasser in Moscow thirty years ago, on August 28.

I got my press card today. I am now an accredited journalist. I feel a sense of power I have never had before.

SEPTEMBER 7

"Can you defy God and his Prophet? Then you women of Islam must veil. That is the only way to worship! The world is looking on us." The message was from the Friday sermon on TV. The worshipers showed on the screen were all men, dressed in civilian clothes, interspersed with some military and children. No women around anywhere.

SEPTEMBER 8

"*Ahlan, ahlan,* Mama Suzanne. Welcome, welcome, Mama Suzanne," was the greeting given to Suzanne Mubarak at the opening of a flower show in Ismailia attended by Arab delegations from Yemen and Palestine. Egypt's first lady, who appears at the opening of charity and social events, is unveiled.

I switched to another channel. Lo and behold, some silent movies of Charlie Chaplin. Then about an hour later, Sheikh Chaarawi, more popular with Egyptians than Khomeini was with the Iranians and more beloved—was speaking about birth control. "There is no need for birth control," he said. "What we need is to cultivate our underdeveloped land."

SEPTEMBER 9

At the health club, the Italian woman I have befriended said today that if the poor people of Egypt decided to "rise up" there would be an eruption nothing could control. "It's as if they were asleep," she said, "but one day . . ." She doesn't understand the culture, I thought to myself. Resignation is built into us. I wonder how I can communicate this to the West? Today I saw a woman crossing from the other bank of the Nile. She had a naked baby in her arms and two children hanging on to her skirts. She was emaciated, and the baby's bottom was dirty. Yet she smiled. She seemed content. Or was it resignation?

One of the local papers reported that for the first time since the peace treaty of 1979, Israel and Egypt have agreed on a joint project: a farm which will make use of Israeli technology and know-how. The paper which reported this is an opposition one and was very disapproving of what it called "normalization" which "defies people's basic feelings."

SEPTEMBER 10

My brother Adel is a Westernized doctor who was educated in London. Even his girlfriends were English. Yet when he married, he chose a wealthy girl thirteen years younger and of Syrian background. Her English is almost nonexistent. She is uneducated and even shuns Western culture. Her favorite pastimes are shopping and viewing Arabic soap operas. Yet she is venerated in our society because she has given birth to a male child and also because she is very wealthy.

My new nephew, Nessim, was baptized "Abram" because his mother had a "vision" that he should be called "Abram." My sister-in-law is very wily, I think. She was just avoiding the name Nessim (my father's name), but she couldn't get away with it. The ceremony was conducted by a Coptic monk complete with rabbinical beard, a handkerchief on his head, and long, white, gold-trimmed robe. He kept on murmuring prayers in Arabic and Coptic, quite indistinguishable to everyone except his choirboy. Now and then the monk would rush out in the midst of the ceremony to conduct some business outside. The little oil-painted room was decorated with reproductions of paintings of the Madonna and Child and two photographs of our Coptic Patriarch, Pope Shenoudah. At one point, the monk interrupted his prayers to look at the family gathered around him, as if to make sure they were all there. Then he said suddenly: "Don't get bored, the more I pray the more *Christian* the baby will become."

The baby lay there wearing some ridiculous organdy dress purchased especially for the occasion from London's Marks and Spencer.* He was held in the arms of a distinctly Muslim nanny, who arrived late and noisily interrupted the ceremony by saying "Is it all over?" At one point the monk turned to my sister-in-law (also demurely dressed by Marks and Spencer) to proselytize, "It's up to you to make him [the baby] practice Christianity and to keep him away from the Devil." He then ordered her to turn eastward and said, "Now I will utter prayers that will keep Satan away and will cleanse you of your sin." Here I interrupted by asking what sin she had committed, since she was married. The monk looked at me in utter astonishment, then after a few speechless seconds retorted, "The sin of childbirth—of procreation."

"But the man is equally sinful," I replied. My brother-in-law tried to pull me away by the arm, as if to protect the monk.

"Well," began the monk, "these are old customs from the Old Testament—we don't question them." When he saw how unconvinced I was, he reiterated, "The mother has to be baptized again. This is her ceremony as much as the baby's. She has to be cleansed to murmur his prayers."

As the ceremony continued, the room filled up with incense until it looked as if the place were on fire.

Later, at my brother's home, there was a sumptuous meal, preceded by hors d'oeuvres and concluded with a large cake on which there was a crucifix drawn from top to bottom and the name "Nessim" smudged on with chocolate cream.

In the evening I met Yussef Cherif Rizkallah, who is in charge of the selection of all foreign films on television. We were old friends, and he greeted me warmly. He had converted to Islam in order to marry a Muslim girl. It is impossible for a female of the Islamic faith to marry a non-Muslim unless he

* This budget store in London is very popular with Arabs rich and poor. Ironically, after the 1967 defeat, the major Arab governments called for a boycott on the store because its two owners were England's largest financial contributors to Israel. This did not deter the Arab consumer.

converts. I asked him if he practiced his ten-year-old religion. "I don't know how to pray," he said. I looked at him in astonishment. For it is truly rare in Egypt to find someone these days who will admit that he is not religious.

Yussef, a short man in his late thirties with a balding head, was wearing jeans. But then a lot of media people wear them. We talked about Islamic fundamentalism. He said that only two hours a week of religious programs had been added in the last year. . . . But that there were other signs: Kissing was forbidden, for instance, and there were certain films he didn't even contemplate recommending for TV. "Like what?" I asked him.

"Like Bertolucci's *The Conformist*," he replied. "We are strictly in family entertainment and Westerns—and then we must not select films that denigrate the United States!"

Tomorrow I will meet the most famous journalist in Egypt.

SEPTEMBER 11

Mustapha Amin

Former owner of Akhbar al-Yom *and* Al-Akhbar; *now Editor in Chief,* Akhbar al-Yom

Mustapha Amin owned two of the major dailies of the Egyptian press, *Akhbar al-Yom* and *Al-Akhbar*. Along with his twin brother, Ali, he belongs to one of the oldest political families of Egypt. They were also the newspaper tycoons of the country. Amin was educated at Georgetown University, where he earned a master's in international relations. He was pro-Nasser until 1965, when the latter had him jailed for allegedly being a CIA agent. Amin spent eight and a half years in jail and was released in 1974 by Sadat. He is still very pro-American, although he has his reservations, as he explained in the interview. He's an aging man, intelligent, with shiny black eyes and a large, egg-shaped bald head. He is almost obese; his large frame is slightly bent and his sagging body talks of fatigue and torture. . . . Yet he is optimistic. I asked him how he could be. "I am a believer," he said simply. "What I like about America is democracy and freedom," he said sincerely. "I wish we could learn that from them. We still have martial law in Egypt. It was imposed in 1939 and still hasn't been lifted." Amin believes that the present Egyptian constitution has to be changed and later admitted that the whole system must go. "All our troubles stem from the lack of democracy and the prevalence of dictatorship," he said, refusing to lay the blame for any of it on the Americans.

While in jail he wrote several books which were published after his release by President Sadat in 1974. His first book, appropriately entitled *First Year in Jail,* was followed by *Second Year in Jail, Third Year in Jail,* and so forth until he had managed to chronicle the eight years. These books are best-sellers. *First Year in Jail* has already seen eight printings.

Mustapha Amin is a modest man who speaks quietly and without any anger. I visited him on the top floor of the Al-Akhbar Building, which was owned by his family before it was confiscated and nationalized by Nasser in the 1960s.

"In the fifties, I used to advocate a revolutionary uprising—King Farouk was still in power. We used to write against corruption and parliamentary dictatorship, and we were making demands for socialism. We used to attack the king, even though prior to this we were all very fond of King Farouk. He was a very popular king, but unfortunately his entourage corrupted him. We assumed that the kind of freedom we had was simply insufficient. For example, in 1951, I was arrested twenty-one times. I would be arrested at 9:00 A.M., court would convene at noon, and the court would decide to release me (on bail) at 4 P.M. In those days I considered this an absolute lack of freedom; to remain eight hours in jail—that was too much!

"Subsequently I have lived to learn what being in prison is really like when I lost my freedom for eight and a half years. But in the king's day, when they simply confiscated an issue of a paper, we thought this was a total infringement on our freedom. Later Nasser confiscated all our newspapers.

"When the revolution took place in 1952, Mr. Caffrey [the American ambassador] received a cable informing him that a revolution had taken place which was seen to be anti-Western and should be squelched militarily. Caffrey got in touch with me and asked me what was happening. So I told him, What you are hearing is nonsense. This is a nationalist revolution and it is not against the West. The free officers sent one of their men over to Washington, and as a result of that, the American government refused to intervene. And based on that so did the British . . ."

"In other words, the British and the Americans allowed the Egyptian military coup to take place?"

"This is how I got involved with the new military regime. Nasser was always in touch with me, and whenever he wanted to relay something to the Americans, he used me as an intermediary. . . .

"Were you an admirer of Nasser in those days?"

"Very much so. First of all, I had been given to understand that he would fulfill all that I had been demanding—they declared that they would preserve and implement our constitution. He fooled me into believing that he wanted real democracy for Egypt. At least that's what he told me and I believed him.

"I thought he was a patriotic and progressive young man who would rule Egypt according to nationalist principles. I made the mistake of thinking that the individual can sacrifice a part of his own personal freedom in order to liberate an entire nation. Then, experience has taught me that it is impossible to liberate a nation when its inhabitants are slaves."

"Has this notion changed now—now that we have had thirty years of a military regime?"

"The change can be symbolized in the three leaders we had: Nasser, Sadat, and Mubarak. At the time of Gamal Abdel Nasser, if you wrote an article which did not please him, he would literally have you hanged (as he hanged the Islamic writer Sayid Qutb because he didn't like his book) or jailed; Anwar al-Sadat, on the other hand, if you wrote something which displeased him, would issue an edict stopping you from working further or simply have you fired from the paper. Hosni Mubarak, if you write something he doesn't like, will stand up before a TV camera and give you hell."

"Is that all?"

"Yes."

"But there are many political detainees in jail."

"Not by order of Mubarak, but by the orders of the public prosecutor—like those extremists, the Jihad people who carry explosives, which would be illegal in any country."

"So to go back, you were considered pro-American, and you were jailed. In other words, do you believe that America plays a powerful role in the Middle East?"

"We need them economically, of course. But above all, I admired America when I was a student there."

"Where did you study in the U.S.?"

"At Georgetown University, where I obtained an M.A. in international relations. The first book I ever wrote was entitled *Laughing America* and it became an immediate bestseller in Egypt! At any rate, I have always felt that Egypt would gain much by having good relations with the U.S. At first, America welcomed this relationship. Then suddenly the relationship failed."

"Why?"

"The reason for this failure was that Gamal Abdel Nasser and his men did not understand the American democratic system. For instance, Nasser would come and tell me, 'When I need something from the Soviets, their ambassador informs me that it will be shipped from Odessa in a week on such and such a day and reach me at Alex on such a day. When I request something from the American ambassador, he returns after three or four weeks and says the State Department has accepted your request—then he returns in five weeks and informs me that the House Foreign Relations Committee is examining the request. Then the Senate gets a go at it—and then some other committee, somewhere else, has turned it down.'

"To Nasser this procedure was an indication that Americans were not serious. He did not have a grasp of the constitutional procedures of American government."

"But wasn't that because of the lack of communication between Egypt and the U.S. at the time of Eisenhower due to the fact that they [the U.S.] wanted military bases in Egypt and Nasser wanted to remain nonaligned?"

"No—they didn't ignore military bases at the time—what happened is that we requested arms. And their Secretary of Defense came over to Egypt and tried to give us a list of what we wanted—but with the understanding that these arms would not be deployed except with the approval of the U.S. The revolutionary council rejected this flatly. So this was the beginning of the first crisis."

"How did the breakdown between us and America take place?"

"In my opinion, everything deteriorated when the U.S. refused to finance the High Dam in Aswan that would have generated electric power for Egypt. They had hoped to bring Nasser down with this rejection. The opposite occurred.

"It made Nasser more popular because he was able to get financing from the Soviet Union."

"But why did the Americans turn Nasser down?"

"They also didn't want to give him arms or wheat. So he was obliged to go to the Soviet Union—but before we bought our arms from the Soviets, we informed them, but they didn't believe us."

"But why did they refuse in the first place?"

"They were afraid lest these weapons be used against Israel."

"Was this in Nasser's mind at the time?"

"It did not occur to him at that time to fight Israel. It was only after Israel invaded Gaza [an incident in the 1950s] killing Egyptian soldiers that the army was furious. So Nasser was obliged to ask for arms [from the Soviets] in order to pacify his army."

"So this was the beginning of the cold war between Egypt and the U.S. Was it at that time that you were jailed?"

"I was jailed in 1965. (President Johnson cut all economic aid to Egypt in 1966.)"

"Up until 1965 your relationship with Nasser was good?"

"Extremely good. In 1964 he came up to me because I was working on American economic aid to Egypt. I used to travel to the U.S. and come back with this economic aid. So, one day he tells me, 'We need twice as much economic aid as they are giving us.' I told him I would try. 'You are going to try just like that, verbally?' he asked me. I said yes. 'Well, you're wrong,' he said. 'I have a report prepared by some consultants who say that the only way to make America pay up is to tell it to go to hell. Then and only then will they increase their aid to us.'

"Needless to say, I didn't agree with the tactic and I told him so. He ignored my advice and informed me that the American ambassador in Cairo threatened the Egyptian Minister of Agriculture with cutting off the wheat entirely!

"Well, I went over and asked the minister, Mr. Steno, if he had indeed been threatened by the American ambassador and he said he had not! So I called up Nasser and told him what I had found out. So Nasser became very angry and said, 'Who told you to do this?'

"Next day, he went to give a speech at Port Said where he declared that American aid to Egypt was worthless and that if they didn't like what he said, then the Americans could drink from the sea [Mediterranean], and if that wasn't enough, they could 'drink from the Red Sea.'

"The crowd was delighted with this bravura, and as we returned on the train—we were in a private car—he was standing and waving, but I sat a little further back in an armchair. Nasser's secretary came up to me and said that the *rais* [boss] wanted to speak to me.

"He was standing with his arms at his sides and, looking straight at me, he said, 'Did you see the impact that my speech had?' So I told him, 'The important thing is the impact that it makes in Washington and not in Port Said.'

" 'No, you will see,' he replied, 'they will double the aid.' But the Americans promptly cut off the aid. He [Nasser] then went around saying that Mustapha Amin knew that they were cutting off the aid because he [Amin] is close to them. He couldn't understand that this was simply a rational deduction on my part. Anyway, he became furious at me. The other thing which got him very angry at me is when I urged him to pursue democracy in Egypt. We were sitting together, and as I explained my views, he remained silent. Finally he spoke and said, 'You are right—I will introduce democracy in Egypt *after* thirty years.' So I looked astonished. And when he saw my astonishment, he got angry. Then he asked me to pursue this business of economic aid with the Americans. Later someone told him that Mustapha Amin said to the Americans that by cutting off the wheat for Nasser you are trying to get him down on his knees. Nasser got furious at me for presumably saying that he could go on his knees. He declared that he would never kneel to anyone."

"Is that all?"

"Yes."

"And you were thrown in jail?"

"Yes. Later, someone, a head of state, asked him, 'Is Mustapha Amin a spy?' Nasser replied that I wasn't. 'So why do you jail him?' Nasser replied, 'Because Mustapha Amin told the Americans that they were cutting off our wheat in order to bring Nasser to his knees, and Nasser never goes down on his knees.' "

"Were the prison years, the eight and a half years, bearable?"

"Of course not. I was tortured . . . Nasser, knowing that I was on very good terms with the Americans, decided to irritate them by jailing and torturing me. But the Americans didn't give a damn—and it also irritated him that America did nothing to help me. I was not America's man. I was Egypt's man."

"But what about Amnesty International and so forth?"

"There were many people who intervened on my behalf but they were Arab leaders. Nothing happened."

"And the torture?"

"I was tortured into confessing that I was an agent for the U.S. Later on, the chief prosecutor of my case, Salah Nasr, was himself sentenced to ten years in jail after Nasser's death. He was sentenced for torturing me, Mustapha Amin, and forcing me to confess that I was a U.S. agent. Of course witnesses were provided from among the revolutionary council who were able to testify that all my contacts with the U.S. were under the authorization of Nasser."

"When were you released?"

"In 1974, by Sadat. He could have released me earlier but he was afraid lest this anger the Russians who were arming him for the 1973 [Yom Kippur] war."

"So you have gone through all this suffering because you were considered America's man?"

"Yes."

"What are the implications of being accused of being America's man? Does it mean that America was hated by the Egyptian revolution?"

"No, it was not hatred at first—only when the U.S. refused to finance the High Dam. You see, the trouble with America is that it put all of the Arab countries in one block and Israel in another. Two million Israelis in one palm and a hundred million Arabs in another. All our demands from the U.S. would take a long time to reach us, but not so with Israel. Of course we have to admit that we are beginners and they know how to manipulate the U.S. better than we do. We did not know how to lobby with Congress, and when our demands were not met, we considered this a hostile act toward us. We just didn't have the know-how."

"But did they make any mistakes toward us?"

"Oh, yes, many mistakes. For instance, when they refused to give us arms. Strange things would occur; we would ask for arms, but they would offer to construct a TV installation for us! Naturally, all of this did not sit very well with the officers who were ruling the country. Walt Disney offered to build a Disneyland at the pyramids. When I told Nasser of this offer, he was quite furious! 'What's this kid stuff?' he said. 'We need tanks, machine guns, planes, not toys!' The Americans evidently didn't realize they were addressing a military man—an officer. Even when Nasser visited the U.N., he did not see America or even sightsee in New York. Nasser never visited a Western country."

"Then he had a built-in suspicion of the West."

"Yes, but this fanaticism is not in the Egyptian people. Anti-Westernism is due to dictatorship. For instance, in 1924, we had real free parliamentary elections in Egypt. There was a province called Armante, whose elected representative was an Egyptian Jew called Yussef Aslan Qattawi. There were three Muslims running against him, but he won. We had the first Jewish senator in Egypt in a district where there were no Jews. That's the amazing thing, I mean, Jews run in districts where there are Jews; but in Egypt, a Jew won the elections being the only Jew! Copts also occupied prominent parliamentary positions."

"So, it was only after the Nasser coup d'etat that the Egyptian minorities began to have a hard time?"

"I believe this emanated from the Nasser dictatorship—never from the people."

"Is anti-Westernism still with us?"

"Undoubtedly. There is a prevalent feeling that the United States aids Israel in an illogical fashion and that although we also get U.S. aid, we are astounded by the promiscuity of Israel in the Middle East: The invasion of southern Lebanon, the destruction of the nuclear reactor in Iraq, the Taba problem, occupation of Arab territories, all compound the anti-Westernism that now exists."

"Can America be of more assistance to the Arabs?"

"No, because the U.S. has budget deficits. Actually, we don't request more aid from the U.S., but we would like her to treat us equally with Israel, respect our identity and our political alliances with the other Arab countries.

"In order to be friends with Israel, we cannot become the enemies of the other Arab countries."

"Haven't we made mistakes too?"

"Yes, our military dictatorship has. Today the prime minister declared that we have lost $100 billion and lost a hundred thousand lives in those wars with Israel."

"Were you initially an admirer of Sadat?"

"Yes, very much. He abolished dictatorship, closed down Nasser's concentration camps, gave the press its freedom, got rid of the Soviet experts, and began libcralizing the economy. His chief mistake is that he jailed everyone who criticized him toward the end of his life."

"Are you a believer in Camp David?"

"I believe his visit to Jerusalem was a good thing, but the Camp David agreements have their limitations. I do not agree that Egyptian boundaries be unpatrolled by Egyptians but by a multinational force."

"Do you think that when Sadat died he was not mourned?"

"Yes, he was not mourned."

"Because he was America's man?"

"No, but because of the corruption that had taken place while he was in power and also his wife's high profile. I remember one day, he fired twelve newspaper editors in one day!"

"So dictatorship returned again with Sadat?"

"Yes, it returned through the back door—it had gone out the front door, but returned through the back door with Sadat."

"Is there freedom now?"

"The opposition papers are free to write what they wish. They may even criticize Mubarak. This has never happened before except prior to the revolution. What remains now is for the state-owned newspapers to exercise the same prerogative.

"I have demanded that the chairman of the board of a newspaper should be elected by his peers and not by the president of the country. Second, I have also demanded the amendment of the Egyptian constitution; it is absurd that the members of parliament are not permitted to discuss budgetary matters. In all parliaments, the budget is discussed and allocated by a special committee. Third, under our present constitution, the parliament cannot decide to vote lack of confidence in the ministership. If they do so, the matter is brought to the attention of the president, and if the president disagrees with parliament, then he gives the prime minister the right to dissolve parliament. There should also be a multiparty system represented in parliament."

"But I have heard that the Islamic extremists have infiltrated all parties in parliament and that they stand a good chance of winning the 1988 parliamentary elections."

"In my opinion, extremism is the natural result of the lack of freedom. Why not have an Islamic party, or even a Communist party? They should go above ground. That is real democracy and freedom."

"What do you think of the normalization of relations with Israel?"

"I believe that Begin vitiated Camp David when he met Sadat in Jerusalem and then bombed the Iraqi nuclear reactor, invaded South Lebanon, and so on. Israel, if it wishes to live in this area, must have good relations with all its neighbors. We in Egypt cannot be the only friends of Israel. We cannot go against our Arab friends and allies. We have the same language, culture, and religion.

"Besides, I refuse the idea of Israel or the U.S. or even Libya becoming the master of the Middle East. America's leadership of the world cost it a lot of blood."

I had been received immediately when I came to interview Mustapha Amin, and he reminded me that he had followed the "tragedy" of my losing my theater. Later, as I left his air-conditioned office, I felt an extraordinary sadness. I was almost speechless with it. As I walked to the open-air parking lot where my car was, I looked up at the rows of dust-covered slums that flanked the dirt road of al-Sahafa Street—the dingy, dark hallways; the crumbling, peeling façades of those slums; and the crowds of men, women, and children who pushed their way, jostling one another in the street—and my sadness deepened.

That evening I leafed through the eighth printing of Mustapha Amin's best-selling autobiographical novel—*First Year in Jail.* The opening line is: "The pen is forbidden—paper is forbidden—ink is forbidden."

SEPTEMBER 12

Dr. Fawzi Abou-Saif
Physician

Today I had lunch with a cousin, Dr. Fawzi Abou-Saif, whom I haven't seen in years. He told me that he had lived with but not married a Muslim woman for a number of years before her premature death from cancer. Her family (she had two children from a previous marriage) wanted him to marry her before her death, but he said he couldn't because in order to do so he would have to become a Muslim. His mistress died brokenhearted, and since she was religious, she was convinced that her soul would roam in hell forever because she had been an "adulteress." Then he spoke of his daughter, who had wanted to marry a Muslim a couple of years ago. Now she is twenty-eight and single—in itself a sizable problem in Cairene society. He had forbidden it. "It's either this Muslim boy or me," he said. I asked him why he opposed the match, and he replied that if she made a Muslim marriage she could be repudiated in a second; she would lose all her rights. Copts can be fanatic too. (Subsequently, his daughter married the Muslim.)

My cousin was a doctor in the air force and was one of Mubarak's colleagues for over fourteen years. "Mubarak was a brave fighter, and he is one of the few air force men who penetrated Israel in 1967." He also told me the Israelis had put a price on his head—they wanted him dead. "The man is a modest man and we don't know if he can make a great leader—at any rate all the political jokes about him describe him as 'slow.' "

This morning the BBC reported that Egypt has been negotiating with the IMF for a whole year over a new loan. The IMF has made new conditions that the subsidies on gas and certain food items be lifted, but the Egyptian government won't implement this because such a move would cause political unrest. In other words, it would shake the present regime. What about the good of Egypt? Nobody seems to care as long as the regime stays in power. One of the intellectuals I spoke to told me that the whole system has to be changed in Egypt. In other words, that the regime of the military junta has to go in order for things to improve. According to Miles Copeland in his book *The Game of Nations,* which was published in 1969, it was the CIA that helped consolidate and put Nasser in power. They thought that the then young officer would be a good player in their game of nations. Today they say the strongest man in Egypt is Field Marshal Abou-Ghazzala, the head of the army. Rumor also has it that it is the Americans who are propping him up.

SEPTEMBER 13

I had a meeting at the Jordanian embassy with the cultural attaché. The embassy is located in the middle-class section of Dokki, not far from the Sheraton Hotel. The entrance is in a garden to a villa which was obviously confiscated in the Nasser days. Once you get by the security—you show your passport—you are received into a spacious, sparsely furnished, somewhat airy, thirties-style house with walls which need painting and old-fashioned, slightly soiled, furnishings which have seen better days. The striking thing about this embassy is that from the moment you set foot in it, you are greeted by photos of King Hussein in various circumstances. As an officer, as the king, as an Arab, with a *kufiyeh,* and so on. Up the wooden staircase and at the landing two men sit idly eyeing the visitors. I mentioned the name of the attaché, and one of the men spoke a few words to an eight-year-old—something about *baba* (father, in Arabic). The boy took me into his father's office, which was also quite sparsely furnished but clean. The man who sat at the desk before me had a small beard and was carrying some worry beads. He asked me to sit down. I gave him the letter even though he said he knew nothing about the matter. . . . Nonetheless he placed it in front of him. Then he said, "This matter is for someone else—the press attaché."

"Can I go in to see him?" I asked. He nodded and then turned away from me and began to chat again with a friend who had come into the office. There was much talk of the swimming pool of the Marriott Hotel, and then the friend got up and dialed the Marriott and asked to speak to the manager. The manager, he was told, was out. But his secretary was in. The friend then told the secretary that she should arrange to give his excellency—referring to the attaché—complimentary use of the pool and to say that so and so [here he gave his name] had said to do so. He, the manager, would know him. Thereupon, there were some more exchanges between the two men and the friend exited. The attaché was now free to examine my letter.

Meanwhile the coffee had been brought in, and I sipped it politely, eyeing him.

"Anything you write will cause sensitivities," he said, "so I must send this letter to the Ministry of Foreign Affairs for their approval."

"Of course," I replied as cheerfully as I could. "How long will it all take?" I added. About three weeks. My face fell. "So long," I murmured.

He nodded. "Your letter will be sent in the diplomatic pouch."

"Of course." After all, Hussein is a king, I thought to myself as I stared up at the picture of Hussein smiling above me. "Don't forget I'm an Arab. I have an Egyptian passport, and I am obviously not biased to the other side," I said. He looked at my passport, then gave it back without a word. I got up and thanked him for the coffee.

"You know, when I receive those foreign correspondents at home, I give them sandwiches."

"Because they do the same in their own country?" I asked.

"No, they do not even offer us a glass of water. But when I receive an Arab, I spread out a proper meal for him."

I smiled and said, "They don't have our sense of hospitality, that's for sure."

Later that evening when I reached home, I switched on the television. They were showing the sports awards from the Liberty Weekend. The show began with "Stars and Stripes" played by a brass band, and then the Statue of Liberty appeared surrounded by blazing fireworks, which synchronized beautifully with the music. I looked at the screen, berating myself for being so incorrigibly admiring. But how could I help it? There she was—Liberty—in all her splendor.

I am languishing without my favorite brand of cigarettes. Finally I pleaded with my newly hired secretary, Salah Abdel Fatah—a retired elderly civil servant—to pull a string. Does he know someone who works at the airport? Yes, his wife's cousin's son is a steward on Saudi Arabian Airlines. He phones him. "The 'More' cigarettes are for my boss," he tells him. "My boss can't breathe without them. There is a large vacuum in his brain. Needs them badly." He puts the receiver down . . . triumphantly. "There is hope," he tells me; "he said he would have them in a couple of days."

You can get only the one or two local brands in Cairo and locally manufactured versions of Rothmans and Marlboro cigarettes. Otherwise the only other thing you can smoke is hashish or the hubble-bubble. . . .

Late that night they showed a movie from the King Farouk period. The director, Togo Mizrahi, and the leading lady, Laila Murad, were both Egyptian Jews. The film denounces modern ways and marriages where women have too much freedom. It was extremely well directed and, though corny and melodramatic, could have stood up to any Hollywood film of that period.

SEPTEMBER 14

The Valley of the Dolls was shown today on the second channel of our TV, which regularly shows American movies. All the kisses and all the erotic scenes had been eliminated, so it was quite hard to follow. Earlier I had a beer in the Meridien Hotel (where, like most hotels in Cairo, they still serve alcohol). I was with a leftist journalist. We talked about Israel. He said he wouldn't mind seeing it, if he were *hijacked* there, but he certainly refused the notion of going of his own free will. The Egyptian left rejects the peace with Israel even more adamantly than the Egyptian right.

SEPTEMBER 15

The Tajamu is the party headquarters of the Egyptian leftists. Although there is no official Communist Party, there is a Progressive Party, as it is called, headed by one of Nasser's officers who staged the 1952 coup which ushered in the revolution. This officer took the leftist direction right up to Moscow, where he was awarded the Lenin Peace Prize in 1971. The gentleman in question is Khaled Moheidin, sometimes referred to as "Ha'dj'i (because he has been on pilgrimage to Mecca). The Egyptian left is trying a rapprochement with the extreme right, and Khaled, for one, claims that there is no discrepancy between Islam and communism. Today at the party headquarters he was referred to as "Bey," a formal term of address which is a leftover from the Turkish aristocracy of Farouk's dynasty. Headquarters is a little apartment on the first floor of one of those tired, peeling downtown Cairo buildings. The lobby contains armchairs which are dusty and sagging, and the walls have not been painted for ages. Opposite the entrance there is a large desk, behind which a kindly Nubian sits. Flanking the desk and almost reaching the ceiling is a large statue—a bust of some personality; I thought it might be Lenin. It is so huge it takes up practically the entire space and is the first thing that greets the visitor upon entering. The statue had a stern look. "Who is this?" I asked a girl who happened to be passing by at the moment.

"Nasser," she replied briefly.

"Oh, it does not look like him," I mumbled as politely as I could. She looked at me pityingly.

I had missed my appointment with Moheidin due to some breakdown of communications. I left my letter of introduction with the secretary and made my way to the Hilton Hotel. On the way, I stopped at what used to be a cigarette and cigar store, and found it quite transformed—they were selling souvenirs and the usual Rothmans and Marlboros. I asked them what happened to the cigars and Turkish tobacco they had been selling for years. "No more imported goods," someone said, disgruntled.

I made my way to my hairdresser, a Coptic Christian girl who had been working there for twenty years and whom I have known for ten years. She welcomed me effusively. As she did my hair, this plump, pleasant-faced woman in her thirties gave me all the gossip of the Coptic community. . . . It concerned the appearance of the Virgin in Cairo. Apparently, she had appeared in a very poor, very small Coptic church in Shubra, a congested district of Cairo, inhabited by lower-middle-class Copts. "There were many who tried to attack the church," she said, "and there have been many miracles."

"Like what?" I asked.

"Well, they said a man went in one day—"

"Who said?"

"The priest from the same church. He tells everything during the service. Well, this man went in carrying two fans for the church as a gift. The priest asked his name and said he would thank him during the service. The man said it was an anonymous gift. Then the man left and apparently was run over by a car. They found nothing on him but a piece of paper bearing the name and place of the church and the priest. The police went to the church. The fans had not yet been unpacked. The priest was surprised that the man had no identity papers and, feeling something was wrong, asked the police to inspect the package. The fans contained explosives! It was the Muslim fundamentalists! Do you see how the Virgin protects her church?" I must have looked disbelievingly at her because she said, "It's a miracle and that's what this is all about."

I nodded. "But are the Christians having a hard time these days?"

"Finding jobs—everybody is trying to emigrate. Do you know when the U.S. bombed Libya, the Copts were not displeased—after all [Qaddafi's] crazy—but the Muslims, they were angry."

"Why?" I asked.

"A Christian country bombing a Muslim one," she replied simply.

"Is the Virgin still appearing?" I asked.

"Yes, but the police are there day and night and no one is allowed in after five P.M."

I walked to my mother's place after that because I did not have my car. On the way, I noticed Cairo's "bag people," older men and women surrounded by parcels sitting on the stone benches of the Garden City corniche. People stared at me because I was walking energetically. Street energy is not a feature of the Cairo landscape—quite the contrary. People ramble on and seem to languish from the heat and the dust. Side by side with the poverty that surrounds one, there is also a lassitude—something worse than despair—a feeling of things that are beyond hope.

I turned off the corniche and into the tree-shaded street where my mother's house is located. My eye caught a slender young girl in pink, unveiled, and walking coquettishly in front of me. One glance and I could place her socially—she could have been a secretary or a maid or even a Cairo call girl—by the way she walked swinging her hips, indifferent to the hostile male stares around us. Suddenly a police car from nowhere appeared and cut in front of her. She objected loudly, asking the men inside if they wanted to run her over. The car slowed down and continued to follow her. Another exchange took place. The car almost drove her to the wall of a nearby building and then came to a halt. I followed rapidly and made my way to the officer who was now angrily addressing the cornered girl. There must have been at least six men in the car, and I didn't like the way they were all glaring at her. As I arrived at her side, I saw she could not have been more than eighteen. I heard her speak defiantly to the police officer. "I have done nothing," she said. "Take me to the police station."

"Now, now," I said, intervening. "Actually," I added, "I saw the whole thing."

The officer replied, "I'm sorry, madame, this girl has to come to the police station. She has just insulted us."

"Is that a crime?"

"Of course. Invective launched at a police officer is a misdemeanor." I looked at the girl. I could imagine what would happen to her if she went to the police station—she wouldn't stand a chance.

"Why don't you apologize to the police officer?" I said quickly.

"I haven't done anything," she replied. The police officer, who had by now left the vehicle and taken a good look at me, said, "It's all right, we'll let her go."

"That's very magnanimous of you," I said. "I really admire your style." He beamed at me and got back into his car. I heaved a sigh of relief. This was actually a nice man. Someone else might not have been so kind.

SEPTEMBER 16

Sheikh Kishk

Famous Muslim preacher

Sheikh Kishk is a Muslim preacher whose name is a household word not only in Egypt but also in the entire Arab world. A couple of months ago, a friend of mine heard a cassette of

Kishk's being listened to in a small Moroccan village. The Bedouins commented avidly upon it and expressed concern about the fate of their beloved preacher in these days. Kishk is not allowed to preach in Egypt under the present regime. The Moroccan Bedouins also informed my friend that he, Kishk, had been blinded by the torture he underwent in Nasser's prisons. But, contrary to the legend that has spread around him, his blindness is due to trachoma, an cyc disease that ravages the children of poor peasants in Egypt.

During the last years of Sadat's presidency, it was impossible to walk in the streets of Cairo without hearing Kishk's sermons. They were broadcast everywhere: in taxis, at street-corner stands, in butchers' shops, on the cassette players of the doormen of Cairo's apartment houses, in people's homes, and, of course, in his mosque, 'Ayn al-Hayat (Source of Life), which lies at the edge of the Qubba Gardens district not far from the poorer, lower-middle-class neighborhoods of Zeitoun and Abassia. Many people traveled from one end of the city to the other to listen to him preach his Friday sermon. They arrived either in Mercedeses or on foot. It is estimated that he had a regular following every Friday of 10,000 worshipers, who sat on the floor on newspapers or on straw mats to listen to his sonorous voice. But Sheikh Kishk told me that about 100,000 people turned up to hear him.* And today, even though he no longer preaches, his cassettes are available and are being listened to from Casablanca to Marseilles.

Kishk was born in 1933 in a small village in the Nile Delta. One of six children, he was brought up by a fiercely pious rural mother and Abdel Hamid. Kishk had to memorize the Koran by the age of twelve. "God has granted me the gift of blindness," he told me, "but he has given me vision." He attended religious schools and enrolled at Al-Azhar University where he excelled because of a prodigious memory and graduated

* The crowds packed not only the actual mosque but additional prayer halls and the alleyways of adjacent houses. Powerful loudspeakers were attached to the walls of the surrounding buildings.

with honors. He became an imam, a leader of prayer, in 1961 and was appointed to government mosques. In 1964, he became a preacher at 'Ayn al-Hayat and was arrested in 1966 on suspicion of being one of the leaders of the Muslim Brotherhood. Although no formal charge was levied against him, he was not released until 1968. He endured enormous torture, of which, people say, he still bears the marks. Despite sporadic prison terms in the subsequent years, he retained his post at his mosque in Qubbah, but in 1981, he was jailed by Sadat along with all the other dissidents of that regime. For Kishk was the most virulent opposer of Sadat's policies.

On January 27, 1982, he was released.

It was not easy to locate Sheikh Kishk. Only his followers and closest friends know where he lives. Nonetheless, I managed to find him, but I am unable to tell my reader his whereabouts.

I took a taxi to one of those lower-middle-class neighborhoods of Cairo where the sewage water floods the unpaved streets and where poverty is half-hidden in the simple, often unfinished three- or four-story tenement buildings with dark hallways and narrow stone stairways. I took along Ahmed Sami Sharara, my friend, assistant, and translator. There were some who said that this was a dangerous mission and that Kishk would not meet me, even if he were friendly. Others told me that he was under surveillance and that my presence in his home would anger "the Authorities."

A woman in her thirties greeted me immediately. Her face was uncovered, and as soon as she saw my male friend, she signaled me to have him step outside because her head was unveiled. I shoved my flustered companion out of the apartment and stepped in. She smiled gratefully. She had the most beautiful face I have ever seen in Egypt. For a moment, I was speechless. I fumbled in my bag for my press card. She nodded as if she knew what it was and said, "He's not here; he's gone out of town, but he'll be back tomorrow. Come back tomorrow." And then she smiled. That's it. My God, I told my companion, as we made our way down the narrow staircase, she didn't even ask me who I was or what I wanted to interview him about. And this is supposed to be one of the most dangerous men in the country!

Next day, I turned up at 10:30 A.M. A small child opened the door, and we were ushered into the living room. As we passed through a dark and somewhat dingy hallway with nothing but a table and sofa, I noticed a small room opening onto the hallway in which there stood an old-fashioned Singer sewing machine. The place was devoid of the usual TV customarily placed in the hallways of such homes.

The room we were taken inside was typical, although poorer than most such rooms for receiving guests. Along the walls there was a *mastaba,* or wooden couch, forming a rectangle; it was covered with white cotton upholstery. On clean, handwoven mats stood several small tables. A Koranic inscription in large Kufic writing hung on the bare, off-white plaster wall. My companion and I sat down and waited silently. I was apprehensive, maybe even a little scared. A few minutes later, Kishk walked into the room. He smiled; no, he almost giggled as he asked us to sit down. I took out my Macmillan letter and shoved it to my friend to translate. Kishk waved his hand. "Don't do that," he said. "Just tell me what's in it and how I can be of service to you." I was speechless.

"I am writing a book which will be published in the United States. . . ." As I spoke, I watched him closely. He was short, stocky, well-built, and was wearing a white *galabiya.* He had a large beard and mustache and, like all blind people here, he wore dark sunglasses. But the face was jovial, almost mischievous. There was no bitterness or tension in the full cheeks, the lips, the smooth, unscarred face. He looked like a man who enjoyed life, and at this moment, he was obviously enjoying my flustered attempts to explain my visit. "Do you wish to keep the Macmillan letter?" I asked as I ended my remarks.

"No, no," he said. "I can't read it. But it's fine. So you live in America? We want to reach the Muslims in America . . ." he added. I nodded and looked at my friend. "But first we must drink tea," Sheikh Kishk said.

"Thank you," I murmured. The tea was handed through the doorway by the wife to the young boy who had let us in. "*Ahlan, ahlan,*" he said as he brought in the tea. "Welcome, welcome."

"I wish to record our interview," I told Sheikh Kishk as we sipped the tea served in tiny glasses.

"Of course," he said unflinchingly.

"By the way," I said lightly, "I have been told you are a millionaire and that you live in a palace, but you live very modestly. . . . What about the royalties from all those cassettes you sell?"

"I do not commission those cassettes; people just record my sermons."

"But it's big business," I reminded him.

"I have never touched a penny from those sales," he said.

"But you are entitled," I said. "You could hire a lawyer," I added.

He laughed and replied, "It is not my style."

I placed my tape recorder on the cushion before him, on which he rested his arm. He took it in his hands and fingered it lovingly, and then placed it next to his face as if to see it, all the while smiling like a child who has been given a toy after having been deprived of it. I did not have to instruct him how to operate it. He knew exactly how far from his lips to place it, and we made several voice tests before he began answering my questions.

"You have been tortured in prison," I began, trying to see if I could draw him out.

He laughed again and then his face suddenly became serious as he replied, "There is no worse torture than the loss of freedom. That is real torture."

"Why do you attack Jihan al-Sadat in your sermons?" I asked. He was famous for his denunciation of Egypt's former first lady.

He cleared his throat, and then, as if he were about to begin a sermon, he said, "*Al-hamdu li-Llah rabb al-'alamin*" (Praise be to God, Lord of Creation), and then added, "Praised be the Lord of the worlds, O Lord, O Lord who has made the Holy

Koran, springtime of our heart, light of our breast, protector of men, I affirm that there is no god but God. Through his thought the heart is soothed, sin is pardoned."*

He cleared his throat again and then began replying to my questions: "It is not proper, according to the Koran, to allude to a woman. The only woman who is mentioned [there] is Maryam [the Virgin Mary]. For a woman to be acceptable in Islam she must take as her models the wives of the Prophet: remain in your homes, pray, give to the poor, and obey God. How painful and shocking when we heard through satellite radio and television that a certain meeting took place in Washington [he is alluding to the signing of the peace treaty]. It had a very painful effect on Muslims all over the world. The Koran advises women to cover themselves, because if they don't, their bodies will be harmed."

"But . . ." I intervened.

He interrupted me and continued, "We are not of the opinion that women should interfere in government."

"But people have heard you attack Jihan," I persisted.

"I never mentioned her name," he said simply.

In spite of myself, I found myself admiring the cunning and intelligence of this blind man who sat fearlessly before me. "But this is the twentieth century," I said, embarking on my second question, "the age of technology, of Star Wars, of computers. Can Islam exist in such an age?"

He cleared his throat again and began his answer by using an analogy. "A straight line is supposed to be the shortest distance between two points, and, as the total number of angles in a triangle makes two right angles, so Islamic life brings about happiness in this world and the next. The former is a mathematical fact and the latter is a religious fact. Neither changes, whatever the times. As for technology, the Prophet was supposed to have said that man should take care of his worldly or practical matters, which is interpreted to mean

* All Koranic verses translated by Ahmed Sami Sharara.

that there is no discrepancy between Islam and technology. After all, the sciences, which are at the disposal of the Western world, are derived from Islamic pioneers as, for example, Ibn Sinna, whose volume on medicine was taught for three centuries in the Parisian universities. Or you have Ibnal-Baytars, the father of veterinary medicine, or Ibn al Hath'am, the founder of ophthalmology. History will tell you who invented mathematics, astronomy, and algebra. Astronomy was invented by Ibn al-Jahez; similarly, botany, calculus, and geography were all invented by Arab scientists. But now our stars have left us and hover over the skies of London, Paris, Washington, Berlin, and Moscow. So you could say that the West is exporting some of its civilization back to us as a way of returning its enormous debt to us. Besides, the Koran is full of allusions to the importance of knowledge.

"How do you like my answer?" Sheikh Kishk asked me suddenly.

"Fine, fine, you are doing just fine." Actually I was quite impressed by his way of maneuvering in answering the questions and his trying to root modern civilization in Islam. In a book published recently in France (Giles Kepel's *Muslim Extremism in Egypt*), the writer devoted a whole chapter to an analysis of Kishk's sermons and this ability to make metaphors, allusions, and puns, and make constant reference to the sciences and technology in order to be on the same wavelength as his audiences.

"What do you think of America?" I asked him now. "Is it a hateful country because its people are non-Muslim?"

He laughed and replied, "I like this question," as if to tell me that he was not intimidated by it. "In Islam you are invoked to take up arms and fight only those who dispossess you of your homes or fight your religions. It is thus forbidden to have relations with those who oppose your religion and dispossess you of your homes. This is the real criteria of the relationship of non-Muslims to Muslims."

"Then you are allowed to kill those who dispossess you or fight Islam?" I asked.

"Islam says do not kill women, children, old men, and do not kill those who are worshipping in their monasteries [an obvious allusion to the massacre the day before of Jews in a synagogue in Istanbul]. They are only asked to pay a tax [djizia] in order to benefit from the protection of Islamic armies. . . ."

At this point, Sheikh Kishk stopped speaking into the tape recorder and announced that we should take a break. He cleared his throat and asked for a glass of water. The water was brought in—again, by the little boy. As the child gave his father the glass, I noticed that he was wearing very Americanized clothes, a pair of blue cotton shorts and a matching T-shirt, with—lo and behold—MICHAEL JACKSON inscribed in big letters on the back. I stared at it and burst out laughing, almost losing my cool. "Your son is wearing an American pop shirt, with a pop singer on it," I said.

Kishk did not lose his cool for a moment. "Oh, this was a gift," he said. "And we have to accept gifts." But he laughed along with me. I was starting to warm up to this blind sheikh who had an answer for everything, but what I liked most was his display of rationalism, his level-headedness and the fact that he never asked me what faith I sported, even though I am sure he realized that I was not of his persuasion.

We settled down again, and I resumed my questioning and asked about his opinion on America and Israel. "We are not enemies of America because it is America. We are not a people full of complexes, we are not a people with inbred disease or bloody wounds, but we are a people with a clear conscience. The enmity we bear toward America is simply because it has established the State of Israel. America has implanted in our Islamic East this long-term evil, and it has nurtured and watered it with its emotion and given it everything from butter to Phantoms. When there will be justice, America will know that we are the ones done wrong to and that Israel has wronged us. It is she who has shed the first blood—witness the incidents of Deir Yassin, Kafr Qassem, Bahr al-Bakar, the Abou-Zaabal factory, and other incidents. When America recognized

Israel, Moscow followed swiftly minutes later, and we became, as the Prophet says: 'Nations are about to fall prey on you as people fall prey on food.' When we fight, it is to the end and medicinal. My recommendation: Remove the blindness from your eyes and read Islam with the naked eye. Islam is a creed and a law. Read Islam, which has lifted racial discrimination and made the Abyssinian slave Bilal, the clerk, a transmitter for the Prophet's inspiration, and read Islam which made the slaves masters. Study the Prophet's biography in depth, and you can understand it because you are a rational people. You are in the forefront of material excellence. You have paid too much attention to the body. Can the body live without soul? Take care of the spirit. The spirit is in Islam. For example, this business of drinking: While America spends billions to prevent its people from drinking, Mohammed came to a society which drank five times a day and replaced drinking by prayer five times a day. Mohammed did not forbid drinks because they were drinks but because they made people lose consciousness. Even George Bernard Shaw, the Irish writer, said if Mohammed were amongst us now, he would have solved all world problems while sipping a cup of coffee. Read Islam from its sources, and don't listen to those who convey it to you with a spirit of enmity or antagonism. Read Islam from its source, and use good interpreters. Read and listen until you learn that Islam has given us a holy book as clear as the sunlight."

When I asked him if he would sit with a Jewish rabbi, if the occasion presented itself, to talk over the Middle East conflict, he replied he had no objection because in Islam it says, "We do not refuse to sit with them because Allah said: 'People of the Book, let us come together to use logic and reason.' On principle we don't mind living with anyone, but God has forbidden us to have discourse with those who fight our religion and who have driven us out of our homes and those who helped those who drove us out [meaning America]. So, Israel is the aggressor, and it is still the aggressor, and it was she who drove the people of Palestine out. Since May 14, 1948, Palestine is a nation without a people, for a people without a nation. There can be no dialogue because they, the Israelis, use force and have dispersed the Palestinians. They have made the Arabs wretched people. But all this does not mean that there cannot be roundtables, and there can be discussions and dialogues in matters of creed with all its implications because Islam is Right, and Righteousness is one of Allah's names." (Allah has ninety-nine names.)

Kishk's views were essentially the Muslim fundamentalist views on for instance the establishing of an Islamic nation, a caliphate to be ruled by a council comprised of representatives from each Muslim country and headed by a caliph (a ruler who traces his lineage to the Prophet). In other words, a religious and not a secular government is the only acceptable form for a state. The solution with regards to Israel and Palestine that he advocated was also fundamentalist: Jews and Christians must live alongside the Muslims, as subjects, in a Muslim state. Israel, he said, though it was an organic part of the United States, would disappear one day, just as all those (pagan) civilizations, such as the Roman, disappeared.

At the end of the interview, he asked me if I would translate for him what had been written about him in the book by Giles Kepel. This I did by translating the biographical data for him. He listened attentively to me and nodded in approval at the correct facts of his life, obviously pleased that the West was paying him so much attention.

SEPTEMBER 17

Pope Shenoudah III

Coptic Patriarch, spiritual leader of Egyptian Christians

"My confinement by Sadat for three years in the desert monastery of Wadi al-Natrun was time spent in Paradise," Pope Shenoudah told me. The Pope is the spiritual leader of the twelve or so million Christian Copts of Egypt. Egyptians were converted to Christianity by St. Mark in A.D. 30. They were inhabitants of Egypt before it was conquered by the Islamic Arab armies of 'Amir-Ibn-Al-'As in A.D. 639. It took centuries of severe persecution to ensure the Arabization and Islamization of the Christian majority of the Egyptian population. The Copts who did not convert to Islam consider themselves the real Egyptians. These Copts of Egypt belong to all strata of society.

"I love solitude and this was a chance for me to be alone to contemplate and to be with God. During that period I wrote sixteen books . . ." he said. I asked him if he didn't mind being away from the society or community of the Copts he had fought so hard for. "I remained in their hearts," he said. When Sadat was assassinated, many Copts celebrated by drinking sharbat, a fruit syrup used on festive occasions. The Copts never forgave Sadat for deposing their spiritually appointed leader and for confining him to house arrest in a desert monastery guarded day and night by a battalion of soldiers.

Pope Shenoudah, his hair concealed beneath a monk's hood, his long white bushy beard contrasting with his black robes, his gold crosier next to him, sat regally before me in his throne room in the papal center at the Cathedral of St. Mark. Like medieval cathedrals, this one is enclosed by a large wall, but its grounds are like fairgrounds. They contain a clerical school and a small Coptic church. Religious stalls sell books and cassettes of Shenoudah's sermons and other religious paraphernalia. The place is heavily guarded, and as I left the papal location after spending three and one-half hours with the Pope, I noticed a police vehicle outside. The officers on duty were sitting out their vigil in front of the late show on TV.

"You must not talk to him about the community," his secretary had told me over the phone. And yet for three hours, the Coptic Patriarch spoke of little else, and he spoke much of President Sadat, who had incarcerated him and humiliated him. Up until 1977, the president had been on good terms with the Pope, and in 1977 they had had a four-hour meeting attended by other bishops, during which the Pope had laid out his grievances to the secular leader of his country. The Copts were not being allowed to build churches, whereas anyone could build without a permit a mosque in any place, even in an apartment house, and that place would not be taxed. But the Copts, whenever they could, would have to get a security clearance preceded by a presidential decree allowing them to build a church. Sadat had promised Shenoudah fifty churches a year, but nothing came of that promise, just as nothing came of the promise to allow the Copts to have their *waqf*—their endowments—returned. Job discrimination against the Copts was also discussed at that historical meeting, and Sadat promised to rectify all wrongs.

But on September 5, 1981, the Pope was deposed and sent into exile. "Sadat had promised that we would have yearly meetings," the Pope told me, "but he didn't even keep that promise. We have not built many churches since that time, and whenever we do try, there are complications."

"Like what?" I asked.

"Somebody comes up to us and says that the land we are building on belongs to someone else and that we need to prove it is ours. We go to court and a few months later we produce evidence. But a mosque has sprung up on the land. We cannot tear down the mosque and so we have to find somewhere else to build on. This happened once on a site, and we then moved to another site. On one occasion we had to move fourteen times."

The Pope also devoted much time to discussing his opposition to the application of Islamic law in Egypt. He stated his opposition to the proposal of a law that made it punishable by death for a Muslim to convert to Christianity—the so-called law of Rida.* A Christian who has converted to Islam and who

* The law of apostasy.

wishes to return to his original faith can also be sentenced to death. The Pope felt very strongly about that law and said that he would continue to oppose it. "If sharia were imposed in Egypt, there would be no secular government," he said. "As in Iran, an imam would rule. A Muslim cannot be ruled by a non-Muslim, according to sharia; therefore there would be no Coptic judges, no ministers, no teachers. The entire Coptic community would have either to segregate itself or become servants."

SEPTEMBER 18

Mubarak and Peres meet in Alexandria. Taba will go to arbitration—and there is now talk of normalization. I called Osama al-Baz over the phone. He took the call and said he would call me back. Maybe there is still hope for the interview with Mubarak. Went to the Jordanian embassy for meeting with the ambassador this time. He received me cordially. A thin, elegant man in his late forties, he spoke smoothly and asked me what exactly I was planning to ask the king. I told him I would show him the Macmillan proposal. We spoke in English. His was excellent. I asked him about the Palestinian problem. Would there ever be self-determination? Never, he said. The Israelis would never agree. The problem will never be solved, he said, but maybe the Egyptian peace with Israel is beneficial to Egypt per se.

Later, at night, I had my first encounter with the Israeli who lives on my floor. It was very late . . . maybe 1 P.M. I had forgotten something in my car. As I stepped off the elevator, he was standing there, almost as if waiting for me. I gasped, startled. He looked at me angrily. "Do you have a dog?" he asked. That question—the manner in which it was asked and his defiant posture, almost threatening—evoked those Israeli officers who have instructions to blow up Palestinian homes and who execute Palestinians without batting an eyelid.

For a moment I was tempted to ask, Are you going to blow

up the building? "Is that your dog littering the floor?" he asked.
"No, it's not," I replied. I was telling the truth. "You'll have to take my word for it," I added and walked away. He glared at me.

SEPTEMBER 19

The meeting with Peres seems to have no repercussions at all. Spent the day at the Meridien pool. It was cool, and the water of the pool was more turquoise than ever and contrasted sharply with the grayish colorless water of the Nile, stretching beyond. The sky was pale blue, and only a couple of supersonic jets interrupted the happy cries of small children in the water. A few foreigners lay around and one Egyptian woman with two children. I knew she was an expatriate from the way she behaved. Not only was she wearing a bathing suit (and not fully clothed), but she talked casually and nonchalantly with a young, blond man on her right. No Egyptian woman here would talk to a man, let alone a foreigner, in public. She smiled all the time and had short-cropped hair. So different from us—her enslaved sisters! A Frenchman in the chaise longue next to mine tried to make conversation with me, but I did not reply. I was scared that it would raise eyebrows. Have I lost my courage?

SEPTEMBER 20

Ahmed Baha' al-Din
Journalist

The press, most of it, is controlled and owned by the state. *Al-Ahram*, the major state-owned newspaper, is housed in a whitish-grayish building that curls around itself several stories high. It was there that my meeting with Ahmed Baha' al-Din, the famous journalist who had exiled himself while Sadat was in power, took place.

Baha' was Sadat's speechwriter but was angered by the president's peace initiative. He left for Kuwait and was subsequently considered an opponent of the late president's regime. In his fifties, he is a veteran journalist who is highly respected. He is married to a Christian Coptic woman. He is widely traveled and speaks fluent English, but our interview was in Arabic.

Baha' is one of those insiders who have invaluable knowledge of the chaos of the Arabic world.

He's a short man with poor eyesight but an all-seeing look.

He is powerful enough to write his own ticket. Baha' is not for sale. Neither the Kuwaitis nor Sadat could buy him.

In addition to his former editorship of *Al-Ahram*, where his weekly column is read religiously, he contributes regularly to publications in Arab countries (such as Kuwait) where his journalism is as revered as it is in Egypt.

Baha' is said to be a friend of Mubarak's. He is certainly a close friend of Jihan al-Sadat, about whom we talked much, and also a friend of most Arab politicians in power. Baha', like other star journalists, has the power to command public opinion that only brilliant journalists have.

His differences with Anwar al-Sadat, who banned his writings eventually, were considered an indication of Sadat's intolerance rather than Baha's opinions.

Baha' blinked at me from horn-rimmed glasses across his large desk in a special office at *Al-Ahram*. He received me extremely cordially, remembering my work as a stage director. Later he was even to accord me two long conversations in his luxuriously furnished apartment not far form the Sheraton Hotel in Cairo.

"You left Egypt for Kuwait because of a difference with Anwar al-Sadat around 1977 and you became outspokenly critical of him," I began.

He interrupted me in English, saying, "No, I left Egypt for health reasons. I resigned my post on the paper because of a brain clot which could have paralyzed me entirely. They told me I must relieve the stress in my life. I must not even work at all and should not remain in Egypt because that's where all my problems were. That's why I left for Kuwait. I received an offer to work for a monthly cultural magazine there called *Al-'Arabi* [*The Arab*]. That was in January 1976. I left on the best of terms with the president, and he allowed me to go on one condition: that I continue writing my weekly column in *Al-Ahram*. He also kept phoning me in Kuwait to write his major speeches for him as I used to do before my illness."

"When did you start becoming a speechwriter for Sadat?"

"In 1974, when I became editor in chief of *Al-Ahram*. The last time I saw Sadat was in December 1977 after the trip to Jerusalem. I came to Cairo specifically to find out what made him go to Jerusalem. We spent the day in his resthouse at the pyramids. He provided me with the background to his decision to go to Israel. That was a Sunday, and I remember he kept me till 6 P.M. on Monday. Then a helicopter came to take him to Ismailia. He told me he is going to Ismailia to await a visit on Tuesday from Begin and his delegation. Sadat told me that on Wednesday he and Begin would have a press conference to declare the main points of the agreement between Egypt and Israel. He was very confident about this. I spent the whole day trying to convince him that this would not happen, that the Israelis will not give in just because he went to Jerusalem."

"Were you opposed to Sadat's visit to Jerusalem?"

"No," he replied dodgingly.

"But you stopped writing his speeches after he went to Jerusalem?"

"Yes, but this was not in opposition to his visit to Jerusalem. Let me put it in another way. I was very close to him when I was the editor in chief of *Al-Ahram*; I used to meet and converse with him every day.* I began to differ with him in 1974 about his economic open-door policy—not in principle,

* Baha' has written a book, *Conversations with Sadat*, which is being publicized and serialized all over the Arab world.

but in the way it was applied. There were two camps: one group—or a tendency, which was in the minority—telling Sadat that after the 1973 war, the people would accept a tightening of the belt in order to rebuild the country. Sadat however was very keen after the 1973 war to convince the people of the peace treaty [with Israel] and that such a treaty would bring prosperity [for Egypt]. He was also very keen to have people feel prosperity after the 1973 war, so he introduced his liberal economic open-door policy [which encouraged the growth of the private sector]. But Egypt can't afford to eat caviar and smoked salmon and to import everything from the West—especially consumer products."

As he talked, it became obvious that Baha' objected to the way in which Egypt's foreign revenues from oil and dollars sent home by Egyptians working in Arab countries were being managed. He claimed that Sadat's economic policies led to corruption and said so in an article he wrote for *Al-Ahram*. The article did not please Sadat, who called him up and told him so. "All I was criticizing was the profiteering that this led to," explained Baha'. In spite of this, he went on to say his friendship with Sadat continued even after Baha' left the country for "health reasons."

Another source of disagreement concerned itself with the food riots in January 1977—massive riots by the people to protest Sadat's attempt to lift government subsidies on certain basic foods. Two weeks after the end of the riots, Sadat rang up Baha' and proposed another speech. "I sat with him from morning till midnight for two days. Again, I had a certain point of view, which was that the rioters were justified in their rebellion." But Sadat didn't agree. "It was a bitter pill for him to swallow." According to Baha', these riots by his people against him were "the turning point" in Sadat's political life. When I inquired why, Baha' reminded me that the food riots had been violent and had lasted for twenty hours, leaving the country virtually in a state of civil anarchy. Sadat, who was in the southern town of Aswan at the time of the riots, watched the burning and looting from his resthouse there. "He sat there, on one side of the Nile, watching the banks of the Nile on the other side being swallowed up in flames. I spent those two days trying to calm him down. But it was the turning point. It made him decide to have a peace treaty with Israel at any cost. Four years had passed since the 1973 war—and the Israelis would not give in one inch. Sadat realized that he must break this deadlock, come what may. The Israelis were occupying the Sinai desert and the Suez Canal was closed to shipping." Baha' took a sip of tea from a cup which had been brought in, then continued with his reminiscence: "To return to the food riots—I told him that the people were justified and that, anyway, everything was over. The army had calmed things down. You see, he wanted me to write him a speech announcing the new emergency laws he was about to impose. These laws, among others, would make it illegal for more than five people to meet at one time, and the punishment for such 'illegal' assembly could amount to twenty-five years in jail. These laws have been imposed subsequently and are still enforced. But I was against these laws and urged him instead to sit with his economic advisors and form a coherent policy and then talk to the people. But Sadat wanted to get up and reprimand the rioters and defend the government's position. So, after two days, I told him, 'Mr. President, I'm sorry, but I think you are going to regret these measures. They will lead you to a new path of repression. I think it is a mistake, and I want to have nothing to do with it.' And he was nice enough to say, 'Okay—forget it and thank you.' So, when I returned to Kuwait, I thought Sadat would never receive me again. But he asked me to visit him in July 1977 [six months later], and he informed me that the twenty-fifth anniversary of the revolution was coming up and that he wanted me to write him a special speech. So I suggested that he make a significant announcement, and I told him about my idea for this announcement: He should declare that he would totally pardon all political prisoners. 'What do you mean by a total pardon?' he asked me. So I replied that it involved pardoning all political prisoners incarcerated from July 23, 1952 [the day of the Egyptian revolution], to July 23, 1977. It would be a coup, and it would also be a new beginning. After I spent many hours debating this with him, he seemed to agree. He even seemed enthusiastic. He like the idea of a national healing. He liked situations like that. And so I wrote the speech and, at the end of it, inserted the announcement of the total pardon, like a bombshell.

"I deposited the speech with him, and on the day it was to be delivered, I sat at home before my television set and watched him read my speech. He read it all faithfully, but, just before the bombshell announcement, he stopped and ended the speech."

"Did you ever see Sadat again?" I said, noticing Baha's irritation with the late president.

"Yes, when he returned from Jerusalem, I went to see him. It was a historical day for him. *Time* magazine had decided to make him 'Man of the Year' and they were using his resthouse at the pyramids to receive the ten journalists who had been sent. The photographers took his picture next to the Sphinx and the pyramids. Sadat was on top of the world. When I began to talk, telling him that the Israelis will never give him anything under pressure, he just laughed as if I were an idiot or a simpleton, and he said to me, 'Ahmed, the world has changed.' "

"Did you ever attack Sadat in your articles?" I asked Baha' pointedly.

"No, never," he replied, "but in my weekly column in *Al-Ahram* I wrote a critical article in the aftermath of the Camp David agreements. It was not critical on the principle—I have always believed we should have an accommodation with Israel," Baha' said quickly. Nonetheless, his article critical of the Camp David agreement was banned and, subsequently, everything that Baha' submitted, including news stories, never saw the printed page. Ahmed Baha' al-Din discovered that he had fallen into disfavor with Sadat through a colleague, Ali al-Gamal, who reported a conversation on the subject with Sadat. "Gamal told me that Sadat asked him, 'Isn't Ahmed on holiday?' So Gamal replied, 'Yes, he's still on holiday.' So Sadat said, 'This means that you don't have to publish his articles.' That was the message. I was never to be published again in Egypt till after Sadat's death."

Baha' looked tired and asked me if we could continue our interview on another day. I agreed and returned a couple of days later.

SEPTEMBER 23

"Mrs. Sadat, though very loved in America, is hated now in Egypt," said Ahmed Baha'. "I believe the gap created by her is due to two factors. The idea of corruption is the first reason. In the final years of Sadat's life, she was reputed to have business dealings. The Sadats were poor and they went out rich. The other thing is that people felt that she was playing a political role, and in Egypt we hate that. This is not America, where a Jimmy Carter and Rosalyn decide on policy matters together. If an Arab leader is known to consult with his wife, people will ask: 'Who has elected her?' Even in Europe, this is the case," he added by way of explanation. "The question we ask ourselves in the Middle East is: Who is the elected or politically responsible person?"

"So, you think Mrs. Sadat was a liability to her husband?" I asked. Baha' shifted in his chair before answering.

"From the point of view of the Egyptian people she was," he replied. "But, in my opinion, she was an asset to him. I am accused of defending her. I knew her very well. I was the only one who defended the idea that her M.A. oral examinations should be televised on our TV in Cairo. I know personally that she worked very hard on her M.A. She has guts and willpower. She is courageous and extremely intelligent. She is quite extraordinary. At the time she had power, beauty, money, and fame—and yet she made the point of appearing on TV as a student, in a student role. At a time when our values have become so materialistic, she wanted to teach people that education is valuable."

"So you are basically not against what she stands for?"

"No, I was never against her. I kept up my relationship with her even after Sadat and I broke off. So I kept on seeing her until his death."

"Why did you continue seeing her even though you were against Sadat?"

"In my opinion, her influence on Sadat was great. Besides, she is a very tactful woman. When Sadat quarreled with someone, she would always try to smooth things over."

"So she was a conduit to Sadat for you?"

"I always let her make the decision about what to tell or not to tell the president," he answered evasively. "She had a tranquilizing effect on him. I admire her very much. But there is a very deep gap between her and the Egyptian people."

"She has also become a target for Islamic fundamentalists, hasn't she? There has been almost a kind of character assassination of Jihan al-Sadat."

"Of course," he replied.

"Is she in danger then?"

"No, I don't think so. Egyptians have a maximum and a minimum way of perceiving things. I don't think a woman would be assassinated."

"But do you think she is seriously deserving of this hatred of her people?"

"Let me say something important. At the time of the making of the peace with Israel, she played mainly to the Western media. To the eyes and ears of the West."

"Wasn't that because she was involved in women's rights on an international level?"

Baha' pondered a little and said, "People perceived her as too Westernized."

"Let's talk a little about what you mean by Westernization and why you think she was too Westernized. Was it her clothes? Her imported wardrobe? Her style? Her jewelry?"

"Yes, to Egyptians this was a comeback of royalty. And besides, look at her friends," he exclaimed. "Imelda Marcos; the Shah's empress. And then kissing Begin in public . . ."

"But didn't he kiss her? What could she do? Slap his face?" I asked.

"But it should not have happened," he replied. "Yesterday, only yesterday, I got a phone call from someone in one of the Arab countries. He asked me, 'What do you think of Peres's visit with Mubarak?' This is a very important man speaking, not a nobody by any means. Anyway I replied and asked this man, 'What about it?' So he says, 'What do you think of this thing which Peres did?' So I replied, 'What thing that Peres did?' 'You mean you didn't see?' he says. So I said, 'No, I did not see.' So the man tells me, 'Peres went and bought a Koran as a gift for Mubarak,' and he says this quite incredulously. 'Didn't you see it on your TV?' 'No,' I said. 'We saw it on our TV,' he replied. 'So what's wrong with that?' I asked the man. 'My brother,' he replied, 'you and I can say, "So what's wrong with that?" But don't you know the people in our countries? A Koran held in the hands of a nonbeliever is no longer pure! Anyway, what does Peres mean by giving a Koran as a gift to Mubarak?' So I replied, 'Maybe it signifies that there is a possibility of coexistence between our two religions.' So the man replied, 'This is our kind of thinking, yours and mine. But what will people say?' So I said, 'But in the Koran, we consider Jews and Christians also as the People of the Book—in other words, as believers.' So he says, 'My friend, in the Islamic street, that man, Peres, is a nonbeliever. Do you know that in the sermons in the mosques this week they speak of nothing else.' So, you see," Baha' added, rounding up his story, "Jihan Sadat broke all our Arab traditions by kissing Begin in public!"

SEPTEMBER 26

Mohammad Sha'lan

Professor of psychology, Al-Azhar University

Mohammad Sha'lan, the ascetic, slender, bearded professor of psychology and psychiatry at the theological school of Al-Azhar, spoke to me at considerable length on Islamic fundamentalism and the desecularization of life in Egypt.

During this meeting, held in his apartment lined with bookshelves and decorated with Koranic inscriptions and handwoven prayer mats, we spoke about Israel. Sha'lan's attitudes and outspokenness about the necessity of dialogue with the Zionist state have made him one of the most controversial figures in the Egyptian public eye. He visited Israel soon after Camp David, when he was in the first group of Egyptian psychiatrists and nonpsychiatrists to engage in the American Psychiatric Association–sponsored meeting of Israeli, Egyptian, and American psychiatrists to "explore the psychological barriers to peace after Sadat's speech." "Of course," he said, "we got stoned by our colleagues and politicians in Egypt, who said that we were abusing psychiatry and psychology, and that we were overreaching ourselves, that we were claiming that all political conflicts are psychological, which is very far from the truth—because half of our team were politicians—on all sides. We made use of these dialogues in order to impress [on everyone] the point that there is no dialogue *without* Palestinian involvement. And this is a point which none of the opposition parties could achieve. *We* achieved a de facto recognition of the Palestinians by our Israeli counterparts, to the point where the Egyptians and the Israelis jointly signed a petition for including Palestinians [in such a dialogue], whereas the American delegation did not take part and did not even understand the significance of our move. But there, you see, we were able to achieve some level of dialogue with the Israelis in which we both had a position against the U.S.A. We were both in favor of the Palestinians."

"I think there are very few Egyptians like yourself who have the courage to dialogue with the Israelis—or who even think along these lines."

"That's very true. That's an unfortunate source of suffering for me. It is not my issue. My issue is: Are we, as an Islamic, third-world culture, able to accept, deal with, tolerate, or talk with Western culture?"

Some say Mohammad Sha'lan is an agent of the CIA. Others, that he is not a true Muslim. When I asked Sha'lan about these accusations, he smiled thinly and his face grew a little white as I said, "I am told that you are being persecuted for your views. Why is that?"

"It's because they have the false impression that I am being supported either by the government or the United States. In both cases, it is not true."

"Could you tell us something about your dialogue with Israel—the fact that you have had encounters with Israelis?"

"The dialogue with Israel originated when I was in the United States and I read many of the expositions and criticisms of the 1967 debacle. One of them was by an American Jew who immigrated to Israel and then came out again. And he said Israel fears peace more than it fears war, that the Israelis were more disturbed by Bourguida's statement that we wanted to have a dialogue with them than by Nasser's statement that we wanted to crush them! And that Israel lives by the threat of war, and that Arabs, if they were able to attack Israel peacefully, could undermine it effectively or just as effectively as by war. And it was a very fascinating viewpoint for me because it was completely opposed to our brainwashing in Egypt: that Israel is our bitter enemy and so on. On another level I was developing internally where I was trying to reintegrate opposites. By opposites I mean my own personal opposites, East vs. West, urban vs. rural, and so on. And Israel represented a polarity for me: Egypt vs. Israel or Zionism vs. Arab nationalism, and that here we are, we have come to a point where we cannot wipe one another out. We have this challenge of how to use this conflict for our mutual development. And I regarded Israel also as the main polarity between East and West, our culture, our Oriental culture and our Western culture. And I took this challenge as a test, a concrete test, for what I was calling for—which is dialogue. But unfortunately, the concrete was misconstrued to mean the abstract, and people regarded me as just interested in promoting peace with Israel and supporting Sadat and Camp David and all this hogwash that they talked about. I am neither for nor against Camp David, neither for nor against Sadat, but the thing is, I am using this opportunity for testing out a hypothesis which is the challenge for our survival: Can we have a dialogue with our enemies? Can we establish bridges with the other? Can we break loose from our own restrictions, our cultural restrictions, our fanaticism, and try to talk to someone who is completely our opposite instead of just negating and refusing?"

"In spite of the fact that the Jews are supposed to be the traditional enemies of Islam?"

"I would say because of the fact.

"The challenge is, Can you dialogue with enemies? The challenge is not can you dialogue with someone who agrees with you. The challenge of a dialogue is to find someone who is completely a polar opposite, who disagrees with you, and to try and reach some modicum of existence because we have to exist with one another—for better or for worse. Furthermore, it is also a test of our own internal tolerance: We have a Christian population and minorities of all sorts. I regard myself as a minority of the population even if I don't have a name called Jewish or Christian. But I am a minority. Unless I am able to live within the atmosphere of tolerance for minorities, of tolerance for the other, then I am subjecting myself to persecution."

"I don't understand your logic."

"I mean, sometimes I find some Christians in Egypt saying: We are also against the Jews. But I reply: Sorry—I am not against the Jews, and I don't go very much for anyone who is against the Jews. And the fact that you are against the Jews doesn't make you any closer to me. It makes you my potential enemy, because just as you are against the Jews, you will be against the Muslims and the Muslims will be against you. What I am talking about is tolerance in its absolute term. It is not tolerance just for any minority. So unless you are ready to accept that, you are condemning yourself, and you are condemning me, because I am a minority.

"So, here it was, a symbol for the cultural-civilizational challenge for Egypt, the Islamic world, the third world in general: Can we develop a dialogue with our enemies? The West is our enemy. They are selling us weapons and letting us kill each other, and they are living off it and they are our enemies and we can't fight them."

"You are talking about the United States in general and not the Soviet Union, I assume?"

"The Soviet Union has changed, even though it sells ideologies. It has become a world power, has become an economic capitalistic nation. It is not a nation of capitalists, but it is not interested in ideology anymore. The way I see it now is that the world is divided into two poles: the pole which supports war and the pole which supports peace.

"War is supported by the Soviet Union as well as by the United States and Europe. And peace is probably, but not yet, supported by Japan. So if we are able as a third-world country to get out of the trap of fighting each other, that's why I think we shouldn't fight Israel—or fight the West either but learn how to deal with them: learn how not to buy their weapons and *not* to fall into the traps that they are making for us, letting us fight civil wars and make revolutions."

"Are we talking specifically here about the U.S. again?"

"I would say the West, including the Soviet Union, because the Soviet Union has ceased to be a preacher of ideology and revolution. Since Trotsky, the curve descends to the state capitalistic society and to the neoimperialistic society. So, what I regard as having been happening is a test of our, Egypt's, traditional role of leading, of taking the initiative. Can we take the initiative in bringing the Arab world, the Islamic world, out of the vicious circle of buying weapons and using these weapons to kill each other instead of really challenging our enemies? We cannot challenge our enemies by fighting them with the weapons that they sell to us! We cannot fight Israel by weapons that are made and sold by the West—it's stupid!

"So logically, let's play judo—they are fighting with weapons? So, we won't use weapons, we'll use something else."

"In other words, dialogue?"

"Unfortunately this position has been misconstrued as being a supporter of peace, of Camp David, of Israel, and so I've been refused many invitations to go to Israel, and I've been cool in accepting any semi-official relations with Israel. Because everything I do is so misunderstood."

"But isn't that self-defeating?"

"I have Israelis as friends, as individuals."

"Can you name a few?"

"Prominent is Shimon Shamir, who is the director of the Academic Center. He is very broadminded, tolerant, and very understanding."

"Which academic center are you referring to?"

"The Academic Center in Cairo."

"I didn't even know such an institution existed," I said, laughing to hide my embarrassment.

"You see, this is one of the funny things," said Sha'lan, smiling. "The agreement at Camp David was to have two academic centers, one in Israel and one in Cairo. Now, they have one here. Why don't we have one there? We are saying, Not until the Palestinians get their rights. What has this got to do with it? They [the Israelis] are inviting us to come and study the enemy—they're inviting you, according to this agreement. And you are punishing yourself. Anyway, my friends include Yaron Hariv, Hak Segeu, people who are in the Intelligence Service—they are all army people."

"Aren't you fearful of having such friends in Cairo? I mean maybe they will think you too are an agent?"

"No, no. The government still is dealing with Israelis, so they can't jail me for something they are doing."

"You were never interrogated by the Intelligence Service in Cairo?"

"No, no. Also, my personal relationship with members of the government is okay. On a personal level, I know many people who are in responsible positions, and they trust my judgment, they trust my sincerity, although they do receive a lot of complaints that I am a spy, yet they know it's not true. And that saves me. I am not supported by the government, but I am supported by individuals within the government. But I am being harassed within the university administration."

"Is it or isn't it possible then to dialogue with Israel and with Western culture?" I asked him, now wishing to return to the original theme of the interview. He was breathless from his long speech but still totally sincere, involved, and enthusiastic as he began his reply.

"The answer that the Saudis have given us is that we wear our veil, but once we get into our private homes we enjoy everything that is Western—furniture, drink, food, morality—all is Western. So what's the point? We are not integrating. We are, in fact, being subdued by Western values in the apparent futile gesture of rejecting those values. The Saudis are the most pro-American, culturally and politically, in the whole Muslim world."

"And America is supporting the Saudi regime, and that is one of the sources of Islamic fundamentalism?"

"Yes, inadvertently, America *is* responsible for Islamic fundamentalism in the Islamic world—by supporting the Saudis or those who are directly or indirectly supporting such movements. They are the safeguards of Islam and they don't want anyone else to speak about Islam. So, within their own culture, they are against fundamentalism and revolution. But outside their own culture they are playing a very dangerous game."

"You mean promoting Islamic fundamentalism in other countries—like Egypt for instance?"

"Yes. They are afraid lest Egypt become a contender for the oil wells of Saudi Arabia so they finance prominent Islamic media figures who serve to interpret Islam in a nonpolitical way, supporting conservative regimes."

"Our military regime?"

"Yes."

"What would happen if we did have an Islamic revolution in Egypt?"

"An Islamic revolution in Egypt would be so unstable that it must find an external enemy—like Iran is fighting Iraq. And since we cannot fight Israel and win, then we must find someone else to fight a protracted fight that will keep the internal regime *proper*, and that would be either Saudi Arabia or Libya. So, it is not in the interest of Saudi Arabia that an Islamic regime takes over in Egypt—because it will seek them, the Saudis, out as the nontrue Muslims and fight them instead of Israel.

"On the other hand, the Saudis support the Islamic fundamentalist wave in Egypt in order to keep the regime weak—always being threatened by Islamic fundamentalism and always seeking the economic support of the Saudis or even their moral support against the fundamentalists. They want Egypt to remain divided, split, and weak."

"And this, in your opinion, is the desire of the U.S. as well?"

"Exactly. Probably it is the planning of the U.S. Such a strategy may be the formulation of the CIA and executed by the Saudis. That is why, if you talk to an official Saudi, they will deny their support for such movements, they will express only love for Egypt, but in fact it is against their interest as a royal regime to love Egypt."

"It is not in the interest of the United States to love Egypt either?" I asked facetiously.

"Yes. Well, the U.S.A. would prefer to have three slaves—Egypt, Israel, and Saudi Arabia, rather than one slave who can be a Spartacus and lead the Arab-Islamic third world.

"And who would that Spartacus be?"

"Egypt. Egypt is the Spartacus of the third world. It's the poor country that has enough dignity to say no—but also has enough slyness to bow, to stoop to conquer, so the U.S. does not trust Egypt."

Nonetheless, Sha'lan believes that everyone covets Egypt—but they all want a weak Egypt. When I asked him about Egypt's dependency on the U.S. for wheat, for the very bread it eats, he said, "Sure, it's like giving someone glucose injections to keep them alive, but you are not teaching them how to eat, plant food, feed themselves."

"What about the population explosion?" I asked him.

He obviously skimmed over that and said that an inherent

weakness is that we are not telling the U.S. we don't want fish; we want a rod and a hook and we want to learn how to fish.

SEPTEMBER 30

I found Sha'lan to be one of the most daring and the most perceptive of all those who spoke on Islam and the role it plays in the Middle East today. Later when I saw him again, his thin ascetic beard had grown as bushy as a sheikh's. I wondered: Is he also changing like the chameleon? But I never asked him that. Instead, I said, "As we were talking, you mentioned that your colleagues are repressed. Other psychologists are repressed? What did you mean by that?" I asked him, starting up my tape recorder.

"Well. What's happening here is that people are not cohesive—they don't feel that they belong to a group that has a goal or a challenge that they are facing together. But really Egyptian society has this quality. Throughout history it has been cohesive, it has its traditions, unity, but I think what we are going through now is a very severe cultural crisis. And I think that the main reason is that the oil money has attracted the allegiance of many people from all classes, so people don't really feel they belong to this society. They belong to whoever pays them, gives them a good salary. So what we have now is a lack of a goal, a lack of leadership, a lack of vision that unites the nation."

"When do you think this disintegration started?"

"I think it started with the infitah [Sadat's open-door economic policy]."

"I see you were not an advocate of Sadat's. You were against his policies?"

"No, I am not for or against because I see it as a natural development. It started after 1967, so I can't say it's Sadat's invention. But he took it over from Nasser, and it had to happen, and I think it was inevitable that Nasser had either to change or to die. But he couldn't continue to be Nasser after 1967. He was dead as an ideological figure. Psychologically."

"Sadat's open-door policy was a reaction to Nasser's closed-door policy and, therefore, it was a necessary step in that direction . . . or that process.

"I look at it as dialectical history. If you go too far in one way and it doesn't work, it can't work because too far means beyond the means of reality."

"But now the pendulum is swinging back again in one direction. Is the door being closed again in Egypt?"

"I think it is. It can never go back. We can never go back to Nasser. But we are swinging away from the extreme open door of Sadat. And it's necessary because you can't develop when you are still a newborn person in a society with all the doors so wide open that anyone can affect you. Some protection is necessary. Not much; too much will make us like we were in the Nasser period. We will become so isolated that we become deluded about our own strength, and we will reach out for goals which we cannot achieve."

"Let's go back to this observation about the feeling of being repressed in Egypt," I said. "I myself have this feeling since I've come back here. I feel this repression. Naturally when one comes from America to Egypt, there is a big cultural change. But the impression is more political. I feel that ordinary people are afraid to *speak out.* People are actually afraid to speak about many subjects, e.g., religion. I know what a brave person you are, even though you are a religious person. Could you comment a little about that?"

"Yes, I think the difference between the repression in Nasser's time and the present time is that in Nasser's time it was a centralized oppression. It was the government that curtailed freedom."

"And now it's a built-in repression?"

"Now, it's built into the social matrix itself."

"What do you mean by that?"

"I mean that the masses have become more fanatic and dictatorial than the government itself."

"You mean they have become totalitarianistic—in that sense?"

"Yes. It's more in the direction of religious fanaticism. Sadat may have facilitated the religious groups in order to counteract the Nasserite socialist groups and the Communists, but in doing so he unleashed a ghost or a *jinni* which he could not control. These religious fanatics, they killed him, and now they are killing the rest of the elite of society."

"So that's what you mean by repression—the repression of intellectuals. In other words, there is a built-in conservatism in this country. People are censoring themselves, making themselves put on a religious garb, not only physically, as in the case of women, but also psychologically—is this what you are saying?"

"Very much so. I think religion has been abused in a way that has not happened in the recent past. If you take the 'Ikhwan' [Muslim Brotherhood] and look at their writings in the 1930s and 1940s and 1950s and then compare this with the writings of the so-called jama'at [radical groups], there is a fantastic difference. What people are writing now, the so-called modern Islamic groups, it's almost delusionary."

"You mean that Jama'at al-Islamiya, which are the much more radical or splinter groups that sprang out of the Muslim Brotherhood, that they distorted Islam?"

"Very much so. It's almost a level of delusions. The idea, for example, of regarding Islam as one and by one they mean 'my one, my vision.' And it reaches comic extents because they have more fights among themselves than they would have between them as a group and the rest of society. Because each one thinks he knows Islam best."

"But when you talk about Islamic movements and the flaws of the Islamic movements in Egyptian society at this moment, at this very moment, are we speaking about the Muslim Brotherhood or the radicals?"

"We are speaking about the Jama'at as the potential disruptive force. The Muslim Brotherhood, no doubt, remains the more organized, the more rational, and the more open—it's more on the *surface.* But the other groups, these so-called Jama'at al-Islamiya, they are like the first spark. They can ignite a revolution. But I don't think they have the organization or the clarity of thought to take over the government."

"You don't think that these groups have infiltrated many aspects of Egyptian social and political life? I have been talking to a lot of people who seem to think they have . . . For instance, they have taken over the syndicates, they have taken over the opposition parties, and they have taken over the student unions on campus. They are very powerful. For instance, on the campus of Assiut University at this moment, and I hear reports of clashes between them and the security police . . ."

"Yes. However, there is also another catch. The regime itself is infiltrated."

"By the Muslim groups—the Islamists?"

"Yes. So we have them in the government party, the NSP. We have them in all the parties, as you mentioned, except the left. But the Progressive Party, the left, is also trying to absorb them."

"And in spite of their incredible infiltration, plus their economic power, you don't think that the Islamic groups are going to win politically?"

"When you speak about political winning, you need a political organization, which they don't have. The only organization is the Muslim Brotherhood, and all the other organizations are small—what they call the grape concept—so they are small cells connected by small strings, so there is no big trunk. So there is no way, now, that they can take over power. They can overthrow a government quite easily."

"But you say they can overthrow the government. That's quite a statement. Do they have the power within the army or the police? Or do they have violent means you know of?"

"No. It's because the government is weak. So all you need is something like the Security Forces riot and they will know how to infiltrate and ignite everybody. The situation is not unripe."

"Is there leadership among them?"

"No."

"But couldn't they find a Khomeini-like leader among the popular religious figures like Sheikh Kishk, or Salama Hafez, or even Metwalli Chaarawi?"

"No, I think all the leaders you mentioned are completely discredited by the public. Hafez Salama and Sabri Islamil and Sheikh Kishk, they are regarded as comedians, really. They are not politicians."

"You mean the person who comes into power should be a politician. But I thought Khomeini thought he should be a spiritual leader."

"Yes, but Khomeini is a politician—a very pragmatic politician, a very crafty, sly politician. We don't have that. Our popular spiritual leaders like Chaarawi are not political. Those who are political, like Sheikh Kishk, don't have enough political credibility on their side. They are not regarded as sophisticated politicians whom we can trust to lead the country."

"But maybe this political figure exists, and he's underground, and we don't know him."

"Well, I have a theory about these figures: They are not individuals. They are individuals in a group. So if the group doesn't exist, they cannot exist. I think if you have the atmosphere that will produce a Napoleon or Hitler, then he will surface . . ."

"But do you think this kind of neo-fascist atmosphere does exist now?"

"Yes, but fortunately or unfortunately it doesn't have the clarity of thought, the ideology that can make it autonomous. There isn't a clear-cut Islamic ideology for politics. Iran is trying to develop such a political ideology. The credit goes to the non-Khomeini factions—the mujahhidin al-Khalq—who theorize Islam in a way that made it complete with Marxism because of the sophistication of their thinking. And yet, now they are being persecuted very badly by Khomeini. So we [in Egypt] don't have that even. The atmosphere is not ripe for an Islamic revolution. It may be right for Islamic chaos—overthrowing the government Islamically. My hunch is that if we do have an Islamic revolution, it will be more co-opted by an army group. Somebody from the army will say: 'I am the Muslim. I will take over and all Muslims listen to me, and the one who doesn't listen to me is not a Muslim.' This is the most likely scenario."

"And the United States will back it, of course?"

"Yes. It will most certainly back it, unfortunately."

"I agree with you completely about the unfortunate business. Do you think the U.S. has played a discernible or indiscernible role in promoting Islamic fundamentalism?"

"Yes, I think so. Although in the second line of diplomacy in the U.S., they are aware of the mistake. The leadership, like the president, the White House, is unaware of this mistake. But when you talk to people in the embassy or people who are second-line diplomats, they are people who think that the left wing in Egypt is who they should deal with and they talk with the left wing more."

"But they are not the policymakers. The policymakers are the ones who helped to kindle this fire, don't you think?"

"Yes, yes."

"I think we both agree that the U.S. has played a very considerable role in promoting fundamentalism in the area, the entire area, in addition to Iran, of course. Would you care to comment on this devious role that the U.S. is playing?"

"Well, if you start from the gross political level, the fact that the U.S. supports Saudi Arabia is *the* key, I think, to what you are talking about. Because Saudi Arabian policy is designed also more or less implicitly with support from the United States. But it isolates Egypt for fear that a strong, hungry Egypt can ask for a bigger share in the oil revenues. We are a growing population, we are a hungry population, we are relatively efficient. We can be violent and aggressive, so for Saudi Arabia and, therefore, for other similar states, Egypt is a dangerous country. So America, in supporting this Saudi Arabian game, is really indirectly supporting Islamic fundamentalism. Because the Saudi regime also depends on this false Islam, which has no real political ideology behind it and uses the so-called sharia only in the criminological sense. They really don't care about adultery or thieves. They care about political opposition. So, in the name of Islam, they suppress any differences. Anybody who differs with them is against Islam."

"Therefore this 'false' Islam is a political system?"

"It is. But it does not claim to be a political system and does not lend itself to political discussion. . . . In its politics, it has a blind spot. So nobody in Saudi Arabia discusses whether the rulership in Islam should be hereditary or should be restricted to a family or a tribe. Although it is completely against Islamic tradition, the whole quarrel in Islam from the very beginning was that they did not give the caliphate to Ali. The Shi'ites think they should have because he is a relative of the Prophet, and the Sunnis, who carried the essential spirit of Islam, said, No, it's the most efficient ruler who should rule, and Abou-Bakr is more efficient than Ali. In the view of many people, Muawiya, whom we regard as an opportunist or a pragmatist, had many good points. He was able to make things work. None of the four caliphs were able to do as well as he did. So the question has not been discussed in Saudi Arabia: Should we have kings? Islam is against kings."

"I thought it was against despotism."

"Against despotism and against rich people. These things are not discussed in Saudi Arabia. There are socialist principles in Islam, as for example, the wealth that is usable by everybody is common property: water, grass [camels drank water and ate grass]. So if you have water in your private grass and someone trespasses, he is not trespassing. Water is common property, and therefore he is not stealing when he intrudes upon you to get it. Now, you have something like oil in Saudi Arabia—it belongs to the king. It's his property."

"All of the oil of the kingdom is a concession of the royal family?"

"Yes. In effect it is his property. Legally, some of it is his property and the other is the state's. You have a very funny situation: There is a price for electricity in Saudi Arabia. And so the people got angry and the king comes out on television and says: I will contribute from my money to pay the difference so you don't have to pay extra for electricity. Imagine a king helps the state from his own money—he gives charity to the state! So nobody discusses this thing. Should the oil belong to the family, to the person, or is it the property of all the Muslims? It should be the property of the Islamic nation."

"What do you mean by the nation?"

"The nation . . . countries where there is a majority of Muslims."

"It should be distributed to all these nations?"

"Yes, yes."

"If you didn't have a Saudi monarchy and if you didn't have America backing it?"

"So this is where I regard America responsible indirectly for Islamic and religious fundamentalist movements in this area."

"Why do you think America props up this monarchy with the feudal system you have described?"

"Apparently they think it's secure enough, like they thought the Shah's regime was secure enough. Secure enough on account of being a very autocratic, domineering regime. So America doesn't want to take risks by supporting the opposition. They supported Marcos, the Shah. That's how they think. Americans don't yet have a political ideology that can be attractive to the masses. So what they end up doing is propping up regimes."

"And the Soviets?"

"The Chinese and the Soviets don't support regimes. They support Communist parties, left-wing parties. They support the masses sometimes. If you look in the streets and ask people, believe me, you would hear such stupid things as: Why don't we give bases to America so that we can get some money?"

"Is this what the common man is saying in Egypt?"

"Yes, the common man. They wouldn't mind selling out to America. Not that they are traitors. The common man or woman in Egypt is very sincere but feels that we are in the pockets of America so we might as well make some more money out of it."

"When you say that we are in the pockets of America, are you saying that you are disapproving of the fact that we are dependent on the U.S.?"

"Certainly."

"Even for our economic survival?"

"Certainly. I am speaking from Egyptian interests but also from American interests. If I were an American, I wouldn't like someone to be so dependent on me."

"How is the backing of the Saudi regime responsible for Islamic fundamentalism? Isn't that what you were saying?"

"It's one factor. It's both direct and indirect. I had the chance to talk to some responsible person in Saudi, and he said, 'We don't support fanatics. We don't like them, they are dangerous to us.' But that's the overt policy. What I am saying is that underneath, unconsciously, knowing it or not knowing, either its secret service knows it and the people don't or maybe nobody knows it but still they are doing it. They *are* supporting fundamentalism indirectly. Just by being there."

"Then it's basically a fundamentalist regime—is that what you are saying?"

"They pay girls in Saudi Arabia to wear the hijab."

"And in Egypt, too?"

"And in Egypt. I don't know if we get the money from the Saudis directly or indirectly; if they do get it directly, it's via people who work in Saudi Arabia, Muslim Brothers who support their equivalents here. And they pay and they support these students. Their fear is communism. They [the Saudis] think that by spreading Islam, the same philosophy that Sadat had, they would counteract the Communists. And by so doing, by counteracting the left and the Communists, they are reinforcing their own reactionary regime."

"What use is it to the Saudis to support it outside their own country?"

"Two uses: It gives them political support—'our system is the system.' Saudis don't look forward to a Nasser in Egypt anymore because the leader in Egypt follows the people. In other words, the Saudi regime would feel morally supported and politically supported by not having socialist regimes around and by not having charismatic leaders of a Nasser type. I think they have learned a lesson twice: one time, during the Mohammed Ali period, and the second time, when Nasser supported the republican rebels in Yemen. He really threatened them. Since then they are very frightened of a strong Egypt. And the only way they can overcome Egypt ideologically is by being the promoters of Islam in the Islamic world. One way to do it is to spread this kind of Islamic ideology into Egypt, an ideology which is really a very superficial school of Islamic thinking with no leftist thought in it. So that's on the one hand. No Nasserism, no nationalism, no socialism. On the other hand, they are weakening the Egyptian regime."

"How?"

"They have a very funny relationship with the Egyptian regime. They don't want it to fall because they don't want an Islamic regime. Believe me, if we had an Islamic government in Egypt, my prediction is that we would have a war, either with Saudi Arabia or with Libya or with both. And the sequence of events will be as follows: You have an Islamic revolutionary-type government. But they are so split up against each other, they want to kill each other. The only way that they can make community is to have an external enemy, like Khomeini did with Iraq. In order to have an external enemy, they have to have someone who will not crush them in six days, like Israel did—so it's either Saudi Arabia or Libya. And the excuse is there: The Saudis are our biggest competitors in Islam, and they are spoiling Islam. So we have to unite our forces and make a good Islamic nation before we fight Israel. This is what the Iranians are saying. They claim that they are against Israel and Zionism, and yet they are buying from Israel. And their known enemy is Iraq, Saddam Hussein, and next to him, it's Egypt, Saudi Arabia, and the rest of the

Arab countries. So the Saudis don't want an Islamic regime in Egypt. They simply want an Islamic *threat* to the present regime in Egypt."

"And what's your prognosis?"

"Well, rationally the prognosis seems bad. We have a weak government, we have a difficult economic situation, and we have a growing population. But there's something funny about Egypt. . . ."

"Please don't give me that mystical optimism!" I said, almost losing my patience.

"Either I'm optimistic, or I commit suicide," he answered serenely.

"You could leave the country, leave Egypt. . . ."

"That would be suicide for me," he said with finality.

Later, as I made my way through a busy street filled with jostling people, sweating faces, cigarette stalls glaring Marlboro, donkey carts, stray cats, screeching brakes announcing a BMW or a Mercedes, I thanked my lucky stars that I didn't have to live in this urban conglomerate nightmare of a city.

But then Connecticut flashed through my mind. The cleanliness, the emptiness in people's faces, the manicured lawns and clean roads, the bleak, sunless days. . . . My heart sank. I looked up. A bedraggled girl with outstretched hand—"baksheesh"—smiled in my direction. Her smile was filled with the warmth of her sun-baked skin and reddened lips. At that moment as I placed the coins in her hands, I knew, with certainty, that leaving Egypt had been suicide for me. She, at least, needed me.

OCTOBER 1986

OCTOBER 1

Dr. Mustapha Khalil

Prime Minister, 1977–1981

"Stability in Egypt and the rest of the area is as important to us here as it is to the West." We were sitting in a magnificent office in the Arab-African Bank in the center of Cairo. The speaker was Mustapha Khalil, Egypt's prime minister during the Sadat years, and now a powerful member of the ruling National Democratic Party.

"I thought it was in the interest of the U.S. to destabilize the area in order to keep Communist influence out," I said. "For they say that Islamic fundamentalism is being nourished by the U.S. in order to destabilize the area."

"This could never be a viable policy," he replied. "We can never accept such fundamentalism because in Sunni Islam, there are no imams—no intermediaries between the Muslim and his God. Political leadership must be in the hands of the politicians and not with religious leaders. We insist on secular leadership. There will never be a rift such as exists between Muslims and Christians in Lebanon."

"So you are against the application of sharia law in Egypt?"

"No, I didn't say that," he replied. "I am saying that I am opposed to political leadership by the religious factions. We already have sharia law. Ninety-nine percent of our laws stem from sharia law. But we cannot go any further. Otherwise we will find ourselves living in tents, riding camels. We Egyptians reject this lifestyle completely."

"Do you have any reservations at all about the U.S. role in the Middle East?" I asked him now. At this point a Nubian clerk, dressed in an immaculate white jacket, opened the door and put a silver tray with lemonades on the table before us. The minister politely offered me one and then resumed the interview. "We would like the U.S. not to be so biased toward Israel. It should be more neutral. Second, American weapons were being used in the Israeli invasion of Lebanon, and we cannot imagine that America can go on backing Israel in its use of military force in the Arab world. We don't believe in terrorism, but we also don't believe in counterterrorism."

Khalil, who has a Ph.D. in engineering from the University of Illinois in Urbana, is a pragmatic man. He likes to see solutions to problems. Maybe that's why he decided to accompany Sadat to Jerusalem. Upon his return from Jerusalem, Sadat offered him the post of prime minister of Egypt. Khalil would like to see Egypt develop along scientific and technological lines. He has no problem with using Western methods.

Khalil impressed me because among other things he was the first leader to speak, or even cite, the population problem, and he said it was the number one economic problem: How can we go on increasing at the level of 1,400,000 a year and still develop economically?

Later, during the taxi ride home, I asked the driver what he thought of America. And the peace with Israel. "America is a superpower with vested interests. It's here not because it likes us, but because it has interests. As for the Israelis—what's one embassy more or less? Nobody wants to go to war anyway. Peace is better. Let's keep the peace."

As I write this I can count five pyramids in the distance, and I think of Mustapha Khalil's words: Egypt has always and will always play an important role in world civilization. Critical of the Islamic movement, he said that Egypt belongs to the international world and stressed that it will go on as such. Egyptians are religious but not fanatic—these were some of the words which cheered me up as I left the interview, wondering why there were not many more men like him in our beloved country.

OCTOBER 2

I have been so sick—one of those viruses or influenzas which assault your knees, your arms, and your throat—the kind of virus which I seem to pick up only in my home country. For a while I couldn't swallow and was feverish. Anyway I couldn't write. I remember keeping an appointment with Egypt's former vice president, Zakaria Muheiddin, the number two man after Nasser. It was absolutely fascinating, but I did not think it wise to record it. Then, nothingness, except a lot of reading. What has left an indelible mark on my imagination is Dostoyevsky's *The House of the Dead*, about a nobleman who survived ten years of isolation in a Siberian prison camp.

Alexander Petravich, Dostoyevsky's hero, tells how mental suffering causes much more anguish than physical suffering. They were not allowed to read in prison, and he felt alienated even from his fellow prisoners, who continued to regard him as a nobleman and treat him as an outsider.

OCTOBER 3

The noon sermon that was televised this Friday came from the mosque of Heliopolis Armed Forces club and was attended by the minister of defense, Abdel Halim Abou-Ghazzala. They say in Cairo that he is America's man. The sermon invoked the worshipers—all men—to have faith in their government and in their armed forces.

Today someone tried to drown a scraggy brown dog by tying it to a long rope and throwing it into the river. Screaming for its life, the dog escaped. "Three people tried to drown it," the guards told me as I intervened. "It's a bad dog, it bites."

"Let it alone," I pleaded. "It will live again." The dog, though wet and petrified, looked well enough. Sure enough, a few seconds later, it ran off. "You see," I told them. "God be with you." They smiled. But I had never seen such terror in a living creature as in that poor dog's eyes.

We need a strong army. Here's why, according to Makram M. Ahmad in *Al-Musawar*.

What would happen if Iran won the Gulf war? "Don't forget," he writes, "the superpowers want an *unstable* Middle East, because that is the only way they can control their spheres of influence here. Meanwhile, the Arabs are disunited. Israel wants to hang onto southern Lebanon; Qaddafi threatens to invade Egypt and to spread terrorism. There is the terrorism practiced under the guise of a cause, such as Palestinian terrorism, or in the name of religion, such as Khomeini's terrorism, or there is the terrorism that comes from nowhere but which finds itself in the instability of the Middle East. Egypt needs a strong army in order to defend itself from the possibility of its catching fire from all those neighboring fires. What would happen if Iran won the Gulf war?" he asks. But he has no ready answer. "What would happen if Israel decided to invade Egypt again?" On this he does have an opinion. "If the Israelis think that the Egyptians conceive peace as a state of lethargy without taking into account the rights of other [Arabs], then they are very much mistaken. What would happen if Qaddafi got a sudden urge to invade Egypt in order to bolster his egomania?

"In spite of the crucial importance of the army, yet Egypt's military budget has decreased from 1971 *from two billion four hundred million pounds a year to one billion 820 million,"* writes Makram. "We are not even as bad as Israel in this respect," he concludes.

OCTOBER 5

Perhaps it's difficult for a Western reader to imagine this sight: about 156 young men in blue overalls crowded into a cage, literally a cage complete with iron bars. The kind which is used in zoos for lions and tigers. Yet there are 156 human spirits in the space I saw today in the courthouse at Abassia. These young men, conscripts who form a special unit called the Security Force, originated by Sadat to protect him, are recruited from the countryside for three-year service stints at a salary of a couple of dollars a month. They are peasants, and most of them are illiterate. Last January, they heard a rumor that their conscription would last for four instead of three years. They rioted, burning and looting choice hotels and tourist sites all over the city. The army intervened, and after three days of almost civil chaos, they were rounded up and order was restored.

A press card, I discovered, is a wonderful thing. It got me into that courthouse, past scores of policemen and plainclothesmen. I even got to interview one of the young men. He said he was innocent, that he had gone straight from his village, where he had been on leave, to the Cairo International Airport, where he was on duty, and that he had been picked up on the way there by the army and jailed. He said prison conditions were dreadful and accepted a cigarette from me. Before giving it to him, I had to ask the permission of a young, muscular man who was wearing civilian clothes and who had decided to hover over me.

After the session—the case postponed to another date a month hence—I asked to interview the judges. They received me in their chambers. One of them was reading a newspaper; the other two, men in their fifties and sixties, looked bored and crowded in that small, bare, gray room with nothing but a wooden table and chairs in it. I asked if this was a political case. One of the judges, the one in the center—that's always the key one—looked up at me sharply and ignored my question. Then I asked when the sentencing would be. These poor men had been in there for eight months. The judge replied by saying that he couldn't tell because their *papers* (the investigations) had to be photocopied! Why was that taking so long? I asked. He informed me that there were about two hundred and fifty cases and about five thousand pages for each case. All in all, about three million pages to be photocopied. And that would take time, he said.

As I left their chambers, I told myself, "It's the perfect bureaucratic excuse to keep them in." Maybe it was true. Things do take a long time to get done in Egypt. But then, why were they not released until the documents were photocopied, since they had not yet been charged formally? "Because we have martial law," a lawyer told me outside when I asked him that question. "We have martial law or emergency laws in Egypt, which means that you or I or anyone can be arrested at any moment, without being charged, and thrown into jail."

"But that's impossible," I said almost incredulously.

"Well, they have to charge you with rioting or with having a political meeting or with destruction of public property or possession of narcotics and that's it."

As I drove home, I remembered the face of the young conscript who was standing just behind the young man who took my cigarette. It was yellow. My people are olive-skinned, so it's difficult to get *yellow*—but his face was yellow. With fear, I suppose. I shall never forget that face. It was an intelligent face, maybe the face of an organizer, a militant, a revolutionary. I can't tell, because he wouldn't open his mouth, even though our eyes had met. His eyes seemed to tell me, I know the likes of you. I was wearing a mauve polyester jumpsuit, but that wasn't it. He could tell my background. But there was, astonishingly enough, no bitterness or resentment in his eyes. Only determination.

The other thing which stayed with me was the social discrepancy between the judges, the police, the lawyers, and the relatives of the conscripts in that courtroom. It was the difference between the rich and the poor, the bourgeois and the proletarian.

When I got to Maadi, I made my way to the Maadi Hotel, a beautiful and luxurious place with an American-style cafeteria. I needed a meal and took my place unthinkingly in the semicrowded, orange-painted dining room. Next to me a group of European businessmen, hosted by some Egyptians, were devouring a meal of steak, vegetables, saffroned rice, fried potatoes, and a mixed green salad. I ordered some cheese and bread and had a difficult time getting through that.

Later that evening, I took my car to be washed and waxed. The owner of the gas station, a big, dark-skinned man, burly, forties, with horn-rimmed glasses, greeted me effusively. We began to chat as I waited for the car, with me asking a lot of questions. He asked me finally why I was asking so many questions. I showed him my press card. He then showed me his I.D. card. He was a major in the Egyptian Intelligence Service! I could have bitten my tongue. I felt scared. He had managed to find out where I live and though he was very friendly, even gave me a discount, he issued a warning: Do not talk to strangers about politics. But I am *press,* I reiterated feebly. Even so, he answered. Everybody is under surveillance. Times are different now. Incorrigibly, I asked him if he had any work to do in our quiet suburb by the Nile, Maadi. Were there any fundamentalists here? Of course not, he said. The only trouble with Maadi was that the Israeli ambassador lived there. People don't like the Israelis, he said. Everyone has someone who has died on the front—in all those wars—so people don't forget that easily.

OCTOBER 6

Nabil al-'Arabi

Egyptian ambassador to the United Nations

I went over to the Ministry of Foreign Affairs to see my friend Ambassador Nabil al-'Arabi, who was our ambassador to the United Nations in New York, and who is the Egyptian representative at the Taba talks with Israel. Security at the ministry was minimal, and I made my way up in the elevator to his modest office without any fuss. He received me warmly. He had given Gloria Steinem her visa to visit Egypt in 1979 and now he was asking about her. "She is well, still fighting," I said in reply.

"What for?" he exclaimed. "Women have all their rights." We both laughed and then he invited me to dinner later that week at his home in Heliopolis.

He said the Israelis had absolutely no claim to Taba. Al-'Arabi is a man of the world, besides being your quintessential charming Arab male. He is about fifty, plays tennis every day.

OCTOBER 8

As I dressed for my first dinner invitation since my arrival, I watched our prime minister, Ali Loutfi, on TV. He said that Egypt had lost thousands of millions of dollars because of the lowering of oil prices and also because of the reduction of the revenues coming into the country from workers in the Arab countries. Then he mentioned the population problem and the fact that we increase at the rate of 1,400,000 a year. He suggested that we should increase our productivity but said nothing about birth control!

Heliopolis sprawls out into the desert and is Cairo's largest suburb. Ambassador al-'Arabi lived in a medium-sized, beige building in a chic, middle-class area of that suburb. The apartment house overlooked a huge Japanese-style villa and was built in the nineteenth century by a Belgian called the Baron Empain. A Nubian waiter ushered me into one of the most tasteful interiors I have ever been in. Turkish and Persian rugs on the floor, a mirror spanning the whole room, Indian cushions strewn on the floor, bronze and silver objets d'art and little Indian statuettes, a wood-paneled bookcase, glass tables, oil paintings by Egyptian artists, and the most beautiful bowl of Egyptian lilies were just some of the features of that room, which took my breath away. In this city of poverty and deprivation, this was a treat for sore eyes. I realized, as I sank into a long couch, that many Egyptians lived in this style. But not enough. Maybe I was moving in the wrong circles, I thought to myself wistfully as I sipped the scotch that had been brought in for me. Maybe I was depressed and overworked and overzealous to see the injustice.

Then the guests arrived, healthy, tanned diplomats and Egyptians who were obviously enjoying their lives in Cairo. A cool desert breeze made its way from the open terrace into the room and mingled with the smell of the lilies and women's perfumes. The conversation was quiet, discreet; the women wore the latest European fashions, and even diamonds and emeralds. The ambassador's wife wore a short, low-cut silk dress and waved her long hair about and smiled from a suntanned face. A lean French woman in an organza dress swished by, while an Italian diplomat displayed his expensive, gray-striped custom-made suit.

Later, at the seated dinner in the peach-colored dining room decorated with oriental rugs and more paintings and candlelight, I made small talk with a French diplomat who posed as the latest authority on Islamic fundamentalism. "The whole thing is completely under control," he informed me. "The government is stable." Across the table, the wife of an American—Robert Sherman, a political officer—talked with great enthusiasm about feminists and feminism. The ambassador's wife kept looking in my direction, but I said nothing. Then there were speeches after dinner, with crystal glasses of imported wine being clinked amid murmured compliments and gentle laughter.

After dinner, coffee and tea, served Arabian style, in small glasses. If you wanted it, you could also have a liqueur, or a Courvoisier. People sat around in groups talking about Peres and the summit recently held in Alexandria. Sherman volunteered the remark that Peres had just given an interview in Paris where he had said that a confederation of Jordan, Palestinians, and Israel should be formed on the West Bank. Sherman thought it was a statement which reflected "vision." But the others didn't agree with him; even a British diplomat said that it might be acceptable to the Americans but it would not be acceptable to the Palestinians.

"I've read your book," said Mrs. Sherman to me, almost furtively, at the end of the evening. But she made no comment about it. I didn't mind. I was enjoying myself too much.

Later I learned that al-'Arabi is also the head of the Egyptian team to the Taba negotiations over that strip of six miles of land which is the source of a border dispute between Egypt and Israel—a dispute which has led to the breakdown of diplomatic relations between the two countries and which will be arbitrated in Geneva in September. Ambassador al-'Arabi will be representing Egypt throughout the Taba arbitration. He was also the Egyptian ambassador to India and the representative to the United Nations in New York.

During the Camp David negotiations, he was the Egyptian legal advisor to President Sadat. He took part in all the Egyptian-Israeli negotiations starting in December 1973 through disengagement talks with Israel in 1974 and 1975, and he also took part in the negotiations that followed President Sadat's visit to Jerusalem in 1977, up to Camp David in September 1978.

When I interviewed him a few days later in the ministry, I sensed in him deep-seated anger toward the Israelis. Did he have any reservations about the peace with Israel, I asked him tactfully. He admitted that he did have reservations. "At Camp David everyone recognized that it would not be possible to have a complete deal on the Palestinian side, in the absence of the Palestinians. So the Camp David framework for the Palestinians was only a transitional period. And it was *not* clarified well. It did require *acceptance* by Palestinians and Jordanians who were not there."

"I believe the talks on autonomy failed completely, didn't they?"

"Yes, and I think it useless to try to resolve them."

"Then how will Palestinian autonomy come about?"

"Autonomy is not the issue; we are talking about self-determination and that should be discussed in an international conference where everyone can sit and sort out their problems. The idea of such a conference has been accepted by both the United States and the Soviet Union in U.N. Resolution 338. The idea of a peace conference has also been accepted by Peres."

"But was the peace treaty good for Egypt if one set aside the Palestinian issue?" I asked.

"The peace treaty is being followed in letter and spirit I think by both sides in the bilateral sense. In the global sense, and the regional sense, I do not think that Israel has carried out its obligations because we entered into peace with Israel not as a separate peace. We thought that there would be other attempts at peace in the area," he replied curtly.

The interview then shifted to President Mubarak. When I asked Ambassador al-'Arabi whether our Egyptian president had reversed Sadat's policies in Egypt, he became extremely angry, saying that it was not President Sadat's intention to make a separate deal with Israel. Egyptians, he said, have now become "doubtful" of Israeli intentions for those reasons. "First of all, just after Camp David, Egypt agreed with President Carter that what was required from Israel was to stop creating new settlements as long as there were negotiations for peace. But Prime Minister Begin began to establish new settlements, and he got into a row with President Carter, who gave in to Prime Minister Begin.

"Second, when the autonomy talks started, they were meant to prepare the way for the participation of the Palestinians, but both Prime Minister Begin and the Israeli government reversed their positions, so much so that Foreign Minister Moshe Dayan and Defense Minister Ezer Weizmann refused to participate in the talks."

Ambassador al-'Arabi paused here to catch his breath, but his anger was mounting steadily as he continued. "Third," he said, "there was the destruction by the Israelis of the Iraqi nuclear reactors, and, fourth, the invasion of Lebanon by Israel. So, President Mubarak, when he took power, had all these factors to reckon with. So, what could he do? He withdrew the Egyptian ambassador [Saad Murtadha] from Israel after they invaded Lebanon in June 1982. He then looked at the balance sheet and said to himself, I am working for peace with Israel because we want peace in the area—but what is Israel doing? And then Israel started this question of Taba," he said, his anger rising to a crescendo.

Before discussing Taba, I asked him why the invasion of Lebanon angered President Mubarak. This was a ridiculous question for me, an Arab, to ask, but I was quite certain that my American readers would want the answer to that question.

Speaking calmly now, Ambassador al-'Arabi was quick to point out the Arabs are of the belief that *any* attack on any part of the Arab world is an infringement of Arab sovereignty. His voice rose in anger again as he asserted that after signing a peace treaty with Israel in 1979, Egyptians thought that Israel would *renounce* the use of force in resolving disputes. "The whole world is now asking the Israelis to withdraw," he added, "including the U.N. Security Council, and let the United Nations take over the security zone which is presently being patrolled by the forces of the South Lebanese army. So no one can objectively say that President Mubarak went back on the commitment to peace with Israel," he concluded. "Peace, to the Arabs," he went on to say, "should encompass the Palestinians, who are the crux of the problem."

The conversation then shifted to the problem of Taba—a six-mile strip of land in the Sinai which the Israelis are refusing to relinquish.

Speaking indignantly now, Ambassador al-'Arabi pointed out emphatically that Taba and the other disputed locations of some boundary pillars were unquestionably Egyptian territory and have been since the beginning of the century. Egypt had this border with the Ottoman Empire. When the Israelis refused to withdraw from it, everyone in Egypt wondered what was going on. We believe in Egypt, he said, that "the Israelis created this dispute as a bone of contention in which the Israelis can give in on something and extract some kind of price. I must say it bluntly," he added.

"What concessions for withdrawal from Taba were the Israelis likely to make and for what in exchange?" I asked.

"I think the Israelis would withdraw from the Taba if we promise them some sort of joint projects in the area." But "bilateral relations," he said, could not be "imposed."

Normalization of relations with Israel, which includes cultural, educational, and trade relations, is a controversial issue in Egypt. Speaking emphatically again and with discernible irritation, al-'Arabi said that "normalization" was a term which was not even "acceptable." "Normalization implies that we have a privileged relationship with Israel. We refuse that concept. We have correct relations with Israel like any other country. We have had peace with Israel for seven and a half years, and we expected the peace to permeate the area. The Likud is not working for that. And there will be no peace until the Palestinian problem is resolved."

I asked him if that was the reason why so many groups in Egypt were now against the peace with Israel. "That is the reason," he asserted.*

OCTOBER 9

Mr. Saqr is one of the lawyers who represents three of the mutineering conscripts in last February's Security Force riots . . . those riots which if it were not for the intervention of the

* In October 1988 an international arbitration panel awarded Egypt sovereignty over the 250 acres of beachfront on the Gulf of Aqaba. Egypt had won its dispute with Israel, and my friend Ambassador al-'Arabi obviously had a lot to do with it.

army would have probably been the cause of the overthrow of the Mubarak regime.

Mr. Saqr lives in a small, dingy, two-bedroom apartment on the third floor of a narrow little building in one of the lower-middle-class suburbs that is so underprivileged that even the streets and roads there are unpaved. The other room in his house he uses as an office. It is poorly furnished and sparse, with the exception of his large desk, over which is a Koranic inscription. His wife and his two young, intelligent-looking, and obviously educated daughters are all veiled. He is a conservative, pious Muslim. In spite of his poverty, he charges nothing, he says, for his defense of the three conscripts. His belief is that there was a plot to overthrow certain people in the government and the Security Force was used by those in higher positions to stir up a civil war. He is a middle-aged man, very average looking, and yet as I listened to him talk, I could sense the passion and enthusiasm of a man with a cause, a man who is dedicated to the poor and the victims of injustice. The conscripts, he told me, were being paid the equivalent of a couple of dollars a month and they mutinied when they heard a rumor that instead of one year they might have to serve three. How can you blame them? he asked.

A documentary shown on TV today on the fifth anniversary of Sadat's death and the thirteenth anniversary of the October War de-emphasized Sadat's role in the victory. The film showed the crossing of the Canal and the destruction of the Bar-Lev line by the Egyptian army. There was a very short shot of Sadat announcing the victory to the Egyptian parliament on October 16 and a very long shot of Mubarak talking about the victory of the air forces in covering the air defenses of the infantry men while they crossed the Canal. Then the documentary went on to show a clip in Washington at the time of Camp David showing Carter and Sadat but not Begin. Begin had been edited out of the clip. Sadat's assassination was *not* shown in this film about October 6, the day he was assassinated; the signing of the peace treaty with Israel was *not* shown; and Mrs. Jihan al-Sadat did *not* appear once! There was some considerably long footage of Mubarak giving a speech in April 1983 at the time of the evacuation of Sinai by the Israelis. Sadat's trip to Jerusalem was *not* shown, although this film purported to show the events before and after the 1973 war that are significant to Egyptian history! Oddly enough the film ended with footage about ten minutes in length showing Mubarak visiting armament factories and other heavy industrial projects. When I saw the film, I was struck by the vast difference between Sadat and Mubarak as media people.

It's like seeing a show, and when Sadat dies, and Mubarak takes over, the fun is over and everybody has to go back to real problems. Mubarak projects an image of seriousness, but it is also anticlimactic. History was being made when Sadat was alive: the October War, the opening of the Canal, the building of the Suez cities, the food riots, the trip to Jerusalem. Now nothing is happening. People have lost not only their optimism but their hopes for something better. Everyone is saying if you haven't made money under Sadat, you never will.

OCTOBER 10

"If sharia is applied in Egypt, the Coptic Christians would have to pay a special, rather heavy tax, or convert to Islam or leave the country," said my lawyer, a Copt himself. Yet, Islamic law has not yet been applied to Egypt, in spite of a strong Islamic lobby to do so. He also mentioned, *en passant*, that there was a piece in one of the newspapers that very day suggesting that some legislation should be applied making it legal to have Egyptian citizenship only if one is a Muslim.

While we were having lunch, Khaled Muheiddin, the head of the leftists in Egypt, walked in with a band of followers, young men carrying briefcases. The restaurant where we were eating is expensive. A plate of shrimps there costs about four times the monthly salary of the conscripts. I wondered if those leftists thought about these things as they took their seats and began ordering their exorbitant meal?

Later on I had a talk with a clerk in my lawyer's office who observed that people were starting finally to regret the passing of the Sadat regime. Of course, the food shortages don't help the present regime—or the inflation of consumer goods prices.

OCTOBER 11

The situation in Egypt is stable, according to a report by the Ministry of the Interior, published in today's papers.

I have been reading Dostoyevsky's *The Devils*, which in many ways could apply sociopolitically to what is happening here: the poverty, the discontent of the elite, the undercurrent of ferment for change, and the overpowering hold of the bureaucracy and of religion. One of the characters, Shatov, even reminded me of Mr. Saqr the lawyer; Shatov makes a long, impassioned speech about the necessity of an autocratic tsar, supported by a strong Orthodox church. That is Dostoyevsky but it could also be Muslim fundamentalists. After all, they want a centralized religious government, too. Mr. Saqr, who obviously hates America and everything it stands for, including the aid it gives Egypt, said that in Islam it was forbidden to take charity. Even the worst menial work is more dignified than charity. "We could grow palm trees all over Egypt," he said, "and live off dates and do without American wheat." I do not think he is a strong supporter of Mubarak either. What he would like is similar to Shatov's dream: a strong ruler who is backed by the Islámic establishment.

OCTOBER 12

The papers today headline the news about a shipment of F-16s to Egypt from the U.S. They are for early detection and surveillance of borders, we read. The story also told that our aerospace industry was manufacturing spare parts for the French Mirage plane.

Meanwhile, according to the leftist *Al-Ahali* newspaper, there has not been a very enthusiastic turnout for the Shura, or upper house of parliament, elections; it reports that only 15 percent of the population turned out to vote, which is not a sign of great support for the present government. Reuters places the turnout at 6 percent. The government, on the other hand, claims that 80 percent of the population turned up to vote. All the opposition parties boycotted the elections because of the "undemocratic way" the elections were supposed to have been conducted. You have to elect a list chosen by the party, but your party can win only if that party list gets at least 8 percent of the votes, and you can never win, because you are running as a party against the government-sponsored party, the NDP, which has a majority in parliament. Anyway, at least I think that's how it goes.

OCTOBER 13

Louis Griess, senior editor of *Sabah al-Khayr*, the government-owned weekly, attacks the Arab regimes that are opposed to Egypt's peace with Israel. "They forget that the peace treaty gave Sinai back to Egypt and that Hosni Mubarak brought together Jordan and the PLO in a dialogue with the U.S. in order to establish a Palestinian state," he writes. Mubarak is also the only leader who is engaging in a dialogue with both the Russians and the Americans, and Egypt is the only Arab country helping Iraq in the Gulf war, whereas there are Arab countries helping Iran. "The Arabs do not consider Iran an Arab country," says the writer, who also attacks those Arabs who "hide behind extremist slogans and smear the reputation of Egypt's peace initiative." The article goes on to praise Mubarak as an "aware leader" who strives day and night for "the simple Egyptian and lives every moment in order to realize the aims of the Arab nation." "The Arabs must solve their own problems and unite before the world pays any attention to them," he says in conclusion.

OCTOBER 14

Went shopping today in a store in Maadi owned by the government. It was about nine in the morning, not the time for the prayer call, and they were playing the Koran on all three floors of the store for the entire hour I was there. Imported goods, perfumes, and gadgets were on sale, though at inflated prices.

Midnight in Cairo isn't what it used to be. Walked my dog in an empty street . . . only two young men talking quietly next to a parked car and some occasional traffic. The Nile is dark and the lights on the other side of the riverbank shimmer like candles in the black-colored water. My dog chases a stray cat; suddenly I find myself next to one of the guard conscripts guarding the Israeli. He is fast asleep, his bayonet in between his legs. I try to find out if he'll wake up. I pretend to take his bayonet, but he doesn't budge. The other soldier sees me and comes toward me. "Too late," I joke, "I already have the bayonet." He grins. It is one of the pleasantest smiles I have received in Cairo to this day. Then he calls out to his colleague, saying, "Hey, boy," but the other young man sleeps on unperturbed.

OCTOBER 15

Mayo, a government newspaper, carries a survey today on achievements of President Mubarak. Apparently the consensus is that he introduced freedom and democracy in Egyptian political life. But the opposition leader, Mustapha Kamal Murad, whom I have interviewed earlier on, claims in the same paper that the regime is to be brought to task for allowing the emergency laws to continue being applied and that real democracy can come about only if Article 144 of the constitution is altered. That article allows the president of Egypt unlimited power. Murad calls for the abolition of this article as well as ratification of a new constitution.

Another opposition leader, Ibrahim Shoukri, whom I also interviewed earlier on, says in the same issue of *Mayo* that a reform of the electoral process of the upper house of parliament should be changed. . . . It seems to me that that they are allowed to publish their views in a government paper is surely a sign of progress. In the Nasser days, if you voiced any criticism, and I mean *voiced*, like in a private party, you could find yourself behind bars the next day. Literally.

OCTOBER 16

The syndicate of university professors threatens to go on strike because they seek an increase in wages. They also complain, in the local papers, about what they call the "infractions" of democracy and torture of prisoners in Egyptian jails. They also protest the presence on the Cairo campus and on other campuses of government security guards.

In *Al-Sha'ab*, an opposition paper, there is an interesting piece of news about Mrs. Sadat. The piece is written by a woman who starts by attacking the late president for fooling the Egyptian people into believing that there would be prosperity after the peace with Israel. But no such thing happened, complains the writer. Moreover, the Palestinian problem remains unsolved. Moreover, "Future generations must oppose and resist Zionism . . . the peace is dishonorable." Then the writer ends her piece by complaining that Mrs. Sadat's "dreadful" photo appeared on TV that day as she was being awarded her doctorate. Her appearance on Egyptian television, concludes the writer, is an "insult to motherhood."

OCTOBER 17

The traffic in Cairo is impossible. Donkey carts, Daihatsu trucks, cars large and small, horse-pulled vehicles, bicycles, and pedestrians, all crowd the thoroughfares at the same time and all make noise simultaneously. I had reached the street where the Ministry of Foreign Affairs is located, opposite the Nile in Gizeh. But where was the Nile? You couldn't see it for all the parked cars—and I couldn't find a place to park. So, like so many of the Foreign Ministry employees, I left my car right there on a bridge. What else could I do? Luckily, as I stepped into the building, someone called my name. It was Ambassador al-'Arabi, my friend, whom I had come to see with a letter for Gloria Steinem. I hoped he would contact her when in New York because he was going there.

After the Ministry of Foreign Affairs, I went over to Cairo University to visit a friend there who has since become the dean of the Faculty of the Arts. Instead I met a lot of old colleagues at the Department of English. One of them, Dr. Fakhri, when asked if Egypt was back to the Middle Ages, skillfully evaded the question by saying that the whole world was worse off than it had been in medieval times: "Who can build those cathedrals now, Chartres, the Milano Duomo?" he asked and then changed the subject. The university was literally buzzing with students. There were so many around, you couldn't walk, and they all seemed busy and happy. Here and there a couple of veiled girls, but on the whole the campus in Gizeh abounded with middle-class students in jeans and European-style clothes, many of them arriving in their own cars. Dr. Fakhri, who said that the department was overstaffed, rushed off to teach a class in civilization—from the Renaissance to the Victorian age. He said he had *six hundred* in class! The English department at Cairo University is one of those enclaves of Western culture which still exist in Cairo. I looked back nostalgically to those days; actually, a student of mine reminded me that I was his teacher there in 1973 when I taught American Drama to the Fourth Year (or seniors) there.

I remember how the students were receptive to and excited by Miller, Williams, and even Albee.

Later I chatted with a colleague, about my age, who has just become the chairman. She is an upper-class Copt who studied English at London University. Very composed and rather withdrawn and old-maidish. I suppose it's a way of surviving in the professional world of Cairo. I mean, to look prim and proper and Victorian and be someone who doesn't look as if she even knows that sex and men exist. Nonetheless, she was quite a close friend when I was teaching there. She told me that she had just finished a piece of research on an American Southern writer by the name of Catherine Woolson, not a feminist, but a single woman who lived by her pen. Then I met another Coptic English teacher, who boasted to me about a recently acquired Ph.D. on Anthony Trollope—amazing!

A strange thing happened at the health club. Although I have tried to remain detached on women's issues, I found myself drawn in spite of myself. Two young, giggling women were pushed inside the steam room, fully clothed and veiled. I looked up without being able to hide my irritation. Finally, I asked if they were Arabs—meaning non-Egyptians. "No," answered one. "We are Egyptians," whereupon she gradually took off the black veil that enfolded her body and hair. Beneath her veil was Western underwear, but her head was still covered by another handkerchief tied up like some sort of scarf. The other girl, also veiled, unveiled and let her underwear fall to her hips and remained in this way, with only her nude back showing. One of them asked me for my body lotion—and somehow, the conversation got started. The one with the black chador informed me that she was married and living in Saudi Arabia. She was married to an Indian; it had been an arranged marriage. I asked her if she had children. "Yes," she said quickly as if it would be disgraceful not to have them. Then the other, a spirited dark girl, told me it was the eve of her wedding night and she had come there to prepare—in other words, to have her body hair removed and her nails done, etc.

"Congratulations," I said.

She shrugged. Then she asked me what I did. I told her I was a university teacher.

Her face lit up at once. "I have a B.A.," she said, "and the day after my marriage I will go in to apply for the M.A. program in business."

I was very impressed and said so. "And what does your husband think of all this?" I asked.

"Nothing," she said. Then she added, "He doesn't want me to work or to go to the university, and he even says I should wear the veil. But I think I will get my own way. I never wanted to get married. I've been engaged for two years, and when I tried to get out of the marriage my big brother threatened me and asked, 'Do you have anybody else? If you don't, then you are going to have to marry this one.' Well, I had no choice, I have just got to get married tomorrow," she said rather wistfully.

"Do you like him?" I asked.

"He's nothing special," she said. "Are you married?"

"Yes," I lied, "to an American, but then, all men are the same." I was thinking of an unfaithful boyfriend in Connecticut whom I was trying to forget.

"That's what I say," she said. Then the three of us were silent, sitting there in our sweat and our frustration, staring glumly at the walls.

As I left the health club, I realized how little I had done for women and how little I could do. Can one change a whole culture? A whole way of thinking? It must come from below, from the women themselves. But anger and rebellion were so alien to the peace-loving, gentle people of my country. Even men could be disarmed with a smile: They endured everything in the name of Allah. They endured it all—cruel rules, heartless dictators, foreign occupations. How can I expect the women to rebel? What anger can be implanted in their submissive breasts if they don't *feel* it?

My mind turned to my own arranged marriage, and again I realized that had it not been for the support of my father, I would be an Egyptian housewife today, bored, fat, and a victim of this society.

Today one of the opposition papers I leafed through reported that Jihan al-Sadat has received her Ph.D. from Cairo University. Her entourage consisted of six Mercedes cars. . . . The notice which alluded to this event was a very short one.

OCTOBER 18
Evening

You can still hear Western music in Cairo. I went to an opening of a sculpture exhibition where the artist—a very talented young man, who was there with his Greek wife and their baby—had sculpted nothing but breasts (or so it seemed to me). Everywhere, white plaster and marble with big round breasts suckling babies. All this took place at the French Cultural Institute run by a very dynamic Frenchman, M. Compte. This was followed by a concert by a young Egyptian violinist who played Handel, Mozart, Fauré, Saint-Saëns, Franck, and Bartók sonatas.

I was the guest of some old friends, a university professor and his wife. The professor spent a lot of time crooning over Egypt's former queen (once married to Farouk) whom he constantly addressed as *"Altesse."* She was elegantly dressed in Parisian clothes and kept a low profile, very soft-spoken and almost modest.* I think if he had just called her Madame, it would have been okay. That's what I called her anyway. There were many familiar faces in the concert hall of the French Cultural Institute—people who used to go to such concerts ten years ago. Professional performers often preside over the cultural scene in Cairo, yet the concerts are free of charge and open to the general

* She died in October 1988. She was apparently so poor that the Egyptian government had to pay her hospital bills.

public. There was a kind of electricity in the audience because our minister of culture himself had come to the concert as an encouragement to the young Egyptian artist, and of course, in endorsement of Franco-Egyptian friendship.

Met an old friend, a Polish woman, Youtka, who had been married to a now-deceased Egyptian painter called Ramsis Younan. Apparently, as she told me, the Ministry of Culture had decided to buy some of his paintings for the state and they had taken them away but nobody had paid her anything! She was trying for access to someone in the ministry to get her money.

OCTOBER 19

Bread is state-subsidized. The young girl who sells it at the government kiosk couldn't be a day over sixteen, and she has a one-year-old baby balanced on the counter. Wherever you go in Egypt now, you see small children. At the noon hour when they leave school, the street is literally swarming with them—so much so that you can't drive your car. Someone said it was the root problem of Egypt. That's putting it mildly, I think. "By the year 2000 we'll be eating each other," someone told me the other day. I remember reading an article in some magazine about two years ago where it said that the density in Cairo is about 300,000 per square mile, more than four times the density of Manhattan. Several thousands live in the city of the dead, the Cairo cemetery, and last night a film was shown that was critical of Mrs. Sadat's law because it gave the women the right to remain in their apartments if their spouses divorced them. In the male-chauvinist film, the husband couldn't find an apartment but had to rent a courtyard in a mausoleum. Actually, this is the fate of many women whose husbands repudiate or divorce them. They end up in the cemetery.

OCTOBER 20

Dr. Magdi Wahba

Scholar, Undersecretary of State for the Ministry of Culture in the 1960s, professor of English literature at Cairo University until 1982

Dr. Magdi Wahba is one of the most intellectual men in the Coptic community. He is a retired professor, with a Ph.D. from Oxford in English literature. He said that the Islamization of Egyptian society had already taken place and that the Copts would soon be living on the margin of society because they simply did not fit in. He also believes that a lot of Christians will convert to Islam for convenience' sake and also because the children go to state schools, where they get an Islamic education—including religious teaching. He told me that many Copts are "copping out" and that there are lines of men wanting to join monasteries as well as nuns—Coptic nuns—for the first time.

Magdi is a handsome man with a wide forehead and beautiful black eyes. He was wearing a galabiya and looked rather majestic in his elegant wood-paneled study, covered with books and Persian rugs and prints. He lives on the thirteenth floor of one of the most exclusive buildings of Zamalek. For me it was like a visit to the past. I had the impression that he still perceived me as that young woman he used to nod at nonchalantly twenty years ago, when I was married to his cousin. As if time hadn't passed and I hadn't changed . . . "Wasn't the marriage your mistake as well?" he asked me accusingly.

"I was seventeen," I stammered . . . but I could tell he wouldn't understand.

Later, I met the BBC correspondent in Cairo, Bob Jobbins, for a drink at the Marriott Hotel in Zamalek. There was a very pleasant, tall, handsome blond Australian there called Peter George, who later gave me some very important phone numbers in Israel and contacts for the PLO. He was in Cairo making a documentary on the economy. He told me that one of the statistics he was quoting on film is that *ten million dollars* a day are spent on feeding the Egyptian people!

OCTOBER 21

Dr. Osama al-Baz

Political advisor to President Mubarak

Osama al-Baz sat curled on a tapestry-embroidered couch in the elegant quarters of the Ministry of Foreign Affairs. He looked like a very expensive Siamese cat. I sat demurely opposite him, in a chair that was also embroidered. "I think President Mubarak has an image problem in the West," I began, after making the usual small talk. Al-Baz, Mubarak's political advisor, listened quietly while I said how concerned I was about writing something positive about Sadat's successor. Al-Baz nodded. "Mubarak is a low-key man," he said, "who is not interested in image making but in doing a job. He meets very few members of the press," he went on. "But we shall see. It might be a good idea since the book is supposed to reach a lot of people." Al-Baz, an American-educated political scientist with a Ph.D., asked me to submit the questions which would be asked of the president, and he would discuss them with me. As he took me to the door of his enormous and luxurious office in the Ministry of Foreign Affairs, he commented nonchalantly that he knew "all about me." "We know you belong to the new left," he said blandly.

"I am a feminist, your excellency," I replied. "That is my only crime," I added.

"It is no crime," he remarked.

Later I submitted the questions. But he did not see me. For the next weeks, I made several phone calls to the chef-de-cabinet of al-Baz. "We have no news for you," they always replied. This remained the case until I left Egypt in February 1987. I am still waiting for al-Baz to discuss the questions I submitted. Maybe it will happen next October, which will be the first anniversary of my meeting with Osama al-Baz at the Ministry of Foreign Affairs in Cairo.

OCTOBER 22

Rifaat al-Mahgoub

Speaker of the Egyptian National Assembly

I had a brief meeting with the Speaker of the Egyptian National Assembly, Rifaat al-Mahgoub. He had left my name at the gate, so I was ushered in immediately.

The antechamber to his office was a large wall-to-wall–carpeted room with a massive desk at which sat Mahgoub's chef-de-cabinet. I was welcomed warmly and beckoned to a large leather sofa opposite the desk. A few minutes later, a dark Nubian clerk brought in a cup of Turkish coffee, served on a silver tray.

A few minutes later, I was brought into a very, very large office. The speaker moved from behind his desk and shook my hand in welcome. Rifaat al-Mahgoub is a silver-haired, brown-skinned, slender and elegant politician. He comes to political life from Cairo University's Political Science department. Mahgoub was reputed to be a Nasser advocate and a socialist. But when Sadat took power, he became a speaker for Sadat's open-door economic policy—a policy which, in effect, was in direct contrast with that of his predecessor, Nasser. At the present time, he is considered a Mubarak man. What that means remains to be seen. The issue preoccupying him most at that time was his initiative in restoring and remodeling and repairing the very shabby, nineteenth-century National Assembly building off Tahrir Square. Therefore he suggested that I be given a tour of the Egyptian assembly. The man's enthusiasm was contagious, and I felt quite excited at the prospect of seeing those restorations.

It was indeed a sight to be seen. Old paintings of pashas, khedives, and kings, dating back to the early part of the nineteenth century, were being diligently restored by young men and women from the fine arts colleges. Gigantic imported taspestries from France's "Aubusson" works were stretched out on tables surrounded by scores of young women repairing their fallen stitches. Embroidered upholstered chairs and gilded armchairs were being given the same treatment. The rooms of the Egyptian parliament were also filled with imported French marble tables with brass legs, oak tables—the kind used for conferences—and an array of elaborate secretaries, bookshelves, and walnut sideboards with gold crescents and coats of arms.

What impressed me was the diligence and the pride with which the young men and women went about their task. As if what they were restoring were a museum or a mosque.

OCTOBER 23

I returned to see Dr. Magdi Wahba. I needed to talk more with him. Such Westernized liberals, who are yet so intensely patriotic, are a disappearing breed.

He was much more relaxed than he was at our first meeting, and I got him to speak about two *very* sensitive subjects: the religious discrimination against the Egyptian Christians in Egypt—the Copts—and his relationship with Mrs. Sadat.

I reproduce this interview in its entirety here because Magdi is one of those intellectuals who doesn't waste a word and who is also the kind of Egyptian liberal who is seldom heard in the West. We began with religion.

"I wanted to ask you how you interpret the events of Zawia al-Hamra and the bloodbaths that occurred around 1980 between Copts and Muslims," I began.

" 'Bloodbaths' is a very big word."

"Is that an exaggeration?"

"Certainly it is part of the general irritation of underprivileged people—or people living too close together, or people living on top of each other—where any little reason, any little excuse, is good enough to row. Like people in crowded buses. There was this element of the row—the quarrel was not between powerful people but between the poor and underprivileged."

"Couldn't it be true," I asked, "that the Copts too, like their Muslim brothers, are becoming aware of their religious identity and also experiencing a spiritual withdrawal?"

"Absolutely. This goes with this sort of attachment to ecclesiastical level and the tremendous explosion of monastic vows. The queues of people trying to get into the monasteries—pharmacists, doctors, engineers, people of the middle classes who've given up life in the world, as it were, and who want to be totally . . . I call it Coptic—is in fact a return to religious life. They are the people whom the poor people look up to, and it's in that sense that you have this spiritual withdrawal in the Sunday School movement, which has become a sort of revolutionary movement. Also, the influx of Copts into the Communist movement, this is another aspect. The lower- and middle-class civilian Copt, who cannot, for reasons best known to himself, believe in a god, wants to find some formula of solidarity, of dialogue with the world around him. And this he does through joining a Communist movement, a feminist movement. These are the invitations to fraternity or solidarity."

"Or a sense of belonging, maybe, with a group which is not going to ostracize him."

"And which is international. Yes, this is important."

"These are all signals or signposts of discrimination."

"Malaise. You see, discrimination is a big word."

"What would happen if there was a religious government? Could you project?"

"I think we would simply become just slightly more withdrawn. There would be (a) more emigration, (b) more withdrawal of the Copts within a more discreet tribal obscurity, (c) a greater attachment to the church rather than to the laity—to the successful laity, (d) a lot of conversions to Islam."

"But no active or overt persecution—going to jail, as has happened in Iran—of religious minorities. You don't think this will happen in a Sunni Egypt?" I asked.

"Not in a Sunni Egypt," Magdi replied. "I don't think so. Because I think they are very much aware of this virtue of tolerance."

"You do know that recently a couple of Muslims converted to Christianity and were thrown into jail and would actually have remained in jail had it not been for the intervention of 'Western influences'?"

"Well, of course. You see, this is the trouble about Islam. It has a door in, but it doesn't have a door out. When you go into Islam, there's no exit. With Christianity, you see, you can be de-Christianized. You can become an agnostic or atheist, or whatever you want to call yourself in Western society."

"But you can't with Islam? You are not allowed to change your religion in Islam?"

"You are not allowed to change *out* of Islam. You are not allowed even if you are out of Islam to say there is no God or 'I do not believe in God.' This is now a crime."

"At this moment in Egypt this could be punishable?"

"At this moment it is punishable to say there is no God."

"To say that there is no God or that you are an atheist?"

"Yes, both."

"How is it punishable?"

"I don't know, but I do know the law came up last year. But this has always been so." He paused a second. "When I became a government official in the faculty of commerce, my first job in 1949 was translations. I remember that you were not allowed to translate the word 'agnostic' into Arabic. This is still very much a society of masks. Traditional societies are societies where the mask is as important as the reality, and I think you have to respect the mask."

"When you say 'mask,' you mean façades, images, appearances?"

"Which the other person can see."

"Which, whatever image you project, is important."

"Very important," he agreed.

"Yes, I make fun of that in my book. I called it the 'comme il faut,' which is being prim and proper."

"You mustn't rock the boat. People can't imagine boat-rocking. You can't be an eccentric in this type of society."

"In this kind of situation, then, where you have a very traditional base, do you think there's any kind of hope for an intellectual, religious, or spiritual foment in man's evolution?"

"Yes, there has been."

"Islam is going backward, rather than forward," I said.

"I don't think you can call it reaction," Magdi answered.

"You called it a retreat in your previous analysis, so in a sense you're going inward and backward rather than opening up."

"Anyway, inward. Because I think opening up is tolerance. Tolerance—recognizing the difference of the other person. The other person is different. We are all equal in the sense that we are all mortal, but some of us are more equal than others. But apart from that, I think, because it's very important to say that there has been this secular tradition in Islam, an intellectual transmission—calling things into question, which is, as it were, the background or the second rank of the line of transmission. Also, this kind of secular Islam is mirrored by the secular minority—Christian, Lebanese, and then Coptic are one secular male development. And that development is itself mirrored by a [secular] feminism, which has the counterimage of itself in this veiling movement, which is also a kind of twisted feminism."

"Yes, I'm glad you say that. It is definitely a kind of revolution in a way, but it's a twisted one."

"It's also a hatred of sex. It's a fear of sex, which is understandable."

"In view of the fact that a lot of women are circumcised, yes, excised," I observed.

Magdi was silent. He clearly was not interested in going into that subject. After a seemingly long pause, he said, "I don't know if you've been on the bus recently, but it is extremely uncomfortable. Very unpleasant."

I knew exactly what he was referring to. In crowded buses women are molested by men. His comment was an observation on that fact and an explanation for the veil. Changing the subject, I said, "When you mentioned Lewis Awad, I remember he had told me that he had had a book banned. He's a Christian intellectual who had a book banned on Arabic linguistics and the fact that there were foreign influences in the Arabic literary language. And he was accused of being heretical and of attacking Islam. How do you think a similar book written by a Muslim would have been attacked by Al-Azhar and subsequently banned, and the author not allowed to work?"

"I'll give you two examples: Taha Hussein's *'Ala Hamish al-Surah* and, not so long ago, Sarwat Okasha's book on the history of Islamic art, which contained illustrations including Turkish miniatures showing the Prophet, showing Ali," he replied.

"They were attacked because they show a secular notion of Islam, obviously," I said. "In the remaining time would you like to speak a little bit, to change the subject, about your very well known, much-talked-about in Cairo relationship with Mrs. Sadat? You were her thesis supervisor, or as we say in America, advisor?"

"It's talked about because it has had some of the most adverse results on people's attitudes toward me."

"Tell us a little bit about that. That will fascinate Americans. Why would it have adverse effects on you?"

"Because everyone thinks I was sucking up to her."

"Wasn't everybody sucking up to her when she was in power and then they dropped her like a hot potato afterward?"

"Unfortunately. But the point is I think she's a very interesting phenomenon. First of all, she's an attractive woman—beautiful, intelligent, and very articulate. Articulate in Arabic. These are things which sort of take her out of the ordinary round of people."

"Would you say she has a kind of power?"

"I don't think so—not really. I think that whatever power she has, she generated herself in two ways. One way was through her experiences during the 1967 and 1973 wars when she really took part in helping with the wounded and with the handicapped, and gave herself a career in that field. It could not be done before. She's a first initiator of that. The second was in her tremendous academic ambition. This is the rather interesting part. Both are the background to her very moderate feminism. I don't think she's one of the . . . she's not a revolutionary feminist."

"Not militant?"

"Not at all."

"But she was considered, even by myself, as a feminist and as a person who raised, as we say in feminist jargon, the consciousness of women. My consciousness, you may be amused to learn, was raised by her at a time when I had no idea what feminism was. And this was in 1975 when she declared Women's Year. So I was not a product of American feminism, because really, in a sense, I was a product of Mrs. Sadat's feminism."

"Oh, I see, yes. Well—"

"In that sense I think she had a very important effect on those who were willing to listen to her."

"But precisely. If you asked a lot of the militant left-wing Egyptian or Arab feminists today if they think that Mrs. Sadat is part of the feminist movement, they would say no."

"Why is that?" I asked.

"First of all, I think there is the resentment of the Sadat role in the peace with Israel and the connection with America, which, of course, raises the hackles of the left-wing militant—feminist or otherwise. Second, I think the fact that no movement—feminist or otherwise—likes to think in terms of heroines or heroes. They like to think that the movement is a movement of the masses—a movement of collective consciousness, collective *prise de conscience*—rather than the invention, or the initiation, or the promotion of one person, or two persons, or three persons. We don't like to think it's Huda Chaarawi or Cessa Nabarawi, or Mme. Sadat."

"Let's go back to your academic relationship with her."

"Well, I was not the supervisor at all. The supervisor was Dr. Suheir al-Qalamawy, and her thesis was about Arabic translations of Shelley and the influence of Shelley on the neo-Romantic poetry in Egypt between the two world wars, and a very thorough analytical comparison of the translations of Shelley into Arabic. Shelley is one of the English poets most frequently translated into Arabic. That was her thesis. I was asked to come in as an examiner of the M.A. thesis from the English side. The examiners were summoned from Alexandria University—a specialist in modern Arabic literature. Her own supervisor, Dr. Suheir al-Qalamawy, and I came into the English side. My connection with her afterward was, first of all, I was very impressed by the thesis. Second, I felt that she had this gift for comparative literature, rather than for, shall we say, going deep into Arabic classical literature. She had the vision, she had the imagination which allowed her to compare literatures, rather than to go into one of them at great depth. That, quite frankly, was my connection. My connection also was admiration for her work. I helped a lot with speech writing when she went around the world to the Far East."

"Were you a close friend or a close associate, then?"

"I can hardly say an associate or a friend. I was a university professor who occasionally gave her a helping hand in writing in English what she thought of in Arabic. But I'm an admirer of her work and a deplorer of the fact that whatever she did is regarded as not hers—is being taken away from her simply for political reasons and sometimes for reasons of jealousy because of this connection with the Western world."

"You mean her work in general?"

"Her feminist work and also her work for the underprivileged."

"Yes. Her thesis was her own work. I mean, she did actually write it? Nobody wrote it for her, as they say?"

"I am sure she used a lot of people to obtain information, and this is legitimate and desirable—that you ask people, for example, who lived in between the two world wars what they remembered, what articles, use them as informants. She used a lot of informants. Because, after all, it was a subject which is not written up in books."

"She had live sources?"

"She had live sources. This was it. People generally, I'm afraid, who express their jealousy tend to express it by casting doubt on her genuine scholarship. But I think they are wrong. She has a tremendous determination to work. She was in her forties when she took her GCE [high school diploma], forty-five or something when she became a B.A., and she must have been in her late forties teaching already. . . . She had a teaching job at the university when she did her M.A. And now I do not know what her age is, but she must be in her fifties."

"Fifty-two."

"Fifty-two—which shows tremendous determination and drive. And if she was simply sort of pretending, she would have stopped halfway. She would have taken an honorary doctorate. She has about twenty honorary doctorates or fifteen honorary doctorates. But she really wanted to prove herself. And it's this drive which is sometimes resented by jealous people."

"What do you think are the reasons why she was or became so unpopular even in Sadat's lifetime?"

"Yes, first of all they thought she was too big for her boots, meaning that she played a part in politics. She influenced her husband."

"And in Islam a woman must not be prominent in politics?"

"Well, she can be in her own right but not through her

husband. That, I suppose, is the real reproach. But, in fact, I don't think she was. Most of her time was taken up in this working for the handicapped and in rehabilitation centers. Most of her time was taken up with teaching and with trying to get on in her graduate studies. And this took up a lot of time. And the rest of the time was spent making speeches either to women or about peace. All in a good cause, really. But I think the resentment was more a resentment of the general policy of the Sadat period than a resentment of her in particular. The connection with the West—at a time when expectations of the connections with the West were a disappointment—made her a victim of that disappointment. The fact that she went on as if this connection were a good thing caused resentment and caused a certain amount of resistance. I think also that people with ideological views different from hers had a stake in running her down."

"You mean the Islamic fundamentalists?"

"And the Marxist left. Both sides were very resentful of her—for different reasons, but resentful."

"What were her crimes, if any? What did she do wrong?"

"Well, the rumormongers had it at the time that she was engaged in business—making *money*—and this was regarded as incompatible with her position as the so-called first lady. Now, whether she did or didn't, I don't know, but I am certain this was what was said at the time. I don't think she made money, but I don't know. I know that she was so busy with other things, but certainly her role with the wounded, with the handicapped after the war, with just children, the villages. She had drive—in social work, in medical work, and in her own academic career—which would have daunted any other woman, I think. But I think there is in handicapped and poor and economically disadvantaged societies, there is the resentment of success. She gave all the outer aspects of happiness and success. And you mustn't be happy and successful. People don't like it."

OCTOBER 24

Dinner with some American expatriates in Maadi. An elder couple who teach at AUC, they were accompanied by a young son, a free-lance writer. "The new freedom that we are supposed to have in Egypt," he told me, "stops short of criticizing Mr. Mubarak."

OCTOBER 27

A weekly magazine reports: "How many people realize that Qaddafi hates Arafat? Libya is trying to influence the Palestinians to kick Arafat out. Libya has even financed a committee which calls itself 'The Committee for the Saving of Palestine . . . from Arafat!' "

How do I tell the good folk back home in Connecticut that their embassy in Cairo is protected by a concrete wall, which looks like the Berlin Wall? That across the street from it there are at least two Ford trucks filled to the brim with security police? Complete with black uniforms, leather boots, and machine guns? That the entrance to the embassy in Garden City is deserted except for the policemen with their machine guns who patrol it? That the same embassy, which used to have elegant wrought iron gates anyone could look through, is now invisible from the street? That the entrance consists of a heavily protected cubicle of a room, filled with electronic devices and guarded by several policemen in plainclothes who eye one suspiciously as one enters? Even a press card doesn't work here. I had an appointment with Mr. Sherman, or so I thought. In a cold, metallic voice, his secretary informed me over the guards' phone that the appointment was for Wednesday. I murmured an apology. I'm overworked, I thought to myself—messing up my appointments like this.

I walked across the street to a pharmacy. I looked back over my shoulder at the wall. It must be twenty feet high and very deep. "I've scraped my heel. Do you have a Band-Aid?" I asked the pharmacist. He said to sit down. I thanked him gratefully. Then he came around from behind the counter and gently administered the medicated gauze to my tired feet. I was so taken aback by this gentleness, this unnecessary kindness, that he smiled.

Made my way to thc Television Building to the Press Office to pick up my permanent card—it's valid for a whole year. Whoopee. The young man who took my photo with a Polaroid camera complained about the corruption in the bureaucracy. "In Sadat's day," he said, "we were getting so much money from the Americans, but where did it go? Who embezzled it? There was a lot of corruption then."

"And now?" I asked.

"Mubarak is a clean man," he answered noncommittally.

OCTOBER 28

Said al-'Ashmawi

Chief Justice, High Courts of State Security

Two plainclothesmen came up with me in the elevator of the elegant apartment house in Zamalek where the Chief Justice of the High Courts of State Security, Said al-'Ashmawi, lives.

After speaking through an intercom with me, another bodyguard opened the front door to the apartment. I was led into a heavily furnished room, with velvet couches, satin curtains, objets d'art, Persian carpets, and an impressive collection of antique clocks. The judge, who had been sitting in a corner of the room, got up to receive me. Dressed in a dark suit, impressive, dark-skinned, and wearing horn-rimmed glasses, he gave me a pleasant smile. The voice was warm and the handshake congenial.

"Why all the security?" I inquired as I sat down on a sofa next to his armchair.

His laugh was soft and throaty. Speaking in English he said, "The Islamic fundamentalists are threatening to take my life," he said. "You see, in 1979 I published my fifth book, *Roots of Islamic Law*, and in this study I discussed the project of the application of Islamic law which stipulated that Islamic law is a main source of Egyptian law. This was amended in 1980, just a little before the assassination of Sadat, to read that Islamic law is *the* main source of Egyptian law. I had studied sharia law and discovered that many expressions in the Koran including the word 'sharia' had original meaning and a historical or developed meaning.

"The word 'sharia' as it is mentioned in the Koran means *method, path, street, way*, and the like. In the Koran there is a very clear concept that there is one religion revealed to all prophets, teachers, messengers, and it is to have faith in God and to be moral in conduct. Every messenger or prophet has his *own path* or his own way to explain to people how to have faith and how to be moral in conduct."

"But where do we get the concept that sharia is religious law?"

"No, I would like to say that the word 'sharia' *developed* in many steps: Now it means jurisprudence. The word 'sharia' has evolved in the same way that the word 'Torah' has evolved. The word 'Torah' means the way of guidance, so I believe that there is a connection between Torah and sharia. Maybe it happened through Jews who converted to Islam. The word 'sharia' was first used to mean the way or the path of the Prophet Mohammed to God. Then it was extended to mean the teachings or legal rules mentioned in the Koran or the prophetic traditions that concern themselves with daily practices. Later the word 'sharia' evolved to imply jurisprudence. Sharia law therefore means the historical Islamic system—or Islamic jurisprudence. The legal rules mentioned in the Koran are very few. For instance the drinking of alcohol is a religious sin, but the legal punishment for it is man-made."

"But I'd like to go back to my original question. What in

your writings made you an enemy of the Islamic fundamentalists?" I asked.

"In my book *The Roots of Sharia*, I offered a new method which consisted of redefining religious expressions. The definition of the word 'sharia' in the Islamic mind, and in our courts, and in the constitution itself was proven to mean jurisprudence and jurisprudence is *man-made*. I then published many articles to prove that Egyptian law is not far removed from sharia law. The government of Anwar al-Sadat adopted my ideas, but for many, this was a shocking revelation. I then angered them further by writing that there is no such thing as Islamic *government*. The word *government* in the Koran simply means justice. It does not mean political power. The religious extremists are misusing words in the Koran. The words 'sharia' and 'government' are used by them in their historical *developed* meaning and *not* in the *original* meaning. So I wrote: let's go back to the original meanings, otherwise we will be distorting the Koran. Furthermore, I wrote that the Koran does *not* consider Jews and Christians infidels. The Koran considers them people of faith—of the Book of God.

"Because I wrote all these things, I was attacked by the Minister of Religious Affairs who considered my blood 'lawful.' In other words, anyone who 'executed' me would have God's praise! Furthermore, a religious extremist magazine, *Al-Daw'aa* [*The Call*], published an article saying that what the minister decreed is a judgment, and every Muslim has a right to execute it! From that time onward the government has assigned bodyguards to me. But I am preparing myself to be murdered. They have tried to put pressure on me. But I didn't surrender. I didn't yield. I am defending the spirit of Islam. They even tried to bribe me. I am living always in danger. Sometimes I go out with a revolver in my pocket. Every night I think is my last. But it is my destiny."

"So your crime is that you interpreted Islam in a liberal way?"

"Yes," al-'Ashmawi replied shortly. "Ultimately, I was trying to make a distinction between historical Islam and authentic Islam. If we did this, then Islam would not be a threat, wouldn't be a bomb. . . . We shouldn't export enmity to Israel while we have a peace treaty with them."

"Before we go on, just let me summarize what you have been saying. Islamic sharia or jurisprudence is actually applied in Egypt, and what is being demanded by extremists is simply application of sharia law—which to them means cutting off hands or lashing adulterers."

He interrupted me here, saying, "Their slogan is that applying sharia will purify society in an instant. In other words, their aim, by demanding the application of sharia, is nothing but a political gesture to enable them to gain power. And after sharia according to them is applied, the extremists will demand a change of the constitution for an Islamic constitution that will then mean they will have full power in their hands to appoint a spiritual head of state."

Al-'Ashmawi believes that his advice to both President Sadat and President Mubarak prevented them from being swept by the powerful Islamic lobby in parliament and aided them in resisting the Islamist demands.

The conversation then turned to the economic power of the Islamic fundamentalists, which is exercised through the mushrooming of Islamic banks all over the country. These banks lure devout Muslims to convert dollars for them by promising *profit* ("Riba") and not *interest*. (Interest is against Islamic principles opposed to money-lending.) They have absorbed an enormous amount of the nation's savings, and some of these banks are so wealthy that they may even lend money to the state in the future. Al-'Ashmawi believes that the Islamic banks are a threat to the government; they could cause the government's bankruptcy. Moreover, he claims that they are infiltrating the media and public life.

My final question to the judge concerned the role of the United States in connection to Islamic fundamentalism. "Most of the educated people believe that there is a plan by Israel and the United States to destroy the stability of Egypt by splitting it into two factions, the Islamic-Arab nationalism, and Iranian-Islamic nationalism. These two axes are working in Egypt through various intelligence services," he said.

This has been a wonderful interview! The judge is a brave man. Tomorrow, a meeting with Robert Sherman at the American Embassy.

OCTOBER 29

A spacious office, clean, overlooking an impeccably well-groomed courtyard, full of palm trees and rubber plants . . . I was not offered any Turkish coffee as one is when one visits or interviews Egyptians. A large clock hung on the wall opposite me to remind me that my half an hour would be counted. With Egyptians, time was of no consequence, and the conversations would ramble on for two or three hours sometimes. Mr. Sherman was guarded. He was the number-four man in the American Embassy in Cairo, as he told me when I mentioned that I had to go through four security checks to reach his office. I had been through international security checks at airports, but nothing compared to this experience at the American Embassy in Cairo. At the entrance they had confiscated my tape machine. Even the ministry of foreign affairs hadn't done that. Then I was asked to walk three times through an electronic door, then through the courtyard to another electronic gate shielding one of the buildings in the compound. Then a young marine looks at me as if I were from another planet. Then another electronic door, and then a secretary took me within the building to yet another electronic device leading to Sherman's office. "We are completely safe in Egypt," Mr. Sherman had said.

NOVEMBER 1986

NOVEMBER 1

Dr. Butrus Butrus Ghalli
Minister of State for Foreign Affairs

Many weeks after I visited him at the Ministry of Foreign Affairs, I was able to get the much-coveted interview promised by Butrus Ghalli, the charming Minister of State for Foreign Affairs. He received me in his tasteful apartment overlooking the Nile. I was ushered by a Nubian servant into a book-lined room, decorated with cushions and expensive carpets. Soon Ghalli cntered, elegantly dressed and charming in manner. He even asked if I would like a drink. Thc minister has known my family, especially my father, for years, and my travails in the Egyptian theater were not unknown to him.

He spoke frankly, discussing confidently such subjects as Sadat and Mubarak's personalities, the differences in their regimes, Islamic fundamentalism, etc. I felt I could trust him, that he was not just giving me a well-informed analysis of the situation in Egypt, he was telling me what he really thought.

Butrus Butrus Ghalli, who has a Ph.D. in political science from the Sorbonne, is internationally known. My first question to him concerned the differences between Sadat's and Mubarak's regimes. Dr. Ghalli spoke officially, on behalf of the government.

"The basic difference is that Sadat was talking to the Israelis before the final withdrawal from the Sinai, and he made a special effort to be nice to them, to say, 'my friend, my friend Mr. Menachem,' to pay visits. I was sent there four or five times during the last few days there was a dispute about Taba and a dispute about many small details. And the day we recovered our territory, we were no longer compelled to do a special effort with the Israelis."

"In other words, we no longer had to 'socialize' with them?" I interrupted.

"It was not so much socializing as a kind of special effort. And then we returned to our nature when we were no longer doing a special effort, neither with the Israelis nor with the Americans nor with anybody."

"But you said in a recent interview in the weekly *Al-Musawar* that there is now a kind of rapprochement with the Soviet Union, which didn't exist at the time of Sadat. . . ."

"But this is something different. I am talking about the reversal in attitude in the present regime. This is the first explanation. The second explanation is that Sadat had a kind of—let us say a kind of personal approach while he was talking to people. Mubarak has a different approach. Number three, during the Sadat period there was no opposition party saying, 'If you talk to the Israelis, you are committing a crime.' Today all the opposition parties are using the anti-Israeli platform. Those three basic elements may explain why there is a perception that Mubarak has a different policy from Sadat. Practically, there is no difference for three main reasons:

"First, the same collaborators of Sadat are the same collaborators of Mubarak.

"Second, the basic elements are exactly the same. We are selling oil to Israel; the Israeli Academy here in Cairo is still working; and we have diplomatic relations with them."

"But I think there is a hardening of attitude toward Israel. I have noticed it," I commented.

"Not from the official side."

"But from the unofficial side. The people in the street?"

"But that is why the perception is that the policy is different. Because there is a change in the public opinion, and the change in the public opinion is due to three things: one, nothing has been done for the Palestinians; two, the Israelis intervened in Lebanon and the aggression against Lebanon was considered an aggression against Egypt; and three, here we come back to our former argument, the opposition from the extreme right to the extreme left have taken it as a political platform to say, 'We are against any policy of rapprochement with Israel.' "

"How about the extreme right, the Moslem fundamentalists? Are they now more powerful, and is that why there is a more vocal expression of this opposition?"

"I don't believe they are more powerful or less powerful. But this opposition was not existing during the period of Sadat, and this opposition is existing now. They have their own newspaper and their *main, main platform*: one of the newspapers is writing a list of people who are talking to the Israelis."

"And you yourself are on such a list, I think."

"Yes."

"You are in danger? You have a bodyguard?"

"I have always had a bodyguard."

"But since Camp David you are on one of those lists, I believe?"

"I am on different lists, unfortunately."

"Many lists? Like what?"

"So, these are the reasons," Ghalli said evasively. " So if you just see the basic fact of the foreign policy, there is no difference. We have never said we are against Camp David."

"But maybe Mubarak is influenced by the vocal opposition of these anti–Camp David people, and he realizes that he cannot act like Sadat did?"

"Again I will add another basic element which is a very important one: We have an economic crisis which did not exist in the Sadat period, and because of this economic crisis, the feelings of the public—public opinion—have to be taken more into consideration. And of course when Mubarak sees that the public opinion is very anti-Israeli, he will just avoid certain manifestations. Sadat used to say, 'My friend Menachem,' and he kissed him. There was a lot of exteriorization, which was one of the special qualities of Sadat."

"There seems to be a lot of discontent. People complain that things have been going downward the past five years, and there is much vocal opposition to the prime minister, Aly Loutfi. The man in the street complains."

"The man in the street has complained all his life and he will complain to the end of his life. The situation is more complicated today than it was five years ago for the very simple reason that we have five million people more. This is the simplest explanation, and the situation will be more difficult in the next five years because we will have six million people more."

"How does one explain to the naïve American public how important solving the Palestinian problem is to achieving peace in the Middle East? The average American is not aware of the link."

"I agree. Like the average Israeli is not aware of the link, and what I have been trying since the first day I saw Moshe Dayan in November 1977 is to explain to them the *Arab* dimension of Egypt. The Egyptians are pro-Arab or feel that they belong to the Arab world, and I give the simplest explanation that can be understood by the Israelis. I say there must be around 2 million Egyptians who are directly or indirectly involved in the Arab world. How are they involved? The mother is ill, there is no medicine in the pharmacy in Cairo. 'But we have our brother,' someone says, 'who is working in Abu Dhabi. Send him a telegram. He may send us this medicine.' Or someone else may say, 'I am unhappy. I can't find the money to buy an apartment for my daughter.' 'Okay, go and work in a hospital in Jeddah or in Baghdad.' So not only do you have twenty million Egyptians who are involved and are very much interested in what is going on in the Arab world, but you have another twenty million who are dreaming about the possibility of going to the Arab world in order to improve their situation in life.

"Now this has changed in the last six months with the price of oil. But I am just trying to tell you what happened in the last ten years. This is the first explanation. The second explanation is, when we are isolated, all the Arab world is less important, and my social situation will not be so good. Thus I [referring to Egypt] am interested in maintaining my Arab dimension. I am interested in having better relations with the Arab world because this will improve the possibility of finding work in the Arab world and being admitted into the Arab world. So, forget about Arab federalism or the leadership of Egypt in the Arab world, which is limited to a group of intellectuals, leftists, or activists in this country. Just take the average Egyptian. The average Egyptian is interested, and we have played the role of leader in the Arab world. How did we play this role? We were leading the crusade against Israel. Because we were leading the military confrontation against Israel."

"Since 1948."

"Since 1948. Suddenly we tried to lead the peace—but we failed, and nobody accepted this. So, the only way to be readmitted in the Arab world is by showing that we are anti-Israeli, or by trying to play a very active role condemning the Israeli intervention against Lebanon, or condemning the bombing of the Iraqi station, etc., etc. But I am trying to give the simplest explanation. We are saying that to 50 percent of the Egyptian population, the Arab world represents bread and butter. When I was sent for one month to Kuwait to help them to make a new program in the Political Science Department, I was paid one belis—a thousand dinars—which represents what I am paid for one year in Egypt."

"I know what you mean."

"So any Egyptian spending one month in an Arab country will be paid as much as what he is paid in one year here in Cairo. So the Arab world represents the bonanza. It is like it was for your young American a hundred years ago: 'Go West, young man.'

"Here it's 'Go to see the Arab world, young man.' If you

want a more sophisticated explanation, you have this: The leftists are using the Arab world as machinery to reinvent their position—their solidarity with the Arab world, from Ahmed Sid Ahmad and Loutfi al-Kholi [noted Egyptian Communists]. They are anti-Israeli because the peace treaty was signed in Washington and not in Tashkent. The rightists—the day they will be in a difficult position is when we have diplomatic relations with the Soviet Union and with Israel. I received the Communist leader five days ago, and I asked him, 'How do you explain that your friends, the Egyptian Communists, are anti-Israeli?' He said, not all of them. And we told them that they will be in a very difficult position when the Soviet Union decides to improve its relations with Israel. So, whatever, they are anti-Israeli. They could have played an important role in the rapprochement with Israel."

"But they didn't. Why?"

"For the reason I told you."

"I see."

"And the extreme right is anti-Israeli because according to the Holy Book, there cannot be coexistence between a Jew and a Muslim. And the Jew represents whatever you want him to represent. They are anti-Jewish for religious reasons."

"Could you just tell us briefly what religious reasons . . . Is there something in the Koran which says you must not cohabit or have a rapport with Jews?"

"In the Koran, without entering into details, you will find many verses, suras, saying that you cannot have any confidence in Jews. So, this is enough. And there are also many suras in the Koran asking that you must continue the holy war with the non-Muslims."

"The right wing uses this as a weapon . . ."

"So both the extreme left and the extreme right are using the anti-Israeli platform."

"Just the other night, a journalist who is covering the Middle East and who is a Westerner—I think he's objective, because he was not exactly overjoyed with Israeli policies—said, 'Look, I want to tell you something. Basically the Arabs hate the Jews and that's why they are making all these wars against them and that's why they don't get together.' It astonished me that this kind of attitude should be held by a sophisticated journalist who is covering the area, but I think it's a very rampant attitude among Westerners."

"The Arabs are anti-Jewish, like the Jews are anti-Arab—there is a basic incompatibility. If you are an Arab in Israel, you are treated like some kind of third-class citizen. There is a kind of incompatibility. It's like being a black among the white settlers in Rhodesia."

"So the two can never get together?"

"No. We have been successful in getting the coexistence of white settler and Negro in different parts of Africa, and there is no reason why we cannot obtain the coexistence of Jews and Arabs. And this is one of the problems of the extreme left in Israel, of the Communists, the program of the Mapai, the program of the Peace Now movements, the program of different Jewish agencies in the States; we are trying to promote a kind of continuous dialogue between Jews and Arabs. So you see nothing is impossible. You see, after all, three wars between the French and the Germans—and now they are on the best of terms. How do you explain this?"

"The fact that we have a peace treaty with Israel is extraordinary. We never thought it would happen in our lifetime," I said.

"Exactly."

"So, I think, as you say, there is a possibility. Do you think that Mubarak can go on with this cold peace, though?"

"There is no more cold peace. I invented the expression 'cold peace.' "

"I am glad you mention it, you should get the authorship rights."

"There is no copyright."

"There is no more cold peace?"

"The answer is—"

"Why did you invent this expression and when?"

"I invented it after the Israeli intervention in Lebanon and when we called back our ambassador. I believe this cold peace came to an end, at least on a formal basis, when we sent back the ambassador."

"I see. So now with the restoration of diplomatic relations, there is no more cold peace?"

"Again, you cannot compare the period of Sadat with the period of Mubarak. You cannot compare the period where we were compelled to *montrez patte douce*, as they say in French."

"Show a very soft attitude?" I asked.

"Because they were still occupying part of our territory. And now, in fact, again, if you want another explanation, the Israelis have not respected their agreement. They were supposed to leave the West Bank, the Gaza Strip. They were supposed to withdraw their armies, to abolish their civil and military installations. And they have done nothing. So we are in a difficult position. Because we are accused, at least we were accused, of having betrayed the Palestinians in favor of the return of the Sinai."

"If we can talk a little about internal problems—the outside world is making a big fuss about the trouble with Egypt's economy. Of course, five million people more in five years, as you said, will create an economic problem."

"I have a very simple image which I have used very often with writers and journalists. I say the problem of Egypt is how to get out of the three circles. The first circle is Cairo, and us spending our whole energy in Cairo at the expense of other cities, so the first problem is how to get out of Cairo. The second circle is the Nile Valley: 96 percent of our territory is a barren desert; 12 percent is represented by the Nile Valley and the Delta. So how we can get outside of the Nile Valley, how we can use two thousand kilometers of beaches on the Red Sea? Thousands of kilometers of shoreline on the Mediterranean Sea? How we can create new cities in the 60 percent of the territory [of Egypt]? So the second circle to get out of is the Nile Valley and the Delta. The third circle to get out of is the Egyptian boundaries. It is not an appeal for expansion, but we must encourage emigration in the Arab world, in the Sudan. We now have one million Egyptians in Iraq. If we can have five million Egyptians there—and they will receive the Iraqi nationality—then we will solve our problem. So, our problem is: the first problem is demographic explosion, the second problem is demographic explosion, the third problem is demographic explosion. The problem is how we can cope with these demographic explosions. You will say birth control—the result of birth control in the best of cases, and this is a statistic given to me by a friend, is that in the year 2000, instead of being eighty million, we will be seventy-five million. Therefore, it's useless. It frightens me even to think of it."

"It is my understanding that Egypt is spending ten million dollars a day to feed the people. Is this correct?"

"We must spend four billion dollars."

"A year?"

"A year."

"So that's around . . ."

"Around ten million, yes, more than ten million."

"This is staggering . . . Is it because of the subsidies and all that?"

"My only answer to this is that this is not the case of Egypt only. This is the case of all third-world countries."

"To go back to an American question. Will terrorism stop if the Palestinians get their autonomous state on the West Bank? A state that is a confederacy between them and Jordan?"

"Certainly, yes."

"You're sure."

"I am not sure of anything."

"But you think this will solve the problem of terrorism?"

"We will still have a certain group of extremists who will not be happy at the solution, but the majority of Palestinians will have a certain kind of identity—they may have a flag, they may have a passport, they may say 'My uncle the ambassador.' The Palestinian of the diaspora, rather than being treated like a refugee, will have a passport and will be treated like a citizen belonging to another country. I can give you just one other example. Look at the Armenian terrorism—sixty or seventy years after the Turkish massacres of the Armenians."

"In Turkey."

"And the Armenians are a small minority. What about the four or five million Palestinians who are surrounding Israel?"

"In all the occupied territories?"

"You have one million on the West Bank, you have a million in Gaza, you have another half million inside Jordan, you have another half million in Lebanon, you have them in Kuwait, you have in Egypt a hundred thousand, etc., so those four or five million will be in the next years six million . . . and so . . ."

"The idea acceptable to the Arabs, of a West Bank state, a state implies an army. The whole idea of having a state with an army is completely unacceptable to the Israelis and the Americans."

"This is the Israeli-American propaganda. We have spent three years negotiating this in the autonomy talks. We were first of all ready to have negotiations, we were ready first of all to have a federation between the states and Jordan—we were ready to have this region which would be completely disarmed."

"Really?"

"Yes, this was discussed for three years. I can give you the working papers of our negotiations—so everything was discussed. We have discussed the existence of United Nations troops. We have discussed—"

"And everything was unacceptable?"

"The Israelis don't want to leave the West Bank."

"So there's a kind of stalemate now, an impasse?"

"Yes, yes, yes, yes."

"So where do we go from here?"

"You have inside Israel between 30 and 40 percent of the population who say, 'We are ready to give back the West Bank and the Gaza Strip in exchange for which we reach peace.' So our option must be to reinforce this number until we can reach the optimum of 50 percent or 60 percent."

"How do we reinforce?"

"Through dialogue, through creating confidence, through having more normalization with Israel."

"You always believed that, your excellency, but I believe that the idea of normalization is totally repugnant to Egyptians and especially to intellectuals."

"Are you speaking of the Egyptian left or the Egyptian right?"

"The left and the right. But isn't that more or less everybody? There are rarely people in the middle like yourself or myself."

"I don't believe so, I don't know. A lot depends on the political climate of the time—on a lot of events—if the atmosphere facilitates that in general, it will work."

"But the atmosphere now cannot facilitate normalization, as a matter of fact it makes it almost impossible."

"Now, now, at present. But wait—maybe in another two or three years it might change."

"So, you are optimistic?"

"I am not optimistic; I am a realist."

"It can all change?"

"It can all change."

"In spite of the Islamization of society that exists at the present time?"

"I think this Islamization is very exaggerated."

"I hope you are right."

"I think it's very exaggerated."

"If you were able to make the Americans do something you wished, what would it be?"

"Ah. What I would wish from the Americans is more objectivity in this conflict. But they are not able to be so. They are pro-Israeli 90 percent."

"They claim that Arab leaders are too radical, and they ask with whom shall we speak? With Arafat?"

"I recognize that the division of the Arab world, the dislocation of the Arab world—"

"Qaddafi, Assad?"

"Qaddafi, Assad, the weakness of the Arab world is encouraging Israeli intransigence and is encouraging American indifference. I agree that there is an erosion not only in American public opinion but also in European public opinion—indeed, African public opinion. Everybody is getting bored by this problem. To whom do you want to talk? To the Palestinians? The PLO? They are divided. To the Arabs? They are divided. How can you talk about giving priority to the Palestinian problem when there is a confrontation between Morocco and Algeria, between Chad and Libya, between North Yemen and South Yemen, between Iraq and Iran? Between Syria and Iraq, so how come? Nobody will pay attention to your Palestinian problem."

"So we are partly to blame?"

"Oh, certainly."

"I think it's important to project to the world that we realize that we are to blame . . . partly. That we do not blame everything on America and Israel."

"I think that we realize that very well. And we say it publicly. The Americans have changed their priorities. Why have they changed their priorities? Because they see that there is no valid interlocutor."

"You mean with regards to the Palestinians?"

"The Arabs in general."

"You mean after the death of Sadat?"

"Not only the death of Sadat. The Arab world is divided. With whom are they going to speak?"

"With Mubarak."

"But it is not Mubarak who is the problem, it is the Palestinians. Egypt has taken its territory. It's over. Now they have to speak with the others. Egypt has signed a peace treaty with Israel, Egypt has created a system of peace with Israel—therefore the problem of Egypt no longer exists. It is the problem of Jordan, of Syria, of Lebanon, of Iraq, and of the Palestinians. We are ready to help in the negotiations."

"But supposing all of Israel and America's dreams came true and somebody shot Arafat? Who do you think would be likely to represent the Palestinians?"

"Don't ask me to answer academic questions based on suppositions."

"What I was implying is that there might probably be someone more radical."

"I don't know."

"Is the problem that there is no one to negotiate with, or is the problem that Israel doesn't want to relinquish the West Bank and the other occupied territories?"

"They don't want to relinquish the West Bank, but we have to encourage them. The agreement of February 1985 is now under reconsideration by both the Jordanians and the Palestinians. You see, the perception abroad is that there is a decomposition in the Arab world."

"An erosion, as you so aptly put it. What would you want to tell the American man or woman in the street about the whole problem? Would you like him to change his thinking about it all? I believe that the average person in America is very pro-Israel."

"And he will continue to be pro-Israel."

"Because he is misinformed or disinformed?"

"They are receiving information from one side and not from the other [the Arab] side."

"So what, as Arabs, can we tell them? You have lived this historical process for so many years. How many years have you been Minister of State for Foreign Affairs?"

"Oh, God," Dr. Ghalli said, "I am beginning my tenth year now."

"And I think the Israeli problem is number one on your agenda?"

"I've spent thirty years in academic life dealing with this problem and then ten years or more in practical life. I really don't know what to say to the Americans . . . to be very honest, because we cannot project a good image of the Arab world. We have nothing to show."

"But we did go to Jerusalem."

"But this was ten years ago. We are now in 1987. We begin 1987 in the next few weeks. This was in 1977. We are very much divided, the price of oil is lower and lower. When the price was high, we projected the image of the ugly Arab all over the States, the fat sheikh with ten women."

"But are there not moderates among us? The middle-of-the-roaders? People who see Egypt geopolitically as lying between the East and the West?"

"The Americans just hear about the Arab terrorists, the ugly Arab, the rich sheikh, and he doesn't see the moderate Egyptian."

"Would you call yourself a moderate Egyptian?"

"I am an internationalist. I have traveled so much, I've worked abroad so much that you cannot present me as the average Egyptian."

"Naturally."

"So this is already a handicap."

"I hope that there are many Egyptians like yourself, at least this is what I would like to tell Americans, who believe that we can have a continuation of the peace with Israel—we can have a moderate attitude."

"I just want to ask you for another explanation: What was the success of the peace process?"

"It's a very good question."

"Why was the peace process so popular? In Egypt?"

"Why?"

"Don't you know the answer?"

"I would like to hear it from you," he said.

"But if I asked you the question, what would be your answer?"

"The answer I have been hearing is that people in Egypt thought that finally with the ending of war, there would be prosperity."

"Exactly. I agree. And this is the first explanation. The peace process was so popular. People said, 'Now we don't have to spend our millions of dollars on arms or war, we will have prosperity.' Now I will ask another question: Why is the rapprochement with the Arab world so popular?"

"Why?"

"Because we are making exactly the same mistake—because we believe that through the rapprochement, maybe we will receive money and we will have prosperity."

"And America has betrayed us in a way. It hasn't given us the economic prosperity which we expected?"

"America has given us billions of dollars, but still, we seem to have failed to use this money intelligently—or we have failed to offer prosperity. The *malentendu* was the belief that prosperity could be obtained by peace—that was an error—as it is an error to believe that prosperity can be achieved by more rapprochement with the Arab world."

"What is the truth?"

"The truth is that we have to work more, the truth is that we must have more austerity, more organization, the truth is that we have to be more serious."

"And we must do something about our population problem."

"This will be very difficult."

"One last question. In a recent interview in *Al-Musawar*, you said that there was an attempt to get the Soviet Union involved in the peace process, that this was brought up in the Alexandria Summit Meeting lately. How can the Soviet Union be brought into the peace process? What did you mean?"

"If we return to the Camp David agreement, it was said in article 6, the last article, that at a further stage, all these agreements would have to be submitted to the five members of the U.N. Security Council, and the members of the Security Council would be asked to adopt a policy to reinforce these agreements. Who are the members of the Security Council? The Soviet Union. So even in Camp David, we have a reference to the Soviet Union, and everybody knows that the Middle East crisis is a cold-war crisis, and there can be no solution in a cold-war crisis unless there is rapprochement between the two superpowers."

"On this issue."

"On this issue. Berlin, Korea, Vietnam, all these cold-war disputes have been solved only by the rapprochement between the two superpowers. So the Middle East crisis has a cold-war dimension; so if we want to overcome this cold-war dimension, you will have to have a rapprochement with the two superpowers. Which means that we must have the direct and indirect participation of the Soviet Union in the peace process."

"In the next summit meeting, if there is such a meeting, will the Soviet Union be present? In Egypt or in Geneva?"

"In a summit or an international conference, it takes two to tango. If the Americans say no and the Russians say yes, or if the Russians say no, and the Americans say yes, there will be no international conference."

The interview had come to an end. Dr. Ghalli saw me to the elevator. As he held the door for me he remarked, "Don't forget to talk to the PLO."

NOVEMBER 3

The Coptic Christians have been forbidden to go to Jerusalem by the Patriarch of the Coptic Orthodox Church, Pope Shenoudah III. They would normally be allowed to go on pilgrimage with special permits . . . but apparently such permits are not available to Muslims who want to go to Jerusalem and therefore the Pope has declared that when both Muslims and Christians are treated equally, then it would be permissible to go to Jerusalem on pilgrimage.

Meanwhile, some considerable bloody fighting has taken place at the campus of Assuit University in the south between Islamic extremists or jama'at and the security police. Thirty-five people were killed. The incident occurred because the extremists wanted their favorite sheikh, Sheikh al-Mahalawy, to preside over the public worship and not the sheikh selected by the government.

One of the opposition papers (*Al-Ahali*) reported that the medical syndicate decided to punish those doctors who teach at Ain Shams University because they allowed Israel to participate in the conference on antibiotics held in Cairo this week. They will be chastized in a disciplinary session. The lawyers' syndicate, for its part, declared that it will not allow those who obtain any credentials in Israel to be listed in the medical register. Meanwhile, the syndicate will present an apology to the members of the other syndicates for Israel's participation in the conference.

The same paper reported that eleven Islamic fundamentalist students had been released by the State Security court on the rural campus of Beni Suef. They had been arrested for alleged disturbances and clashes with the Security Police. They had been found innocent of charges of "misusing the campus mosque" and of hanging posters that stir Christians against Muslims.

NOVEMBER 6

Had a meeting with the chef de cabinet of the prime minister, who has lived in the U.S. and who shared the confidence with me that it took him months to get used to Cairo when he returned here. But he now likes it very much and feels very relaxed, he said.

"If you stay here long enough you'll get used to it—it's laid back, as they say in the States."

"Don't you mind the crowds?" I asked.

He was smoking a pipe and occupied one of the most spacious, high-ceilinged offices I had ever been inside, except of course for Butrus Ghalli's office. "No," he said. "I can never, never get used to the swarms of people in Cairo."

I replied, "But the street life is wonderful. There is always something going on, and people come up and talk readily and show an interest in one. You don't find that in the U.S.," I said.

He smiled approvingly and said, "Welcome abroad."

NOVEMBER 13

The Egyptian press reported today that four Israeli leftists were summoned for police questioning with regard to their meeting in Romania with representatives of the PLO. The meeting had taken place on November 6 between twenty-nine Israelis and fifteen Palestinians. Apparently this meeting constitutes a violation of an Israeli law banning contact with the PLO. The four Israelis were questioned and then ordered to post a $330 bond. One of them, Yael Lotan, also gave an interview to the BBC in which she said: "We did not go to Romania in order to break the law, but to carry a message of peace." Good for her, I say.

NOVEMBER 14

What is the difference between an F-16 and a Mirage 1000? Maybe some Americans know the answer, but today many Egyptians were given a lengthy demonstration on television of air exercises of both planes on the memorial Aeronautical Day here, assisted by the president and Field Marshal Abou-Ghazzala. Mubarak got all fired up talking about Egypt's arsenal. The air force is obviously his passion.

The prime minister, Ali Loutfi, met with the Grand Mufti of Egypt to discuss the propagation of Islamic learning in the country. I suppose Sunni Islam is infinitely different from Shi'a. Where else but Cairo would you be shown a film of Elvis Presley on late night TV followed by reading of the Koran, which concludes the programming?

NOVEMBER 15

If you want to know a country, search for its poets and artists. There are two plays showing in Cairo this week, sponsored by government-subsidized companies, which seem to represent a portion of public opinion. *The Planet of the Rats* and *The Dream of the Knights* deal with a theme that is preoccupying the country. At least that's what their admiring reviewer seems to think, and he is a leftist Ph.D. from the Egyptian Institute of the Theater. What is preoccupying Cairo? Its relationship with Israel, says this reviewer. The government is telling us that normalization is "in," i.e., the normalization of relations with Israel. But that is a very painful reality to accept, he writes in *Al-Wafd,* a major opposition paper. The "rats" in question are the Americans, who invade a small Egyptian village and put up the Star of David there. To the Egyptian man in the street, there is no difference between Israel and the United States.

NOVEMBER 27

Israel has launched its *seventeenth* air raid on Palestinian camps this year. Israeli war planes attacked Palestinian guerrillas fighting Shi'a "Amal" militiamen to control a strategic village in South Lebanon today. The Red Cross appealed for a cease-fire to evacuate civilians. Meanwhile, Yassir Arafat had sent a message to President Mubarak condemning the Shi'a Amal, Syria, and Israel for this latest atrocity being committed against Palestinians living in refugee camps in Lebanon.

Cairo is bustling with an international book fair—the Children's Book International Fair, which was inaugurated by Suzy Mubarak, who even appeared on TV for the event. Many speeches were given at the opening by important officials of the Ministry of Culture. An Iraqi representative said that the children's books were the "pen and the sword" of the Arab conflict in the Gulf war. Mrs. Mubarak herself gave a speech in which she said, "The process of reading is the sound foundation for any cultural policy drawn for the future of the new generation."

It was also reported today in the press that assassination threats have been made on the lives of members of the Israeli embassy by extremists or jama'at groups.

There was a short documentary on TV on the occasion of the U.N. Solidarity Day for the Palestinians. It showed the role the U.N. played in that conflict and particularly the support Egypt lent to the cause, with a considerable amount of footage showing Mubarak with Arafat and Hussein. Sadat was not in any of the footage and, of course, neither was his peace initiative.

It seems there is some kind of conflict between Egypt and the U.S. over the interest rate charged by the U.S. to Egypt on arms purchases. Egypt wants the rate reduced from 14 percent to 7 percent. The papers here claim that the U.S. has refused to do this for the coming year (1987) but that this reduction is being studied by Congress for subsequent years. Egypt apparently is also asking for "facilities" in importing spare parts for its F-16s and also an increase in financial aid to the country. Apparently Mubarak's forthcoming trip to the U.S. will depend on the American reaction to Egypt's requests.

"Reagan's Scandal" fills the papers of the opposition press. He is being called a liar and a hypocrite. The papers claim that the U.S. supplied arms to the Iranians in order to prolong the Gulf war, in other words, to help America penetrate the area while everyone is busy with the war and also too busy to pay any attention to Israel. It's some sort of conspiracy against the Arab world. "America's interest is to weaken the Arabs and the Muslims and to safeguard Israel and also to dominate and exploit the area in the international confrontation," said *Al-Sha'ab.*

NOVEMBER 28

Everybody in Cairo is reading the opposition press. *Al-Wafd* ran a very interesting article today about how the Israelis are trying to "corrupt" the minds of Egyptians through the normalization of relations with Israel. According to this piece, a book on the subject, *The Israeli Conspiracy Against the Egyptian Mind,* has recently been published. The book contains details of these various attempts at normalization from the time of the signing of the peace treaty with Israel until 1986. Normal cultural relations between the two countries were supposed to have been set up after the gradual withdrawal of forces from the Sinai by Israel.

But what's the real story behind all this protocol? The signing of these various agreements was to take place on May 8, 1980. The event, however, was blacked out in the Egyptian press. The names of the Egyptian delegates to the signing of the agreements were not published. It all happened in utmost secrecy in "order not to offend Egyptian sensibilities." For instance, the Deputy Minister of Cultural Affairs, Mr. Saad al-Din Wahba (who, it is reputed, holds twenty-two cultural posts), categorically refused to be at the signing of these agreements.* The task was assigned to the first deputy of the Ministry of Foreign Affairs and other minor officials from the Ministry of Culture.

Trouble also seems to have arisen over who should foot the bill of the Israeli visitors. The Ministry of Foreign Affairs refused to do so, and the Ministry of Culture finally gave in and picked up the tab. There was also a problem as to where to house them. One Cairo hotel turned the Israelis down for security reasons. Finally they were taken in by a small hotel owned by a Lebanese investor in downtown Giza.

Who was responsible for the Committee on Cultural Nor-

* Mr. Saad al-Din Wahba has since been dismissed from the Ministry of Culture.

malization? We do not know who made the decision, according to *Al-Wafd*, not to allow them into the Egyptian National Library. And, according to the aforementioned book (from which this information is derived), most of the Egyptians who had to accompany the Israelis were unenthusiastic. One of them even boycotted a luncheon in order not to jeopardize a job he was being offered in another Arab country. The Egyptian delegation also did not turn up at a luncheon given in their honor by the Israeli ambassador in Cairo. At one point someone seemed to suggest that it would be a good idea if some Egyptian art troupes would be invited to Israel. This suggestion was met with a singular lack of enthusiasm by the Israelis, who claimed that it would cost too much money.

NOVEMBER 29

Yussef Walli

Deputy Prime Minister; Chairman, National Democratic Party

Had a brief meeting with the deputy prime minister, Yussef Walli, one of the most powerful men in Egypt. It took place at the impressive headquarters of the National Democratic Party, which he chairs. The building was empty except for the security guards, as far as I could tell. I walked along an endless light-blue corridor to the secretary's office, and after a few moments he received me. He knew of me, he said. I was offered coffee. The floor was covered with an expensive oriental carpet and a very large gilt-framed portrait of Mubarak. He asked me to write my questions down and added that I could ask any questions, and he promised to have the answers delivered to my home. "I used to work with your mother on the Horticultural Society," he suddenly added. "She's a tough lady."

NOVEMBER 30

It's getting chilly in Cairo. I have a very bad cold.

I received the following in reply to my questions to Egypt's deputy prime minister, Yussef Walli.

Q. *What are the long-range projects or policies for developing agricultural acres in Egypt?*

A. Agricultural development in Egypt is based on two major considerations. First, emphasis is given to improving biological technology such as high-yielding plant varieties, fertilization, pesticides, improved irrigation, better seeds, and other modern technologies. Second, emphasis is also given to mechanization and other nonbiological practices. Where mechanization might have biological effects, such as greater production from improved multiple cropping systems, it should be encouraged. However, where mechanization's main effect is a labor substitute, it would not be wise to encourage it unless it is clearly appropriate to the socio-economic conditions of Egyptian agriculture. In other words, technological changes in Egypt should be related to specific conditions such as it is in India, Taiwan, Thailand, South Korea, and Japan. Strengthening and supporting research centers for generating domestic nonbiological technology best suited to Egyptian conditions is a basic long-run objective.

Horizontal and vertical development of agricultural land and human and capital resources is considered the main function for long-term policies. There are also opportunities for improving productivity in existing and reclaimed land areas by solving the problems of soil salinity and alkalinity, increasing water retention capacity, and improving field irrigation methods.

Supporting, strengthening, and establishing more governmental and nongovernmental agricultural institutions is a major goal for long-term agricultural development.

Strong and powerful institutions capable of providing services and inputs in correct quantities and timing are necessary for overall agricultural development. Well-functioning and efficient cooperatives, agricultural research institutes, agricultural extension services, agricultural authorities at the local level, and credit and marketing institutions are primarily goals of institutional development programs. Also, agricultural producer and exporter unions are currently being promoted to catalyze self-help within agriculture.

Q. *There is much talk on the part of the government of the development of Egypt's resources. What kind of resources and how soon can this development make an impact on the economy?*

A. Egypt's resources are primarily a relatively cheap and intelligent labor force; the consumer, the real basis for expansion as there is a forced market; the proximity of Egypt to the key international markets; and the untouched natural resources.

The real development of Egypt's resources shall be achieved through the encouragement of private sector initiative and the improvement of relations with the outside world to attract both technology and private capital, whether domestic or foreign. I believe the next five-year plan, 1987–1991, will witness the impact of such development on the economy as the share of investments allocated to the private sector has increased to 50 percent of the total investments versus 25 percent in the present five-year plan. This would be more indicative if we know that the private sector's contribution to GNP is presently around 60 percent.

Q. *What is being done about the population explosion?*

A. Serious birth control programs are being adopted under the sponsorship of a special government body known as the "Birth Control Authority" that was formed to assume this national responsibility.

Q. *Is the present regime continuing along the lines of the infitah or open-door policy?*

A. Talking about open-door policy, policy intentions are not sufficient to create the proper economic environment and the healthy investment climate conducive to an increase in private-sector activities, especially in the productive sectors. To optimize the benefits of such opening of the economy, the government is simultaneously creating the proper climate and infrastructure—in terms of policies, legal framework, and procedures—and evolving the financial markets to support expanded private-sector investments. The government is currently engaged in a more careful analysis and in-depth review of all laws, rules, and regulations enacted in the past, with a view to eliminating deterrents to private-sector investments. The private sector is viewed as the real dynamo of growth in the Egyptian economy.

Q. *Do you have any reservations about the role the U.S. is playing economically in Egypt? Can it be improved?*

A. Talking about the role the U.S. is playing economically in Egypt, I must admit that the American investments in Egypt do not go hand in hand with American wealth and abilities. It is rather a pity that the total U.S. direct investments in Egypt did not exceed US$200 million in all sectors and fields of activities, apart from oil exploration, in which the U.S. has employed some US$1.3 billion.

Egypt and the U.S. should deal as partners and not just as friends, as this partnership did not develop out of thin air; it has developed on the basis of experience and trust. I believe this will be more and more reflected in the U.S. economic role in Egypt as we are really concerned about making our cooperation a two-way street.

Q. *What is the policy of the government toward Muslim extremism?*

A. Egypt is a country that has never known extremism. We

are for all religions, but we refuse extremism in Islam as much as we refuse it in any other religion.

Q. *What would you like to communicate to American investors and American tourists?*

A. I would like to communicate to American investors that we welcome any American endeavor to channel some of their offshore investments with full guarantees of security and in the manner that could lead to mutual benefits to our two nations. Let's make use of the latent economic forces of Egypt. Egypt can also assist U.S. enterprises by offering an export base from which these enterprises can reach out to wider world markets.

As for American tourists, I would like to address to them the slogan that was introduced by the American Chamber of Commerce in Egypt (AMCHAM): "Egypt loves you. Come see for yourself."

Q. *Can you tell us something about your personal career and your goals while in government?*

A. I believe one's personal career passes through phases. I make the best out of each phase. Politics requires adaptability. There is also what I would call planned adaptability.

NOVEMBER 30

Field Marshal Abou-Ghazzala is back from the U.S. He had talks there to "boost military cooperation between Egypt and the U.S." The U.S. Congress has already approved $1.3 billion in military assistance through 1987 and $815 million in economic aid to Egypt. One of the ways of "increasing productivity" that is the theme everyone in government is talking about is to reclaim land. Accordingly, the government of the new prime minister says it plans to reclaim 200,000 acres by the end of the five-year development plan.

You can watch *The Big Valley* every afternoon at 3 P.M. and *The Survivors* at 8 P.M.—two soaps that are extremely popular with Egyptian audiences. There is also a very popular Arabic soap about corruption in the construction business. Obviously another way of knocking the open-door economic policies of Sadat, when people supposedly made money in unlawful ways.

DECEMBER 1986

DECEMBER 1

It rained in Cairo today. For the first time in the five months I've been here, the air seems lighter and fresh. I read once that if you breathe the air in Cairo—and how can one avoid doing that—it's like smoking two hundred cigarettes a day. No wonder I've been feeling ill. My cold has become worse.

I was amused by people's reactions to the rain. Everybody rushed to shelter even though it was a drizzle—the gentlest, shortest downpour you ever saw. Suddenly the streets were empty and the crowds, the hooting cars vanished. Where were they, the people, the noise, the unrelenting sunshine?

Meanwhile, the Nile and the overcast bluish-gray sky seem to melt into one another. Only the sharp peaks of the pyramids in the foggy distance interrupt this embrace. I am going to stay in bed and read the papers.

The Egyptian press today reported with much disapproval Israel's connection in the arms shipment by the U.S. to Iran. All the papers condemn Reagan—some of them gleefully.

DECEMBER 2

There are rumors, a highly placed official told me yesterday, that Mubarak and even his wife have business investments with the Arabs and that is the explanation for why the government apparatus is penetrated by the Muslim fundamentalist movement.

"Do you think this is true?" I asked him.

"When one of your former ministers of the interior works as the P.R. man for the biggest Islamic bank, when the Sheikh of Al-Azhar is given first-page coverage to denounce birth control in a *government-owned* newspaper, when normalization has not been applied with Israel, and there is the beginning of an estrangement with the U.S.—when the Islamic lobby is allowed free reign in public life as if nothing else mattered—then you can safely say that the government has been infiltrated," he said.

Ahmad Baha' al-Din, whom I have interviewed, wrote in *Al-Ahram* in his daily column (on Nov. 27) that the whole Arab world looks as if it were groomed for an auction sale. He was referring to the Lebanese who offered up his eleven children for sale because hunger and poverty in Lebanon have made him incapable of supporting them. "Each country under a façade," he writes, "of meaningless clamor and clangorous slogans is seeking the protection of a big power that would save it from civil war, or a clash with a neighboring country, or a stifling economic crisis, or . . . What is surprising is that all such problems are the work of Arabs themselves."

Another writer in another government newspaper takes a less self-critical view. He writes, "Though a peace treaty exists between Egypt and Israel, this does not mean that Egypt should accept Israeli viewpoints without argument. The Israelis insist that a type of censorship be imposed on Egyptian newspapers in order to make sure that nothing is written to criticize or censure Israeli policies. Israelis want Egyptian newspapers to depict them as angels and to lavish praise on their policy of expansionism! The peace treaty cannot change the course of history. It cannot, for instance, turn the massacres perpetrated by Israelis into acts of humanitarianism. Indeed, the crimes perpetrated by Israelis will always appear as crimes no matter what the Israelis want. It is not the peace treaty which can create bonds of friendship between the Arabs and Israelis, but it is Israel's *intention* which can. If the Israelis wish to improve relations, they have to demonstrate good intentions."

On December 1, the Egyptian newspapers reported that President Mubarak has declared that "the talks Marshal Abou-Ghazzala held with officials of the Reagan administration were positive," and "I expect, God willing, a response shortly." Replying to a question on whether PLO leader Arafat planned a visit to Cairo, Mubarak replied that "Mr. Arafat is welcome here at any time." Asked about the prospects of a fresh move in the peace process, seven weeks after the Alexandria meeting with Peres, Mubarak replied: "The views floated by Mr. Peres were not his own but represented his government." "When Mr. Peres accepted the idea of an international conference, he was, in fact, expressing the views of the Israeli government," said Mubarak. President Mubarak also called for Arab countries to unite behind the Joint Arab Defense Pact because of the danger of the escalation of the Iran-Iraq war. President Khomeini, he said, has threatened to expand the hostilities to other Arab states. The Egyptian press describes the Iranian system as "a fanatical system unrelated to the needs of tolerance and fair dealing." "In view of the fact that the war is a threat not just to Arabs but to the world as a whole because of the dangers to shipping which it poses in the Gulf, especially to tankers which take vital oil supplies to the West, it should now be the duty of the international community to do everything possible to bring the war to a speedy end. Washington must do everything in its power to reverse the situation," the article said.

DECEMBER 4

Two Palestinians were shot dead by Israelis on the West Bank today. Israeli troops fired at demonstrators near Bir Zeit University. Bir Zeit is the second biggest West Bank university. The Palestinians said that the clashes began when troops closed a main road leading to the university. The students retaliated by staging a sit-down strike in front of the roadblock.

Also in the Cairo press: "As if the attacks on Palestinian

camps in Lebanon were not enough, Israeli occupation forces, clearly feeling under no constraint, carried out a murderous action yesterday against Palestinian students at Ramallah in the West Bank." According to reports, Israeli troops fired into a crowd of students without a warning, following a protest against the occupation and attacks on Palestinians in Lebanon. At most students appear to have thrown stones at Israeli soldiers. "If gunfire is the Israeli answer to stone-throwing in a legitimate protest, then it is only fair to say that the U.S., with its lavish no-questions-asked supplies of arms to Israel, is virtually an accomplice in the murder of civilians." End of quote—need I say more?

Must find a way to get to Arafat.

On December 2, the day of the opening of the International Film Festival in Cairo, in which fifty countries are represented, Mubarak sent a message through his prime minister which read, "Just as art needs freedom, freedom can flourish where there is art, for art is freedom and freedom art."

DECEMBER 5

Majid abu Dirah, a Palestinian, was killed today. The papers are full of the news: Israeli soldiers today shot and killed a fourteen-year-old Arab youth at a refugee camp near the West Bank city of Nablus. He was shot when a group of stone-throwing Arabs attacked an army patrol in the Balata refugee camp. Then the Israelis arrested a teacher trying to cross a roadblock, and when students began to chant slogans after the arrest, the soldiers responded by firing tear-gas canisters. Then rioting broke out and the soldiers began to fire at the students. That's how they shot the fourteen-year-old boy.

DECEMBER 6

There was an interesting piece of news on the second page of one of the papers today. It concerned the Security riots. The state security court yesterday ordered the release without bail of 162 police conscripts pending their trial on charges of rioting last February. The conscripts, most of them in their late teens and early twenties, rose in the crowded courtroom shouting, "Long live justice," after the three-judge panel announced its decision. They have been held for ten months under emergency laws. This brings to 546 the number of suspects released since last month out of a total 1,324 conscripts facing trial for their alleged part in the riots.

DECEMBER 7

Still very sick with a bad cold. Have nothing to do but to read the papers.

Arab oil producers face a predicted income drop of $60 billion this year. The fighting in the Palestinian refugee camps in Southern Lebanon was strongly condemned here and the upper house or Shura council of the parliament, which said that it "regretted the planned warfare carried out by Amal Shi'ites, supported by the Syrian regime. This is a clear-cut attempt to eliminate the Palestinian existence in Lebanon and to weaken its legitimate leader, Yassir Arafat." The statement said that it is regrettable that these incidents are currently being launched in collaboration and in coordination with Israel, which is currently waging air and sea attacks against the Palestinian refugee camps. Thus the aim of Israel, by allowing Syrians to deploy their offices in the south of Lebanon, is the liquidation of Palestinians. The statement concluded that *a lasting and comprehensive settlement of the Palestinian issue is the only way of restoring stability and peace in the Middle East.* Message: Keep hands off Lebanon since those massacres will harm the Arab cause.

Finally some news about Mrs. Mubarak. She gave a speech at the opening session of the sixteenth annual symposium of the Demographic Center, in which she stressed the importance of a long-term national program to face the population problem. Egypt's population, she said, increases by 1.3 million per year. And, wonder of wonders, she even said, "There is still a lot of work to be done in order to improve the status of Egyptian women, especially in rural areas." She also referred to statistics by UNICEF: 230 million women in the third world suffer from anemia and 500,000 mothers die every year due to causes related to repeated pregnancy. She emphasized the need to work out a clear-cut "national policy for the population and in following up studies conducted in the field of population."

DECEMBER 10

Egypt and Israel today set up an international tribunal in Geneva in order to resolve the dispute over the control of Taba on the Gulf of Aqaba. Taba consists of a 760-yard beachfront. The Egyptian team leader is none other than Ambassador Nabil al-Arabi. The tribunal's decision on this dispute is to be final. Also front-page news in the Egyptian press today was an item about an Arab girl who was shot in the arm by Israeli troops. Israeli soldiers opened fire to disperse a group of schoolgirls in the Gaza occupied territory. The Israeli military spokesman said she was trying to "whip up anti-Israeli anger."

Have been making several phone calls to find out how to contact the PLO in Cairo.

DECEMBER 11

Said Kamal

Palestine Liberation Organization

It is not easy to meet the PLO, even in Cairo. They have an office here, but after Camp David that office was closed down. For obvious reasons. The telephone number of that office is unobtainable, and it was only thanks to the goodness of the

Jordanian ambassador's secretary that I was able to get it. Abou Yehia (a nom de guerre) answered my call and promised me to relay to the Fatah contact the message to call me. How was I to find out if the message was relayed? I asked. Call me tomorrow at noon. This I did. The phone was busy and went on being busy all morning. I tried again the following day. Abou Yehia took the call. Yes, he had passed along the message and Fatah would call me at my office between five and eight in the evening as I specified. When? I asked. In the next couple of days, he replied.

Four days went by and no phone call. So, I decided to send my assistant. "Get his home number," I instructed him. The assistant went over to the former offices of the PLO and came back with two numbers. One of them was supposedly a home number. We called that but got a recording saying the number had been temporarily disconnected. Then my assistant said he managed to find out by "inquiring" (my assistant has all kinds of contacts) that the man I was looking for had left Cairo and gone to Baghdad. When would he return? No one knew, said my assistant. I give up, I said.

Then it occurred to me to phone my Australian friend, Peter George, who had managed to track down Arafat for an interview with Australian TV. I spent a couple of days thinking whether I should do this from Cairo or wait until I was back in the States. One thing led to another, and I decided to wait, having at least temporarily given up all hope of making contact with the PLO. Yet Abou Yehia had been friendly on the phone, especially when I said that I was being referred to them by none other than his excellency Butrus Ghalli, the minister of state for foreign affairs.

Frustration set in. And with it paralysis. I busied myself with other tasks, and more interviews here in Cairo, and with writing and having material sent to New York, which is no easy task. First, I had to type out the material, then drive over to the typist in Maadi, one of the few who actually knew English and could type my stuff without massacring it, then return, make corrections, wait for the corrections, then take the material to the post office and mail it to New York. This procedure took up the better part of two weeks. It is three weeks since my last frustrated attempt to contact the PLO in Cairo.

Then one day the unexpected happened. I was sitting languidly in my office when the phone rang and a strange but friendly voice said, "Is this Doctora Laila?"

"Yes," I answered.

"I have been trying to contact you for some time but your phone does not answer. I almost gave up . . . you are very difficult to reach."

"Who is this?" I asked.

"I am Said Kamal."

The phone almost dropped from my hand. That was the inside man whom I had been trying to contact; the man closest to Arafat—at least within Egypt—whom I was supposed to meet for the Arafat interview. "I am delighted you called," I said, trying not to sound overexcited. "I am very anxious to meet you."

"All right," he replied in a warm and gentle voice. "When would you like to come over?"

"As soon as possible," I replied.

"How about tomorrow?" he asked.

"Perfect," I said.

"What time would you like to come?" he said.

"Any time that suits you," I replied.

"Ten-thirty in the morning, then," he answered, and gave me his home address and his phone number! When I put the receiver down, I thought I would jump for joy.

Kamal lives in one of those luxury high-rises in Cairo overlooking the Nile. A bodyguard intercepted me at the entrance and seemed quite aware of the visit. Most of the floors and the entrance of the building were far from being completed, and as the elevator took us up, I noticed that most of the apartments were uninhabited and that their doors and windows had not yet been installed. Yet by Cairo standards it showed promise of becoming one of the more prestigious buildings of the city. The neighborhood was excellent, but as my reader can imagine, I am not at liberty to divulge it. We rang the bell (unfortunately, I was ten minutes too early), and after a while a voice answered from the intercom."Can he see us from inside?" I asked the bodyguard who stood close by. He nodded his head. A few minutes later the door was opened, and the PLO Palestinian stood before us.

Kamal is very tall, over six feet, broad-shouldered, handsome, dark, and in his late thirties. I was quite taken aback because I thought he would be an older man. He gave me a disarming smile and ushered me into a very tasteful, trendy, modern interior.

"Would you like a Nescafé or tea?" he asked.

"Nescafé," I replied. "But are you going to make it?" I asked for no reason.

"It's all right," he smiled. "I'll just put the kettle on." He came back a few minutes later and sat opposite me on a couch.

"Did Dr. Ghalli tell you about me?" I couldn't help asking. I couldn't imagine any other reason for all this friendliness.

He nodded. "Yes, he said we should see you when I asked him." I heaved a sigh of relief. Then I showed him my Macmillan letter. We talked for a while about the Palestinian situation and Arafat.

"How much time will you need with Abou-Amar?" he asked. Abou-Amar is Arafat's nom de guerre.

"Well, as long as he can spare," I said.

"He will be here in Cairo in the beginning of January, and you can see him then."

I couldn't believe it. So simple. "Are you sure?" I asked stupidly.

He smiled and said, "Of course, and when you sit with him, then he will decide how long he wants to spend with you because he will feel things right away. Right now, of course, he's dead to the world [he was alluding to the recent massacre of Palestinians in Southern Lebanon at the hands of the Shi'ite militiamen and the Israelis, but he did not mention any of that], but when he comes to Cairo, then I will speak to him."

"You know, books are more important than articles," I said.

"Yes." He nodded. "Arafat appreciates books." A few minutes later, he showed me to the door with a promise to ring me up in a couple of days to make further arrangements before my projected trip to New York.

Said Kamal was not only a dashing man, but also there was something secretive and mysterious about him which caught my imagination. I was told by an informed source beforehand that he had remained in Egypt even after the breaking of relations between the PLO and the Sadat regime and that he had had various meetings with Sadat during those stormy years. I was also told that the previous regime and the present one have used him to convey messages to Arafat, rather than the official PLO representative, who regarded Kemal with considerable envy because of his diplomatic skills. Kamal is also extremely close to Arafat.

DECEMBER 12

Two foreign ladies stand chatting outside a butcher shop in Zamalek, unperturbed by the at least ten decapitated lambs with paper streamers in place of their heads that hang upside down from a grid overhead. It is a common sight to see beef and lamb carcasses displayed in this fashion in the streets of Cairo. Meat here is slaughtered kosher style, and the beheaded animal is a sure sign that it is kosher. Islam and Judaism have similar laws regulating how animals are slaughtered, and Muslims, like Jews, do not eat pork.

Zamalek is the most affluent suburb of Cairo, an island in the middle of the Nile, rows of beige and off-white luxury apartment houses that overlook the Nile or the polo fields of the Gezira Sporting Club. It bustles with street activity. Since the open-door policy of Sadat, the proliferation of boutiques selling luxury items is particularly discernible in Zamalek. You can buy anything here, from a computer to the most trendy French clothes and perfumes.

The Tenth International Film Festival takes place at the

Marriott in Zamalek, with films being shown all over town. The films shown during the festival by fifty different countries (Israel is not one of them for obvious reasons) are uncut, and only ten films have been banned for political reasons. *The Color Purple* is one of the American films which was shown here with great success. Among the people one could see walking in the tropical paradise that is the Marriott garden, with its exotic palm trees and manicured lawns and marble fountains and alabaster courtyards evoking Andalusian architecture, are film director Agnes Varda, actors Dominique Sanda and Yves Montand, and celebrities from the Arab film world. Inside the Marriott, sheltered from the outside world, I think of the gulf between Cairo's two worlds—truly, it is the gulf between the rich and the poor.

DECEMBER 13

John Rodenbeck, an expatriate American who teaches English at the American University in Cairo, has been living in Egypt forever. At least for as far back as I can remember. He was teaching when I was a student there. Married to a very congenial journalist we call "Duffy," he has two children and has always lived in Maadi. He is a white-haired gentleman with sharp, small features, and an excessively refined intuition, which I think was refined from living in the Middle East. His friends and contacts in Cairo range far and wide, and his affinity with the country is such that I sometimes feel that he is more Egyptian than we are.

"Laila," he said to me as we were having dinner, "be careful not to let the New York publishers use you to write an anti-Arab piece."

"Why do you say that?" I asked.

He avoided answering my question and replied instead that there was nothing but anti-Arab stuff in the U.S. papers, novels, and on TV and that what the Arabs needed was something like the B'nai B'rith–Anti-Defamation League to enable Arabs to go to court every time they detected prejudice against them. I greeted his remark with enthusiasm, although I did not share his view that I was being "used" by my affable New York publishers.

DECEMBER 16

Everyone is talking about AIDS. It has become a scandal here because the first case of AIDS was discovered only a few days ago. According to government reports, *there is no AIDS in Egypt*. The case that was discovered was "imported." From where? From the United States, of course. Who else would bring us such plagues? First the peace with Israel, now AIDS . . .

AIDS did not exist in Egypt before this interference, for Allah has protected Egypt because of its adherence to religion. So spoke a learned doctor at the special meeting of the People's Assembly, or parliament, when this issue was brought up by a member of the Wafd party opposition. How is it, inquired the opposition member in the televised session, that the people of Egypt are not informed of the facts of this "occurrence of AIDS?" The very prominent doctor referred to above got up and gave a special speech to *inform* the parliament and the people of Egypt.

According to the doctor, the whole thing started at the American University in Cairo. A certain professor with "perverse" sexual habits had brought his lover of fourteen years, also a man with "perverse" sexual habits, with him to Cairo while he was on a teaching job at AUC. The young man was evidently contaminated with the disease and died a few months after his arrival. The professor announced to his class the fact that *he* had AIDS, and all hell broke loose. The class was far from sympathetic. Everybody tried to make for the doors and windows. The disease, they thought, was contagious by air, by food, water, and even breath. But this is not the case, said the learned doctor. The disease is only contagious through sexual contact and through blood transfusions. Nonetheless, the Egyptian authorities immediately intervened and sealed the professor's flat, and had him extradited five days after his lover had died. The lover *was not buried* in Egypt (emphasized the doctor) but was sent back to the States *with all his belongings* as well as, of course, those of his friend.

The doctor then referred to a "memorandum" before him: The outbreak of this one case of AIDS would not make it necessary to quarantine people coming from outside the country to examine them for AIDS. AIDS is only contaminating in the aforesaid cases. Moreover, God has protected Egypt because of its adherence to Islam, concluded the doctor. "To all religions, including Christianity," intervened the silver-haired Speaker of the Assembly.

Meanwhile, as the doctor spoke, there was a continuous roar in the chamber, but the Speaker banged his fist on the podium and stated that according to a certain article number something, this matter would not be discussed in the Assembly. And that was that.

At the end of the learned doctor's speech, the Speaker announced that the whole matter would be relegated for further study and examination to the "Health Committee" of the People's Assembly.

The next item on the agenda was United States aid to Egypt. . . .

DECEMBER 27

A weekly magazine reported that students at the American University in Cairo protested a trip organized by the university to visit Israel. They also protested any cooperation between AUC and the normalization of relations with Israel.

I have finally been contacted by Said Kamal of the PLO. He promised to phone me at Scribner headquarters in New York to make the final arrangements for the interview with Yassir Arafat.

Will he keep his word, I wonder.

JANUARY 1987

JANUARY 5
New York, the Waldorf-Astoria

The sushi bar at the Waldorf-Astoria is one of those rarefied New York restaurants that are so luxurious they defy description. A mini-skirted, long-lashed Japanese waitress has ushered Robert Stewart and me to the bar. Robert is my enthusiastic editor and publisher. It is he who has been urging along my valiant efforts in Cairo and whose long-distance telephone calls either made or destroyed my days there. "What about Mubarak? When are you going to see him?" he was forever asking. Robert knows a lot about the Middle East. But he has never been there. . . .

Right now he was looking about uncomfortably. He did not like being placed at the bar. "When can we have a table?" he asked with a note of irritation.

"In about fifteen minutes," said the waitress nonchalantly. Did she realize how precious this publisher's time was or that I had flown especially from Cairo for this meeting? I suspect not. And she didn't care. This was the Waldorf at lunch hour.

I looked around me at the elegant crowd. They poked gently at their overstuffed plates, as they were pushing the food away. Memories of Egypt still clung to me: the poverty-stricken children playing in the streets, the stray dogs, the smell of burning garbage.

"What would you like to drink?" asked the waitress mechanically. Against my better judgment I ordered a martini. "How would you like that?" she said with only a slight movement of her eyelashes.

"On the rocks, please. And make it with vodka."

Robert ordered iced tea.

As we glanced at the menu, Robert mentioned how glad he was that I was able to get an appointment to meet Arafat. Said Kamal had kept his word. "When you get Qaddafi, then you will have the two wildest characters there." I looked at him silently. Did he forget that I was an Arab, I wondered. Was I supposed to feel flattered or what? The waitress placed our drinks before us. I took a big sip of my vodka martini. I sat back.

"Robert," I began, "it's so difficult to communicate the chaos, no, the tragedy, the tragic reality from which I have just come."

"Yes," he murmured softly. "But that's the challenge you have set for yourself."

JANUARY 11
Cairo

I am busy making preparations to go to Iraq. I cannot contain my excitement. Oddly enough, I feel no fear. Only anticipation.

Said Kamal has made all the arrangements in Baghdad, including hotel reservations. All I need to do now is to book my airline ticket on Egypt Air.

JANUARY 15
Baghdad

Baghdad. It is almost impossible to fathom that a war is going on as one enters the Saddam Hussein International Airport in Baghdad. It is a modern, futuristic steel-and-glass building with pointed Islamic Abassid-style arches holding up a domed roof. On the two-and-a-half-hour Egypt Air flight from Cairo, another woman and I were the only females on board—with the exception, of course, of the flight attendants. My reason for coming here was to interview Yassir Arafat, the PLO chairman. A date and meeting had been arranged after six weeks of negotiations with Said Kamal. And after several phone calls from New York, the meeting was finally set.

As soon as I set foot in the airport, I was searched. It was a routine security search. The young woman even emptied out my lipstick. As I stepped into the hall where everybody lined up for passport control, a friendly young man with a rather chubby face and a worn tweed coat approached me as if he knew exactly who I was. "Hello, Laila," he said, dropping the customary "doctora." "I am M from the Munazama 'Organization.' " He was the Palestinian Liberation Organization man sent to meet me at the airport. He took my passport, looked me up and down, and proceeded to pass me through the long line of my waiting male compatriots. The passport control man took a look at me, my passport, and the arrival card I had filled out and then threw them all back at me and said that he couldn't read my writing. I really don't need this, I thought to myself, snatching the card and going over it once more, then I shoved it rudely and impatiently at the mustached man behind his glass cubicle, saying with quite a bit of determination that I was a journalist and didn't like to be kept waiting. He looked at it silently, examined some kind of computer in front of him, waited, then shoved my passport and papers back at me. I was free to enter Iraq.

I looked around, but M had disappeared. I proceeded to lug my suitcase to the customs "Nothing to Declare" official in the almost deserted arrival hall. I showed him my press card. He searched my bag and then nodded politely. I looked around again for M, but he had vanished. I was later to discover that PLO officials always had a way of suddenly vanishing. I wheeled my luggage through some kind of glass gate to the exit. As I walked, someone called out, "Laila."

A thin, well-built, wavy-haired, very dark-skinned, very masculine man in casual clothes waved at me. "I am X," he said. "From the Munazama?" I inquired. He nodded. Another man, dressed in a quiet gray suit, came up to me and shook hands and said they would see me to my hotel as soon as the other guests they were waiting for came out. No more exchanges. I looked around. The empty airport glistened with cleanliness. A few people in Western clothes went by. A large, well-lit, almost life-size color photograph of Saddam Hussein smiled at us. Outside it was pitch black; inside there was hardly any sound except a clear, pleasant voice coming from an overhead microphone announcing the arrival of a plane.

My companions soon moved again to the passenger gate to welcome two men dressed in sober gray suits who looked like academics. They all shook hands and then kissed one another. One of the PLO men then waved at me to follow, grabbed my suitcase, and made for the outside to the large, deserted parking lot. The two men followed, after nodding briefly in my direction. They spoke softly to the other PLO man in Arabic. When we got to the car, I placed myself next to the driver. "Would you like to sit back here?" someone asked me in English.

"No, this is okay," I replied, also in English.

As we sped along the dark highway, the men continued to chat quietly. The driver listened to an Arabic song. The streets were bare. No people, nor any cars, except occasionally a police patrol, a long antenna on its roof. Otherwise, everything was quiet—as if we had entered a ghost city. Here and there at various points on the highway were posters of a smiling Saddam Hussein, welcoming one to Baghdad. The driver drove hard and fast, as if he were being pursued. About twenty minutes later we pulled into a car park adjoining some large modern building. It was the hotel. But it looked more like a fortress.

The austere exterior of the building contrasted with the very luxurious interior: electronic guitar and organ played soft Western music. At the reception desk, a smiling young man and woman offered me a pink card to fill out. Meanwhile, my PLO hosts stood by and asked me to give out their phone number as a reference. One of the three men, the tough-looking driver, took my room number and left with the other two men, who had also been assigned rooms in that hotel.

The room was very modern, almost luxurious, and had a very large TV set, but when I turned it on, I noticed that there was only one channel. I freshened up and went down for dinner. The pale, elegant lobby with its blue-gray velvet sofas, soft lights, and lush plants was quite empty. The dining room was beautifully decorated with a large Christmas tree, and at the far end of the room was a tall, layered wedding cake. The buffet offered everything that buffets in the West offer: lamb, chicken, beef, salads, oriental specialties such as kebab and rice, and a lot of fancy desserts and puddings. But there were more waiters than customers. It was late. A young man, an Egyptian I soon realized from his accent, approached me and asked me what I wanted to drink. He asked me a few questions. Just trying to be friendly, I thought to myself, but later I was told that in Baghdad, they keep an eye on you—wherever you go. A Christmas tree with decorations hung side by side with a huge crescent (the Muslim religious emblem) from the ceiling. I turned to my compatriot who was hovering over me and asked him how he liked it in Baghdad. His reply did not astonish me. "It's like Egypt was after the 1967 war—you mustn't look, touch, move, sort of situation—everything is out of bounds."

After dinner, I went up to my room. Something was literally howling. I looked out. At first I thought it was a siren. Then I realized it was just the wind.

Earlier, in the long, empty corridors of the hotel I had noticed the word SHELTER hurriedly painted on a placard; in the elevator there was a sign, in English and Arabic, warning non-hotel guests not to loiter or walk in the corridors . . .

I settled down in bed fully clothed and waited for the phone to ring. I was told that maybe I would be called in the middle of the night. Arafat was known to receive the press at three o'clock in the morning.

I fell asleep fully clothed.

JANUARY 16

A gay marchlike tune came at me from the direction of the TV set, which I had forgotten to turn off. As I was about to turn it off, I noticed a lot of marching—and singing. Then Saddam Hussein came on to give a speech. He sat with a bowl of red carnations on one side and an Iraqi flag on the other. "My dearest, most cherished fighters," he began. "I salute you with the salute of love. And the men and women of Iraq salute you, too. You have achieved a great victory in the conflict, O heroes of Iraq." Then he went on to say, "The conflict which has gone on for seven years with the collaborators of Zionism, the servants of imperialism . . ." Saddam Hussein spoke softly. He faced the camera quietly and relaxedly. He is a well-built man, slightly stocky, with curly brown hair and light brown eyes, and a rather swarthy but handsome rugged face. He read from several sheets of paper as he gave his speech. But even though he spoke softly, his speech was filled with strong recriminations against the Iranians, whom he called "the shameful ones."

"Are there any messages for me?" I asked the phone operator hopefully.

"No," she replied.

I dressed and went for breakfast in the hotel coffee shop. "We have everything here," said the waiter, "except eggs."

"Are there food shortages?" I ask.

"Sometimes," he replies. "Today it's eggs."

Nonetheless, I enjoyed marvelously well-brewed coffee and croissants. Then I took a brief walk around the hotel compound. I don't know if this area is representative of Baghdad. It certainly did not seem to be affluent or a shopping area. The buildings were run-down. There was sewage water in the streets and very few people about. Small stores with few goods were scattered here and there. Once you walk out on the street, you realize immediately that there is a war going on. The city had a neglected look. Nonetheless there was a semblance of normalcy. A barber in his shop shaved his one customer while the Koran blasted from a nearby radio. A fish shop displayed two small fishes on a wooden table in front of the store. Someone was frying at the back. A couple of bedraggled children played near an open doorway that revealed a rather shabby interior with a stone stairway. It all seemed strangely familiar. And, I suddenly realized, what all this was evoking for me was Egypt in the sixties, when we, too, had a war going on and a socialist system. For the Arab Ba'th Socialist Party or Renaissance Party which rules in Iraq operates on a socialist economy. Here too there were very few cars, and most of those I saw were older European models. The traffic was light. Now and then, a woman shrouded from head to foot in a black chador would pass by. I hailed a cab and went to downtown Baghdad. Again that neglected look. The store windows were empty. I went into a pharmacy and asked for shampoo. There was none. Did they have cotton wool? No. Did they have aspirins? Also no.

People crowded the shopping area and seemed to be buying essentials like shoes, clothing of the cheapest kind, and other basic commodities. The local restaurants were empty. One pastry shop had nothing to display and nothing to sell. It was as if everything had not been replenished for years.

They say the city is no longer in danger of being hit by missles, but obviously Baghdad is still in danger. (One week after this was written, the center of the city was hit by Iranian missiles that caused civilian deaths.) But the headlines in the local newspaper are reassuring: MORE ENEMY EQUIPMENT DESTROYED, etc. The other thing which reminded me so vividly of Nasser's Egypt was that even the store windows displayed photos or posters of Saddam Hussein just as they displayed posters of Nasser in Cairo's stores in the sixties. Here, the only other visible advertisements in the street were a couple of handwritten placards with WE SHALL TRIUMPH scrawled on them. Prophetic words.

I returned to the hotel and busied myself with reading the papers, looking out of the window, and waiting for the phone call which was to summon me to the presence of the PLO leader.

I turned on the TV. Nothing but patriotic songs sung by colorful choruses of men and women sitting or kneeling on the ground in heavily embroidered kaftans. The songs that I listened to all paid tribute to Saddam Hussein, eulogizing him and the army. Sometimes arsenal was displayed: One sequence accompanying the songs was of a glittering yacht, decorated not only with strings of marvelous colored lights and flowers but also with what looked to me like a real live missile jutting out from the prow of the gliding boat.

There is very little American influence in Baghdad. Unless, of course, you count the Pepsi-Cola they serve you at the hotel. But today they showed a John Wayne movie. It was shown around three in the afternoon, and then the TV went blank. Needless to say the TV is government-owned, as are all hotels in Baghdad. Only small businesses like cigarette stores or food shops are not government-owned. One of the waiters in the hotel told me that there was a great deal of private wealth in Iraq. The waiter, like a lot of the hotel personnel, was Egyptian. At one time last year there were three million Egyptians working in Iraq, and we were told in Cairo that one million mercenaries are enlisted in the Iraqi army. The Egyptians are not as well regarded as, say, Europeans or other expatriates because they are impoverished rural or urban laborers. Iraq welcomes Egyptians without even an entry visa, and for many years Baghdad has been a source of employment for thousands of Egypt's otherwise unemployed.

JANUARY 17

Yassir Arafat

Chairman, Palestine Liberation Organization

I was starting to worry about the interview. Had they forgotten me? I realized that Arafat is a busy man. Peter George, the Australian journalist, told me that he had had to wait for three days in his hotel before he was allowed to interview the PLO leader. Maybe I should wait another day before calling? I decided against it. I picked up the phone and dialed the PLO headquarters. "Hello?" A friendly voice answered.

"It's me, Dr. Laila . . ."

"Where were you today? We looked all over the hotel for

you. You hadn't even left a message or your key to say where you were" came the rejoinder.

"I am very sorry," I mumbled. "You see, I had run out of shampoo." It was the only excuse I could think of and it was true.

"The Chairman wanted you to have lunch with us," said the voice. "Oh, dear, I'm so sorry," I muttered, feeling very angry and very sorry for myself. "But we'll call you again this evening, after six." And the phone clicked.

I heaved a sigh of relief and switched on the TV again. They had not forgotten me. I did not mind the monotonous programming anymore. A state poet came on the screen to read a very patriotic poem in classical Arabic. As a background to his recitation were stills of Iraqi soldiers on the front. "O Soldiers of Saddam," he began and then continued by eulogizing Saddam Hussein and the Iraqi soldiers fighting the "Khomeini Zionists." I looked at my watch. Time for dinner. At the coffee shop, I was served with an extremely creditable chef's salad, complete with Swiss cheese. The place, as usual, was deserted. But from the outside came the sound of gay trumpets and hand-beaten drums. I asked the waiter what the sound was about. "It's a wedding procession," he said, and then added: "The war has not dampened their zeal for marriages. And on Thursdays, you will find one procession after another, with all the traditional fanfare."

Suddenly the phone rang. "I am downstairs in the lobby waiting for you," said a voice.

"I will be right down," I replied. It was the PLO man who would accompany me to Arafat.

As I shook hands in the lobby, I noticed that he was a very handsome young man, dressed in a gray silk suit and red tie. He led me to a chauffeured car and, contrary to my expectations, I was not blindfolded or asked not to look out of the window. Later we arrived at a guarded checkpoint. The car was recognized and a roadblock lifted. It was dark as we parked next to an unpretentious-looking villa guarded by two Iraqi soldiers holding machine guns. I was ushered in.

Yassir Arafat was standing at the entrance with an official but warm handshake. "Welcome, Laila," he said. His tone conveyed friendship. He wore dark green army fatigues with a pistol strapped to a leather belt at his hip. On his head was the famous Palestinian headdress, the kufiyeh. Arafat is not a tall man, but he evokes the dignity of a head of state—maybe because he is so short and yet so imposing; there is something Napoleonic about him. His movements and gestures are swift and decisive, like those of a commander in the midst of a campaign or a general on the eve of a crucial battle. The jaw is firm, the face resilient.

If you are not an adamant Zionist, I doubt that you could escape being impressed by his charm and charismatic personality. Standing before him now, I was suddenly able to undertand why he is loved by Palestinians and Arabs alike. Arafat is perceived by millions, in and outside the Arab world, as the embodiment of the Palestinian cause. His physical presence only reinforced that perception.

In spite of his imposing appearance, the smile that he flashed at me was oddly fatherly. I was then ushered into a tasteful interior of soft colors, wall-to-wall carpeting with matching beige velvet sofas spanning the room on all three sides. The sofas were backed by contemporary stained-glass windows depicting different scenes of Arabian folklore. On a low, modern, rectangular table was a bowl of pink chrysanthemums. Two members of the Palestinian Executive Committee shook hands with me and beckoned me to the sofa. Arafat left the room and disappeared for a while. One of the men, about fifty, dark, stocky, and confident, began to talk to me about Iraq. I mentioned briefly that I had been downtown that morning and couldn't find any shampoo. The dark, stocky man said Iraq had everything to offer, even Western consumer goods, even at this particular time of crisis. Then I was told what were the most interesting tourist attractions of the city and how to get there. The conversation rambled on politely. I was being treated as if I had come to pay a social call; tea was brought in, and a few other people entered the room and introduced themselves by name and shook hands. I had the feeling I was being received in an extremely hospitable, warm, extended Arab family. Later, I came to realize that this is basically the psychological makeup of the PLO. It is a close-knit family hierarchy, and Arafat, who is referred to by all as "the father" (*al-walid* in Arabic), is the head of this family. He concerns himself with strategic policymaking as well as with the smallest details of his family: for instance, Was the tape recorder in good working order for the interview?

Once or twice some uniformed Palestinians came in, but they were very unobtrusive and went about their business silently. On the whole there was a kind of salon atmosphere about the place and the people which really staggered me; I had expected to be blindfolded and taken into an army trench where the PLO would be in hiding! Where on earth, I asked myself now, did I get this impression? No doubt from the U.S. media. It was this preconception that I was about to walk into a heavily guarded, secretive, terrorist group that had been quickly dispelled.

A young man wearing a very attractive custom-made suit walked in and inquired politely where I had been that morning, since I was supposed to be having lunch with them. I gave the shampoo excuse and was very apologetic. He grasped my meaning immediately and reiterated that I would have discovered that the PLO eat with knives and forks. We all laughed at that; the ice was broken.

About forty minutes later, Arafat re-entered the room and like a gracious host placed himself next to me on the sofa. "So where were you this morning? We were looking for you in the hotel today." I explained what had happened and again gave the shampoo excuse. At this he replied without any irony, and very politely, that he was sorry he couldn't provide me with any shampoo. He just didn't use it, he added, pointing to his obviously bald head. We both laughed.

He then got up and ushered me into a stylish modern study. He sat behind a large, attractive desk and asked me a few questions about the interview. He explained that he was very busy, almost by way of apology for not seeing me sooner, and that he had a dinner for the Chinese ambassador but could we meet after that? I mentioned that I was fully prepared to work late in the night because that's when I heard he gave his interviews. He smiled at that. He asked me what kind of readers I expected for the book, and I mentioned that we would be addressing ordinary people in the United States rather than politicians or specialists. I added that in America there were many who are open to getting the views of the PLO and the Palestinian people. I also said that among the 200 million Americans of the U.S.A. there are some who were not Zionists. His reply was that there are 230 million Americans who were not Zionists. "It is the American government which is misguided," he added. The conversation suddenly took a different turn. I was carrying an almost full pack of English Players cigarettes. He asked me why I smoke so much. I replied that I smoked so much in order to control my appetite. Everybody in the room laughed politely at the observation, but Arafat admonished me in a fatherly fashion, saying that I should really cut down on my smoking.

Meanwhile a man entered the room with Arafat's coat. As he was helped with his coat, he asked the man why no message had been left for me at the hotel when they went to look for me that morning. The man stammered something. Then Arafat addressed another man in the room and ordered him—literally ordered him—to "take Laila out to dinner."

"That's quite unnecessary," I said. Arafat waved his hand as if to say he would not take no for an answer and swept out of the room majestically, surrounded by three of his men.

I was taken back to the hotel for dinner by a very affable looking man in his late thirties who confessed that he had had dinner. When I suggested that we should forget about it, he said he'd never hear the end of it if he disobeyed al-walid's orders.

The coffee shop in the hotel was, as usual, empty. We took our seat in a corner. I ordered a salad and he obliged me by doing the same. At first we made small talk. Then the conversation turned to Arafat. "Arafat *is* the Palestinian people," he said. "For us he embodies the fatherland." Then he began telling me anecdotes about the way Arafat adores the children whose fathers or relatives were killed in *fedayeen* incursions or the wars. "He treats them as if they were his own immediate family." Then he spoke about Lebanon and how brutal it had been to leave it. He said that he had spent all his life in Beirut. He also mentioned that there are 450,000 Palestinians inside Lebanon who face possible extermination. They were left behind when Arafat and the PLO evacuated that country in 1982. Apparently Arafat had been given a written document signed by Philip Habib asserting that the U.S. would safeguard the refugee camps as well as Palestinian civilians in West Beirut. But as soon as Arafat left, the massacres on the camps of Sabra and Shatila were started by the Israeli-backed Southern Lebanon army commanded by Eli Hebika, and then by Amal (Shi'a) forces supported by certain Arab and Iraini factions.

Then he spoke about his own daughter and how when she was three she was almost blown up by a bomb placed in his car. I asked him then what he would say to the accusation leveled at the PLO that it was a terrorist organization. He shook his head sadly. "If you even hit or hurt a cat, it will go away into a corner and then spring back and maybe scratch you. If you continue to hurt it, even in its corner, it is bound to lash back." The conversation then turned once more to Arafat. Why was Arafat not married, I asked. "He was in love with a girl once and she was killed. He never got over that. Besides he has no time. You know he seldom has time to sleep. Actually, he sleeps very little, from about five in the morning to ten. Rarely gets more than four hours' sleep," he said.

As I listened, it became obvious that this man and probably many like him were ready to give up their lives for Arafat. It was clear to me that the personality of the man was crucial to understanding the excessive loyalty of his followers. I had read that a survey had been conducted on the West Bank and Gaza in which Arafat's popularity was queried. Among the millions living in Israeli-occupied territories, he remains unquestionably the leader they have chosen. The survey was made a couple of months ago.

It was getting close to midnight. "I'd better go up to my room and freshen up," I announced as we finished our salads.

The moment I stepped into the room, the phone rang. Arafat was back and was expecting me. I rushed down. The young man with the silk suit was there and I was chauffeured back to the PLO headquarters. Arafat was waiting in his study. I pulled a chair right next to his and we began to tape the interview.

"Ask me any questions," he said confidentially. Since I knew nothing of his early life, I asked him to talk about his beginning. He hesitated and then speaking slowly in English said, "My mother is from Jerusalem, my father is from Gaza. Needless to say, both are under Israeli occupation to this day. But I lived in Jerusalem with my uncles. The house in which we lived was directly beside the Wailing Wall, and it was one of the first houses to be demolished and exploded by the Israelis because they knew it was Yassir Arafat's house. It was a big, ancient, old-style house. The whole family of my mother, all my uncles and aunts, used to live there. I was living with them. They took out all my relatives and blew it up!"

"Did the Israelis already know of and dread Arafat then, in 1967?" I asked.

"We started working in the resistance movement in 1965—but I had (before that) worked with the Egyptian resistance against the British. My small family, most of them are still living in Egypt," he added. Arafat has four brothers and five sisters in Cairo. Then I asked him if they all left at the time of the demolition of their home by the Israelis and he replied that he wasn't there when it happened. In place of the Arafat home, there is now a vacant lot, a square, not far from the Wailing Wall.

Arafat then went on to describe his schooling, which all took place in Cairo, both on the high school and college levels.

He graduated with a degree in civil engineering from Farouk University (now Cairo University).

As he talked, I was able to get a very close look at him. Arafat is fifty-six years old but actually looks ten years older. The face is jovial, smiling, even warm, but there is something glassy about the eyes—they are the eyes of a man who has seen death thousands of times. "It makes no difference to me how old I am," he said when I asked his age, "because my heart is very young. I have never been married, and I have no children, although I consider all Palestinian children my own . . . Maybe that's why I feel young. It's something in the mind." I mentioned that he is called "al-walid" by his men. "They call me different things," he said. "They call me the old man but they mean the village elder . . . and this name was the name given me in 1967 and 1968 when I was in the secret resistance in a village near Nablus, when I couldn't be referred to under my own name."*

Arafat went on to tell how he was a reserve officer in the Egyptian army, and how he fought in the 1956 Suez War on the Egyptian side as a bomb disposal expert. His job was to dismantle unexploded bombs from captured and fallen planes. When I asked him if he had been scared of death, he replied quickly, "There is no one who is not scared of death, and if you don't fear, others will not fear you. But I am a strong believer."

Arafat also fought, as early as 1947, in the Palestinian army, when he was the youngest officer among them. "I have lived in battle and strife, my family fought, the homes around me fought, and after the catastrophe of 1948, I remained in this

* After the defeat of the Arab armies by Israel in 1967, Arafat began a series of Fatah operations against the Israelis in the now-occupied West Bank. From Nablus, grenades were thrown at Israeli patrols, bombs were detonated in village squares and bus terminals, and soon explosions were going on at the rate of thirty a month. By the end of 1968, Arafat had to flee his secret headquarters in Nablus and take refuge across the Jordan. In March 1968, however, Palestinian morale was boosted when Jordanian and PLO forces inflicted severe losses on Israeli retaliatory forces in Karameh in the Jordan Valley. This resulted in a PLO congress in Cairo in which Arafat was promoted to PLO chairman.

atmosphere of combat in Egypt." (In Egypt he was fighting guerrilla warfare against the British occupation.)

By the "catastrophe" of 1948, Arafat meant the establishment of the State of Israel. In 1945, President Truman had endorsed the Zionist demand that 100,000 Jews should be allowed immediately into Palestine. But the British government, which had a mandate in Palestinc, stipulated that the 65,000-strong Jewish underground army be dismantled first. A widespread campaign of Zionist terrorism culminated in Jerusalem in 1945 with the blowing up of the King David Hotel, which housed the military offices of the British government. The British handed the whole matter to a U.N. Special Committee on Palestine, which issued a report recommending that Palestine be partitioned into Arab and Jewish states, with Jerusalem under international control. The U.N. General Assembly voted for partition in November 1947. The Arabs totally rejected partition, but the Zionists accepted it. The resolution provided for a Jewish state at a time when Jews formed 30 percent of the population and owned 8 percent of the land of Palestine. The U.N. partition resolution consequently touched off violent protest from the Arabs, and it was then that Arafat became the "youngest officer" in the Palestinian army, which began to fight the Zionist Haganah and such groups as the Irgun. Instead of implementing the partition, Britain in the meantime declared that it would relinquish its mandate in Palestine on May 15, 1948. Meanwhile, Palestinians living in Palestine were terrorized into leaving their villages by reports of massacres by the Zionists such as the well-known bloodbath of the village of Deir Yassin, where women and children were slaughtered by the Irgun. Thus began the mass exodus of Palestinians from their villages and their homes. Meanwhile, the British left Palestine on May 14, when their troops evacuated the country. On the same day, the Zionists proclaimed the State of Israel—which was promptly recognized by the U.S. and the Soviet Union. The exodus of Palestinians resulted in their number decreasing in the area from 750,000 to 165,000. Moreover, Israel now controlled 80 percent of the area of Palestine. Of the 20 percent of Palestine which remained in Arab hands, a semi-desert area called the Gaza Strip was placed under Egyptian control and the West Bank of the Jordan River (which is a substantial area, including Jerusalem) was annexed by Transjordan (with strong opposition from the Arabs) to form the Hashemite Kingdom of Jordan. Incidentally, Transjordan originally framed a part of the British mandate in Palestine. In 1946, the mandate ended and a kingdom was proclaimed. More than half of its population is made up of Arab refugees from Palestine. It would be well to keep in mind that Palestinians as well as other Arabs feel very bitter about the injustice which, they say, has been perpetrated on them—the indigenous inhabitants of Palestine—by the U.S. and by Britain. Both these two Western powers aided in the creation of the State of Israel at the expense of the Palestinians. This feeling of injustice has been the one most significant factor in radicalizing the Arab world and engendering anti-Western feelings among it.

Britain had contributed to the creation of the State of Israel in the Balfour Declaration of November 1917. The British gained control of the area after it was lost by the Ottoman Turks. In a letter to Lord Rothschild, Balfour wrote, "Her Majesty's government views with favor the establishment of a National Home for the Jewish people and will use their best endeavor to facilitate the achievement of this objective." At about that time there were about 700,000 Arabs and 56,000 Jews in Palestine. Therefore massive Jewish immigration into Palestine started and continued for the next thirty years under the auspices of the British military. There are some who conjecture, like the historian Arnold Toynbee, that had Palestine remained under Ottoman Turkish rule, it might have become an independent Arab state in 1918, i.e., after World War I. But with the British controlling it and opening the door to Jewish immigration, the Palestinians didn't have a chance. This may explain why many Arabs and Palestinians feel that Israel is just an extension of British and Western imperialism in the area after World War I.

As for the U.S., from the very first it became Israel's chief supporter and friend. To the Arabs, America simply replaced Britain as an imperialistic power which desires to dominate the Middle East. Israel, as a powerful client state, helps it in this goal. That may explain why, for many Arabs, America is the enemy and the most important reason for this belief is the Palestinian refugee problem.

These historical facts were being taken for granted by the PLO leader as he spoke to me.

Arafat continued to relate how he established contact with the Free Officers, who, under Nasser, later overthrew the Farouk monarchy in Egypt. It was then, in 1946, that he met Anwar al-Sadat as well as all the other leading figures of the Egyptian revolution. "I even knew Sadat before he was married to Jihan," he said with a smile in his voice, as if to say "We go back a long ways." While he was in Egypt in the late forties, Arafat also established the Palestinian Student Union or Federation, which developed into a powerful political organization. The student federation enabled Arafat to make contact with Palestinian students all over the Arab world. Guerrilla activities against Israel were begun. Meanwhile Arafat participated in the 1956 war against Israel within the Egyptian armed forces and was also employed as a civil engineer in the textile town of Mahalla. Another student group comprising Palestinian university graduates was formed at that time. In 1957 Arafat moved to Kuwait, where he also worked as a civil engineer. It was in 1957 that his organization, Fatah, was started. The name "Fatah" indicates the National Movement for the Liberation of Palestine. Al-Fatah then was only a cell, but it created an important base for the movement. Although Arafat did not mention the means of financing Al-Fatah, it is well known that it was backed by wealthy Palestinians in Kuwait. The organization also had its own magazine and training bases in revolutionary Algeria. In 1954, when the Muslim Brotherhood tried to assassinate Nasser, Arafat had to leave Egypt because he was suspected of being a member of that organization.

Although Egypt did train Palestinian guerrillas, at that time they were being led by an Egyptian called Mustapha Hafez in Gaza. But Mustapha Hafez, according to Arafat, was training an Arafat-initiated group which as early as 1954 was penetrating Israel in what Arafat calls "resistance" incursions. When I asked Arafat if he could describe one of the military operations of the Palestinian guerrillas in 1954, he said he couldn't remember anything precise, "but it was against their Israeli colonies around Gaza," which is a Palestinian border. Assisting Arafat at the time was Abou-Jihad, who was in charge of the military operations of the PLO. Abou-Jihad was assassinated by the Israelis in 1988.

"Fatah has the support of all the Palestinian people," said Arafat. But when I asked him how many were actually members, he evaded the question.

"But what about the other Palestinian organizations?" I asked.

"They are different kinds of ideological movements, like the Popular Front for the Liberation of Palestine under the leftist George Habash.* The Syrians also have a Ba'th Palestinian group called 'al-Saiqa' and here the Iraqis have another group called the 'Arab Front.' " When I asked him what their relationship to Fatah and to himself was, he replied that they were

* The Popular Front for the Liberation of Palestine is run by a Christian Palestinian, George Habash. Habash started with an organization called the Arab Nationalist Movement in 1953. This, like the early beginnings of Al-Fatah, was also a student organization. At that time, Habash was studying for a medical degree at the American Univeristy in Beirut. At first an advocate of Nasser, he gradually lost faith in the effectiveness of the Arab states to liberate Palestine. He began to move toward a Guevara-style revolutionary guerrilla action as well as intelligence operations by agents inside Israel. The defeat of the Egyptian armies in 1967 in the Six-Day War against Israel confirmed Habash's view that the Arab armies were ineffective. His PFLP was further radicalized. He believes that the struggle for the liberation of Palestine must be pursued by every single means including hijacking and acts of terrorism inside and outside Israel. Anything which would harm the Israeli state is justified, and if innocent civilians have to suffer, that is tragic but unavoidable. Therefore, he and Al-Fatah, which is far more moderate, parted company, and any attempts to bring him under the leadership of Arafat failed. Habash, according to some, can never be leader of the Palestinian movement because he is a Christian. As a Marxist, he believes in the need for total revolution in Arab society before the Arabs can stand up to the State of Israel.

all members of the PLO. "We have democracy in the PLO," he asserted. "Sometimes we are very near to one another and sometimes we are very far. Democracy is one of the main sources of power for the Palestinian revolution," he stressed.

Some coffee was brought in at this point by the young man who had taken me out to dinner. Arafat drank tea he flavored with honey. "Sugar," he mumbled, "is white poison."

"The Israelis," I began, trying not to lose the momentum of the interview, "wanted to destroy the PLO when they invaded Lebanon in 1982, and I have even read that they wanted to kill you. To many, you are the PLO." There was a silence. I tried again: "What would happen if you stepped down and decided to retire on the French Riviera?" I asked humorously.

"I would like [to retire] with a beautiful wife," he said, smiling.

"But what would happen?" I asked once more.

"Our people are stronger than all their leaders, they are stronger than past leaders, stronger than this leadership, and they will be in the future stronger than the next leaders. I am proud of this fact."

"If a bi-national state solution exists one day, would the PLO cease to exist?" I asked.

"The PLO is one of the means," he replied. "We are working for the masses, our people, their future, and their homeland, Palestine. Once a homeland is established, let's say on the West Bank and Gaza—a purely Palestinian homeland—let's suppose this is a possible dream . . ." He interrupted himself here and said, "It will come and I will invite you. I have no doubt," he said confidently and optimistically.

"Can we go back to talk a little bit about the financing of Fatah?" I ask now.

"There is no difference between Fatah and the PLO—Fatah is the mainstream PLO—so we have to speak about the PLO. The PLO is the sole representative of the Palestinian people," he said. The PLO was recognized as the sole representative of the Palestinian people by the Arab League in 1974 in the Rabat Conference, and also by the U.N. in the same year, the year Arafat addressed the General Assembly. The PLO was given observer status at the U.N. and recognized as a full member of the Arab League as well. Speaking proudly but quietly, Arafat was now saying, "We have full membership in many international United Nations establishments, like UNESCO, for example."

I then asked him why he thought the U.S. was so intransigent about giving its recognition to the PLO. He was quiet again and then replied, "This is a very difficult question. But you see the American administration and the American public opinion have been raped by Kissinger. That hypocrite called Kissinger, that hypocrite who placed certain conditions on the American administration which do not do the American people or American policy any good. When Kissinger resigned he said, 'History will prove that I have not betrayed my people.' He did not say my *nation*. And when he was shuttling in the Middle East, there was a demonstration against him which led him to comment, 'History will prove how I have served Israel.' And he has. Look at the Sinai agreement which he drafted: There is a clause in it—nonrecognition of the PLO—that still afflicts us.* Because the PLO does not recognize Resolution 242. What do I have to recognize it for? A war between Arabs and Israel. A cease-fire resolution was passed in the U.N. between Israel and the states fighting Israel. There is nothing in there about the Palestinians [in Resolution 242] and they ask that I recognize it. There is in 242 *no* indication about the Palestinian refugees. Dayan, at the beginning of October 1977, made an agreement with Vance and

* I believe he is referring to the second-stage interim disengagement signed by Sadat and Rabin on September 4, 1975, to ensure a cease-fire after the October War of 1973 between Egypt and Israel. Israel was to continue withdrawing farther into the Sinai beyond the strategic Mitle and Gidi passes and including the Sinai oil fields, with each side agreeing not to resort to military force. Kissinger, who was mediating on behalf of Washington, was asked by the Israelis to give "meaningful compensations" for their losses of the passes and oil fields. One of these "compensations" was America's assurance to Israel not to pressure it to withdraw from the Israeli-occupied Syrian Golan or from the West Bank of Jordan and also to withhold recognition of the PLO as long as the Palestinians would not accept U.N. Resolution 242. The agreement was signed on September 4, 1975, in Geneva.

Carter which he called 'my six-hour battle,' in which Carter and Vance confessed that what was meant by 'the refugees' in Resolution 242 was not an allusion to the Palestinian refugees but to Jewish and Arab refugees . . . they had cancelled out the word 'Palestinian' from the resolution," he exclaimed indignantly.

"But in fact, you don't recognize 242 or 338 to this day,"* I said.

"I recognize all U.N. resolutions," he replied.

"All of them?"

I looked at him somewhat skeptically, which made him say, "I recognize them as a block. And then I ask you, Why don't they force Israel to recognize the U.N. partition resolution? If they would, they have to withdraw from all the territories they have occupied." Arafat paused. He was getting angry. But then he continued with the same calm as before. "Then Reagan came along, and history cheated us. We received two blows. The first blow came from Sadat. We were three partners in the 1973 battle, the Egyptian fighting force was the first, the Syrians were the second, and the Palestinians the third. And then there was also a supporting force, the Arab force, which came to our assistance in the fighting . . . anyway, Sadat comes along at a time when we had also decided to go to Geneva.†

* In Algiers, on November 15, 1988, the Palestine National Council agreed to hold a conference based on U.N. Resolutions 242 and 338. But at the time of this interview the PLO, including Fatah, *did not* recognize Resolution 242 on the ground that it involves the acceptance of the State of Israel in its present form. What the Palestinians have always demanded is a *non*sectarian, democratic state that would include Muslims, Jews, and Christians.

Arafat has also gone on record as stating that he would settle for a Palestinian Arab state, which must include the West Bank and Gaza Strip.

† In October 1973 there was an American-Soviet plan for a Geneva peace conference. The format was that Israel and the Arab states involved would confer under American-Soviet auspices. The conference was to take place at the end of 1973. The meeting took place without great success. The idea of a Geneva conference came up again in 1976 at the instigation of President Carter, who also insisted that the Palestinians be represented at Geneva. The Israelis, of course, rejected the idea of talking with the PLO or the idea of a Palestinian homeland on the West Bank or Gaza, which Carter pressed. This was in September 1977. Meanwhile secret negotiations between Egypt and Israel were taking place, and in November 1977 Sadat decided to visit the Israeli Knesset on his own. Thus Geneva was abandoned.

"It was our agreement. A decision made by the Arabs. We had all agreed together to go to Geneva."

"Before 1977?" I asked.

"No, in 1977," he said and added, indignantly, "I was even being asked who the Palestinian representatives were to be. And they told me there is a problem with the Americans and this business of 242 and the Sinai agreement. So I put a limit to it all and said, All right, one Arab delegation. And it was agreed between us that it would be just one Arab delegation and I even named the Palestinians—professors who were teaching in American universities, like Dr. Khalidi, Ibrahim Abou Loghod and other Palestinian professors who are teaching in American universities—I was about to name them to be in the delegation. But then Sadat went to Jerusalem." Here Arafat's voice dropped and suddenly became very mournful. "And Egypt's huge power withdrew from the struggle and left us out in the cold. That was the first blow." He paused here before continuing.

Before he resumed I said, thinking I knew what he was about to say, "The second blow was Israel's occupation of Lebanon in 1981."*

"Oh, no, no, no, I don't consider it a blow. It's a battle. The second blow was the betrayal [of the Palestinians] by al-Assad [the President of Syria] . . . In 1977 it was betrayal by Sadat—he went and made a separate peace—and the second betrayal was from Assad, who made an agreement alone and left me beseiged, blockaded. The bombing began on June 4, 1982; June 6 was the day of Ishtiyah, and on the tenth he made the Philip Habib–Assad cease-fire accord." He paused, breathless. His

* The Lebanese civil war between the Christians and the Muslims was first helped by Arafat (on the Muslim-progressive side), then led by the PLO. Originally the civil war in Lebanon was said to be encouraged by the Soviet Union and Syria. The Russians wanted to put an end to the American-Israeli attempts at the creation of a Maronite Christian satellite. As for the Syrians, their aim was to destablize the country in order to make it easier to control all or most of Lebanon to form a Greater Syrian Commonwealth.

When Israel did invade Southern Lebanon in 1982, it occupied more than half of Lebanon; killed more than 20,000 men, women, and children; displaced another 100,000; destroyed the south; put Beirut under seige; and half-annihilated the capital.

anger mounting once more, he said, "It was an agreement between Hafez al-Assad and Philip Habib. The battle against me continued even while I was under seige. I was told that the agreement did not include the Palestinians." He paused and then said more quietly, "That was the second betrayal."

"And why did Hafez al-Assad do this?" I asked.

"And why did Sadat do it?" he said, replying with an angry question.

"As an Egyptian I can only tell you that Sadat wanted to liberate Sinai."

He was angry at my response and said, "Tell me, if you please, does the most trivial peasant in Assiut agree that Sinai be liberated without Jerusalem?"

"No," I replied quickly. Who was I to speak on behalf of Egyptian peasants?

"Besides," said Arafat, speaking very fast now, "we fought together, so why not solve things together. But you go and liberate your land [referring to Sadat] and leave me all alone?" He paused and then said with much anger, "At least he could have returned Gaza to me." There was a pause. Arafat was obviously livid with anger, even at the memory.

"But why did Hafez al-Assad betray you?" I persisted.

"Kissinger fooled him," he said. "There was an agreement between Kissinger and Assad in 1976. *Le Lion de la Grande Syrie,*" Arafat said, speaking in French. "Don't you remember in *Jeune Afrique*?" He referred to a periodical, issued in Paris, about the Middle East and Africa.

"There was an agreement between him and Kissinger, who told him, 'Assad, I will make you the Lion of Greater Syria.' That was the time when Assad invaded Lebanon.* Kissinger was fooling him."

* Various waves of Syrian forces entered Lebanon during April and June 10, 1976, advancing toward areas under the control of the Lebanese army and the Palestinian resistance in order, according to the Palestinians, to change the balance of power in favor of the Christian Lebanese Phalangists and their allies. On October 16, 1976, Arab heads of state met in Riyadd and agreed to create the Arab Deterrent Force from various of their states. At a later stage only the Syrian forces remained in the ADF.

"Greater Syria?" I asked.

"It comprises, historically, Syria, Lebanon, and Palestine." There was a pause. What he had been saying brought to mind what the novelist Naguib Mahfouz had told me: The Arabs have killed more Palestinians than the Israelis have. I ventured that remark to Arafat as he sat before me now. He nodded sadly.

"But how does it feel to be betrayed by your own Arab brothers?" I asked.

"What am I to do? This is the Arab nation. Can I get another nation from outside?" He seemed to be resigned to the fact that he had to suffer the betrayals of his fellow Arabs as a brother tolerates and endures the iniquities of another brother. It was his tribe. What could he do?

"I want to tell you something," he said quietly now. "Sabra and Shatila*—the butcheries there. Only one was Israeli, the other three were Syrian-Arab. And the massacres continue. It is all too painful. Don't remind me. The Palestinian people received two blows in five years from traitors in the Arab nation."

"And yet the PLO has made an astonishing comeback in Lebanon?" I ventured now. He made no comment to this.

Returning now to the Lebanese war, he said, "After the battle of 1982 from which we emerged victorious, Alexander Haig and Sharon's agreement that they would finish us off in three to five days hadn't worked. They sent us three-quarters of the Israeli army with its air force and its navy with the aim of finishing us off. They didn't finish us off. It turned out to be the longest of the Arab-Israeli wars and the most heroic. It was not Sharon who got me out of Lebanon. It was the Lebanese. They said to me, 'Abou-Amar, this is enough. We can't take it

* The massacres of Palestinians in 1982 and 1985 in the refugee camps of Sabra and Shatila and Burj al-Barajne in southern Lebanon are thought, by Palestinians and others, to be a plan jointly worked out by Syria and Israel and the U.S. to put an end to the Palestinian presence in Lebanon and hand over Lebanon to the joint control of Damascus and Jerusalem so as to carve up Lebanon into confessional mini-states.

anymore.' Together [with the Lebanese] I lost in eighty-eight days 72,000 dead and wounded. That's what made me leave. They said they couldn't take it anymore. You see the Lebanese were our allies. Beirut is not a Palestinian city. If it had been, no one would have been able to make me leave it. I would have stayed to the death."

"You didn't want to leave Beirut?" I said.

He interrupted me quickly: "Because it was the city of my leadership. But I gave the Lebanese and Palestinian heroes—the Arab nation—who fought that war, I gave them glory. And then to compound my wounds, I discover that the Syrians, as I leave Beirut, seize and confiscate all my weapons and my [military] warehouses and sell them to the Iranians."

"You mean they made them inaccessible to you?"

"No," he replied angrily. "They *sold* them to the Iranians. Those thieves, the leadership of thieves in Damascus, took these weapons and *sold* them to the Iranians," he reiterated, emphasizing every word.

He took a deep breath like a man in pain and continued, "And then they came and beseiged me in Tripoli. Tripoli was cruel; ninety-six days of seige, the Israelis pounding me from the sea and the Syrians from the shore." He paused again and then said quietly: "For the first time, an Israeli military force and an Arab military force fight side by side against the Palestinians. For the first time people finally came to recognize the conspiracy. What Sharon couldn't finish off in Beirut, Hafez al-Assad tried to do in Tripoli."

"Was there some kind of agreement with the Americans? Is that what you are trying to tell us?"

Tapping on his desk, Arafat answered swiftly, "The secret agreement was not between Philip Habib and Hafez al-Assad for a cease-fire, but it was a secret Israeli, Syrian, and American agreement. There is documented proof of this. The agreement was to expel the PLO from Lebanon," he said in measured words. "And the agreement is ongoing," he continued, "between MacFarlane and Assad."

"What is this agreement?" I asked.

"The dividing of Lebanon into two spheres of influence, one Syrian and one Israeli." He then proceeded to describe in geographical terms exactly where these zones were to be and then asserted that Lebanon was to be divided into religious cantons, that the PLO would not be permitted to return to Lebanon, and that the agreement also provided for the guaranteeing of the northern Israeli border from attacks by the fedayeen and their allies. The next step, according to Arafat, was the implementation of the idea of the division of Lebanon into religious cantons: Christian, Maronite, Orthodox, Shi'a (in the south), Druze, and Alawi (in Tripoli). In addition, Arafat told me that there are seventy-three different Islamic sects in the Middle East (not in Egypt) and twenty-nine different Christian sects. "Our enemies know us well. There are nineteen officially recognized Christian sects in Lebanon alone. Therefore, our Israeli and American enemies got Egypt outside the conflict through Camp David and then divided up the eastern area into religious entities in order to control it. The experimental field is Lebanon. It is there that the seed had been planted that will spread all over the rest of the area. And the crime of Hafez al-Assad is that he participates in this conspiracy. Treason! To want to create ten states in Lebanon! Look at the Chinese. With all their diversity, they are *one nation*. As for us Palestinians, our hope is to get a little piece of land; therefore, we cannot possibly accept religious divisions among us. Such division would be a total breakdown of the Palestinian people."

He paused here, as if to catch his breath, and then continued quietly and deliberately. "The Zionists took our land, but the Palestinian nation remained; we succeeded in maintaining the unity of the people of Palestine. In Lebanon they [the Zionists] hit the people and the land," he said forcefully. "The unity of the people was destroyed and that of the land, and that is the future of the eastern area. And, therefore, the danger is not the camp wars. What are the camp wars? The camp wars are the implementation of Sharon's plan, which was to destroy the infrastructure of the PLO and especially the refugee camps in Lebanon. They have to be demolished and shifted to Jordan in order to establish an alternative country for the Palestinians. We refuse an alternative homeland completely. We have one homeland: Palestine. And we have one capital: Jerusalem!" Arafat said these last words with implacable firmness. He meant every single syllable of what he was saying.

Arafat believes that the continued presence of the PLO in Lebanon will help offset the two conspiracies: the plan to divide that country into religious areas and the plan to displace those half a million Palestinians in Lebanon to Jordan in order to create an alternative homeland for them.

After a few minutes of silence, I asked him, "What about your relationship with Saddam Hussein?"

"Saddam Hussein and I are fighting to preserve the Arab nation from further deterioration. I am sorry to say that the enemy has entered the bedroom. There is a nervous breakdown in this nation. The enemy has penetrated the bedroom. Our enemies have not just entered the home but the bedroom as well." He was silent after he spoke those words as if they needed no explanation. For an Arab, the sanctity of the home and family is symbolized in matrimonial relations. When that bond is broken, there is not only disintegration of the family, but honor is lost. To Arafat, the Arab cause is symbolized in this microcosm.

"You refuse any peaceful solution with the Israelis, that is until they return all the occupied territories won in the 1967 war?" I asked him.

"At least they should accord me what the whole world has accorded me—the U.N. resolutions." I looked at him questioningly. "I am speaking about international legality," he said calmly. "International legality cannot be divided," he said in English. "You can't have international legality with one or two resolutions. International legality is one unit," he said emphatically. "Self-determination cannot be divided. How can the American administration accept the self-determination of the people of the Falkland Islands who do not number more than 1,800, and reject, at the same time, the self-determination of six million Palestinians?" There was a pause. "And self-determination, Laila, is one of the main principles of the American nation," he said with astonishment.

"And, of course, you can't be practicing self-determination if you live under Israeli occupation," I said.

"And, of course, 40 percent of our people live in the occupied territories under this oppression, under the oppression of Sharon and people like Meir Kahane, who are judaizing the Muslim and Christian holy places. How can this be accepted?" he asked, again with indignation.

"You are saying then that to continue living under Israeli occupation is untenable to you, the PLO."

"Yes," he said. "We have 50 percent of our people living in the diaspora," he added.

"Then what you want is that the military occupation of the West Bank and Gaza be lifted before you make peace with Israel?" I asked.

"According to the Fez Peace Project, we wish to get rid of the entire *occupation* of lands acquired by the Israelis in the 1967 war." As he spoke, the door was opened and a very slender and small-framed young woman of about twenty-five entered. Arafat's face lit up. "This is ———," he said by way of introduction. "Do you know who she is?" he asked. I shook my head. "She was the assistant to our ambassador in a European capital, but they kicked her out on the grounds that she was a terrorist. But she is not a terrorist," he said with sincerity. I looked at the girl. I didn't know what terrorists look like, but this girl had the saddest, most beautiful eyes I have ever seen in my life. A nervous laugh emanated from me, nonetheless. "You know," said Arafat, like a proud father, "she can speak their European language. But unfortunately there were Zionist elements in their country," he said. Meanwhile, the young woman said nothing. "She is like my daughter," Arafat added proudly. I looked at the girl again. Nothing. The sad expression did not change. She's a tough cookie, that one, I thought to myself as I glanced at the determined unsmiling jaw. I cleared my throat. The girl had almost thrown me off with her silence. She was not hostile to me. It was nothing personal, I realized. Those eyes were looking reproachfully at the whole world.

"Of course, there is an internationally recognized principle that the Palestinians have the right of self-determination—in other words to have a state," I said, resuming.

Arafat broke in. "We are human beings."

"But I think," I continued, "that the Israelis will not relinquish the occupied territories . . ."

Before I had finished my phrase, he broke in again, saying emphatically, "There will be no peace, no settlement, no security."

"So what happens?" I asked.

"As long as the rights of the Palestinians are ignored, the rights which were determined by the international legal community, and as long as the international U.N. resolutions are not implemented, there will be no future peace, no stability, and no security in the area." Arafat spoke these words sadly, almost mournfully. Suddenly he raised his voice and declared: "There will be no security for the other if there is none for me, no stability for the other if there is none for me, and there is no peace for the other if there is no peace for me." After he spoke there was a long pause. It was as if he had spoken his last.

"What is the absolute minimum that you will accept?" I asked now.

"The United Nations resolutions," said Arafat shortly.* In a statement he made in June 1986, Arafat said that he would accept the implementation of *all* U.N. resolutions and that the PLO (according to a resolution made in 1977) would be willing to accept the setting up of a Palestinian national state

* This is what Arafat did in fact accept in Algiers on November 15, 1988. At a special meeting the Palestine National Council adopted by a majority of 243 to 46 a new PLO peace policy which included accepting Resolutions 242 and 338 as a basis of negotiations at an international peace conference with the participation of Israel, the PLO, and the five permanent members of the U.N. Security Council.

on *any* part of any land from which Israel would withdraw or which would be liberated. This too was rejected by the Israelis. Nonetheless, Arafat asserted that a Palestinian state was a concrete possibility: "We will have it, very soon," he said. When I asked him how this was to come about, he replied that it would happen by "all means," in other words, by military and political fighting. His hope is based on the conviction that all military dictatorships must come to an end: "Where is Hitler?" he asked. "Where is the British occupation of India? Where is the British occupation in America? Where is the Spanish occupation of Latin America? Where is the French occupation in Algiers?" To Arafat it is only a matter of time before the Israeli occupation comes to an end.

"This Israeli military junta," he told me, tapping lightly on his desk, "is the naughty baby of the American administration."

"You mean spoiled baby?" I asked in English.

"They *spoil* all the American interests in this area," he rejoined in English. To him, Reagan's administration was also a "dictatorship" which had not been awakened.

"Yet the Americans have so much power," I said, trying to bait him.

He shook his head in defiance and said slowly, "The Palestinian people are one of the most important realities of the Middle East situation. It is a fact." He paused again. I was silent. I knew he wanted to say something else.

"You see," he continued, "four years ago, Begin, Haig, and Sharon declared that Israel will have peace for the next forty years! They called it the Peace Galilee Campaign. Where are those forty years that Haig, Begin, and Sharon mentioned now? Vanished! Because it's not easy to liquidate four or five million Palestinians." He spoke in English now, emphasizing every word with quiet confidence. "And we are not alone," he added.

"They say in the West that you are becoming much more moderate, compromising . . ."

"Yes, yes, yes," he replied.

"And," I continued, interrupting him, "you have spoken to Israelis in the Peace Camp, face to face." If I thought he would deny this or protest, I was mistaken.

"We have our democracy," he said calmly, "and we are proud of our democracy. Since I have been elected through this democratic process, I have to follow all the political programs which have been accepted by our representatives. In one of the most important resolutions of the Palestine National Council since 1974 and 1975, it says that we have to start a dialogue with the democratic and progressive forces in Israel and even *outside Israel* which accept the Palestinian rights."

"Such as?" I ventured. "The Communist Party?"

"The Communist Party [of Israel], the Peace NOW movement," he replied.

"So you have actually dialogued with Israelis?" I asked.

"Yes, yes, yes," he replied as if it was the most natural thing on earth. "For your information," he continued, almost smiling, "twenty-four members of the Knesset [out of 120] have signed a very important document stipulating self-determination for the Palestinian people."

"When did this happen?"

"This year," he replied casually.

"Then there was the Bucharest meeting," I reminded him. In November, several PLO members and several Peace NOW members had met face to face in Romania for direct talks.

"This was not the first time Emad," said Arafat, pointing to one of his aides who was present at the moment, "had a dialogue [with the Israelis] in Bonn. Before that there was another dialogue in Prague. And before that in Rome."

"Were these meetings only with the Peace Camp?" I asked.

"With democratic and progressive forces: the Peace Camp, the Progressive lists, the Black Panthers, the Orientals for Peace and certain parts of Mapam, some personalities from Mapam."

"So, in addition to the change in your position, and your new moderation, do you see a change in their camp?" I asked.

Emad volunteered the observation that there were two changes in Israeli public opinion. On the one hand, there was a desire for more dialogue with the PLO, and on the other hand, there was a law, newly passed in the Knesset, sentencing anyone who dialogued with the PLO to three years in jail.

"You see, they are afraid of peace," said Arafat.

"Your dialogue with Israelis, is it a tactic or a strategy?" I asked.

"It's part of our political program," he answered and added, "I myself have met many of them."

"Like whom? Uri Avnery?"

"Avnery is just one of them. Many, many."

"Did this bring about any results?" I asked.

There was a pause. The PLO chairman was choosing his words carefully here: "This is a principle," he said finally and added, "*I am not against the Jews*. They are our cousins. We are not anti-Semitic. *They* are. If they are against the Palestinians, then *they* are anti-Semitic. *We are Semitic.*" He paused here and said very quietly and slowly, "We are not against Jews. And many of our leaders *are* Jews. Did you know that?"

"Like who?" I asked.

He mentioned some names and said that these leaders were now in Israeli prisons. "They are not only members of the PLO but members of Fatah," he asserted proudly.

"So they are Jewish Palestinians who were jailed by the Israelis?"

"Yes," he replied. Arafat then told me that he had appointed a Palestinian Jew by the name of Illan Minedi to replace the assassinated PLO representative Issam Sartawi.* He mentioned that three months earlier there had been an assassination attempt on the new representative's life as well. "I think many Americans don't realize that people are jailed in Israel

* Sartawi, the PLO's leading diplomat, was assassinated by the Syrian-backed terrorist Abu Nidal because of his dialogues with Israelis. Sartawi paved the way for several meetings between the Israeli Peace Camp and Arafat.

and the occupied territories if they are even *suspected* of being members of the PLO. You have no idea how violent they are with the Jews who work with us . . . far more violent than with Muslim or Christian." He banged the desk before him quite vehemently as he said that. Then he mentioned an incident in 1974 when three PLO sympathizers—a Muslim sheikh, or man of the cloth; a Christian bishop; and a Jew—all found themselves in jail at the same time. Subsequently, the Christian and the Muslim were freed, but the Jew still serves his sentence in an Israeli jail.

Speaking quietly once more, he said, "In 1974 [at the U.N.], I said a very important thing: Why do I not have the right to dream? To dream of a democratic state where Jews, Christians, and Muslims can live together on equal footing?"

"But wasn't that exactly what Sadat wanted? Didn't he also dream of a time when Jews and Christians and Muslims could live side by side?" I said.

Arafat's anger mounted rapidly with his reply. "Live where?" he asked loudly. "In the diaspora? In the diaspora? In the diaspora? He has betrayed us."

"Because he made a separate peace?" I asked.

"A separate peace," Arafat asserted.

The atmosphere in the room was tense. The mention of Sadat's name had made Arafat uptight. He was still banging rhythmically on his desk.

"So you would find it acceptable, as a Palestinian leader, to live within Israel if it were not a religious state?"

"If it were democratic Palestine," he replied with military bluntness. "I have declared this many times. They live in *our* homeland. But we accept living with them—as *equals*. As fellow citizens. Look at the Sephardic Jews, they are tenth-class citizens. So what do you think *we* will be? Number fifty?" he asked sarcastically.

"So, therefore," I said, trying to change a subject which had obviously inflamed him, "it is better to have two states, Israel and Palestine?"

"To me it makes no difference. We have resolutions concerning the two. Either we can live in a democratic state—all of us. Or we are ready to establish our independent state in any part of territory evacuated by Israel or liberated. This is one of the most important resolutions of our PNC [Palestine National Council]. And for this we have accepted the idea of going to the Geneva Conference." He was silent.

"Well, that's obviously very clear," I ventured.

Arafat was still tapping on his desk, but he had calmed down considerably.

Someone walked into the room, and a book was brought in. Arafat glanced at it. It was in English. The book was then handed to me. It was called *Flashback* and it was by a colonel in the Palestinian army called "Abou al-Tayib" who served in the Lebanese war against the Israelis and who had chronicled that battle in a handsome volume which even included photos. The book was to be published in London. Arafat insisted that I should have the copy in my hand for future reference. I accepted this gift.

"What about your relationship with America? Is that ongoing or is the file closed?" I asked, now trying to phrase the question in a tactful fashion.

"It's not me who is closing it. It is the American administration that is trying to break with six million Palestinians."

I looked at my watch. It was past three in the morning, and Arafat was starting to look tired. But I knew I had to press on. I had kept some crucial questions for the end.

"But what should America do? Specifically?" I asked.

Arafat replied that America should recognize the U.N. partition plan, which he claimed it had not done. "The first item of the partition plan resolution. There are two items—one stipulating the creation of an Arab state, and the other of a Jewish state. They only recognized the second part of one resolution," he said in total amazement. In other words, he was blaming the U.S. for not implementing the November 27, 1947, U.N. partition resolution which the Arabs had originally rejected but which had subsequently become acceptable.

"But you have to recognize the State of Israel first, not so?" I said.

"You mean the victims recognize the aggressors? I will not accept it. I am no Sadat. He gave everything and he took nothing. Disaster."

"What about the liberation of Sinai; wasn't that something?" I asked.

"Sinai is demilitarized. And do you know that I am *not* allowed to visit Sinai! We have a camp there and I can't visit it. It's against Camp David! Can you believe such a thing?" he asked unbelievingly. Then he was silent. But there was much in that silence. Pain and suffering were the least of it. Arafat obviously carried around deep wounds from his fellow Arabs.

"You are being accused of being a terrorist, at least from the American point of view," I said finally.

"It is beneath my dignity to answer such a petty question," he replied with controlled anger. I looked at him silently. He calmed down a little and said, "De Gaulle was a terrorist to the Nazis; George Washington was a terrorist from the point of view of the English . . . You can fool some of the people some of the time, but you can't fool all of the people all of the time," he said, quoting Lincoln. "Sooner or later . . . The Americans are a superpower, but the downfall of great empires can be violent. Once upon a time, they used to say 'Our [America's] strongest base in the Middle East is the Shah's Iran.' Today they are paying a price. Not just their power, their reputation, but their *honor* has been lost in Irangate." He stressed the word "honor" as only an Arab will do—as the most valuable thing that could be lost, the greatest thing to forgo . . .

He had somehow evaded the whole issue of terrorism, and I was determined to get back to it. I felt that people in the West had a real need to understand *why* terrorism. I tried to get this through to him now: "Can you tell us *why* you do not consider your operations as terrorism?"

"You are speaking to a Palestinian," he said and repeated it again. "You are speaking to a Palestinian."

As an Arab, I understood what he meant: Palestinians had been expelled from and deprived of their homeland. It was their right to get it back—by any means they had. But the West did not understand this. Therefore I continued to pound him on that issue: "Why do you say you are not a terrorist?"

He began his answer quietly and spoke with patience, as if he were trying to teach a child a difficult lesson: "The U.N. Charter says that, for any nation or people, if it is faced with persecution or with dictatorship or with occupation, then it is the right of that people to employ all means to confront their occupier and/or aggressor. The constitution of the United Nations, which is in New York, says this. The principles on which the American nation is based say this. So why is the Palestinian nation the sole exception? Give me peace and give my people peace."

There was a silence after this. "You know, every age has its Romans who throw their Christians to the lions," he said suddenly. The fact that he was making this sort of analogy did not surprise me. Arafat saw himself and his people as the martyrs of the American Caesar. "Every age has its Caesar and its Reagan," he declared animatedly.

I tried once more to steer the conversation back to the issue of terrorism . . . "What is the aim of your military operations? Not civilian targets, I hope."

"The military operations are against . . ." He faltered here. The sentence remained suspended. Instead he said quickly, "We have issued the Cairo declaration against terrorism . . ." And he did not finish the sentence. I looked at him. He had suddenly decided to shuffle some papers on his desk.

There was a brief, rather embarrassing silence. Then, to my surprise, the young woman who had been sitting silently throughout all this spoke. Her voice was soft and subdued: "The Cairo declaration of 1985 is against acts of terrorism outside the occupied territories." Then she was silent again.

"Does that mean that there are to be no acts of terrorism except in territories occupied by Israel?" My question was totally ignored by Arafat, who was now quite engrossed in his papers.* Emad, the aide, volunteered the remark that the PLO was not known to conduct terrorist acts outside the occupied territories. I looked at Arafat. He simply ignored the remark and seemed to have completely withdrawn from the interview.

A long and painful silence followed. It was their way of letting me know that the subject of terrorism was not going to be expanded any further. I finally broke the silence and turned to Arafat. "In spite of all this fighting, and the ongoing struggle of the Palestinians, not a single inch of your territory has been liberated." He continued to shuffle his papers. "Would you like to comment?" I asked, persisting.

"Rhodesia remained Rhodesia for ever so long. But today it is Zimbabwe and Mugabe is a leader of the nonaligned movement," he said. He shifted uninterestedly in his chair and remarked airily: "The same thing happened to Algeria, and to George Washington . . ."

"Do you think that peace will ever come about? And if so, how?" I asked.

"Only by the implementation of the U.N. resolutions," he said, laboring the point. Arafat was obviously adamant in his insistence that resolutions other than 242 are pertinent and relevant. But ultimately the only solution really acceptable to Arafat was, as he said, "One democratic state. We are ready to accept one democratic state." Obviously, in this state which Arafat envisions, the Palestinians, who number over six million, would be the majority. To Arafat, this was a goal worth working for.

[On December 14, 1988, at a press conference in Geneva, Arafat denounced terrorism and accepted Israel's right to exist. Four hours later, U.S. Secretary of State George Schultz announced an end to the thirteen-year policy of ostracizing the PLO. Thus the dialogue between the U.S. and the PLO was to resume. Arafat had come a long way. But would the Israelis?]

* I think he was shocked by my question. The word "terrorism" is not in the Arab vocabulary. The phrase we accept is "liberation through armed struggle."

JANUARY 20
Cairo

Coming back to Cairo after Baghdad was like coming back to "gay Paree." For whatever its shortcomings, and despite the poverty that inundates it, Cairo is still a normal city—a city which goes about its day-to-day business. In Baghdad one had the impression that everyone was waiting for the next air raid.

At the airport I sank back into the Mercedes limousine and let the soft winter breeze of the dry, crisp, moonlit desert night caress my face. There was a kind of gentleness in the atmosphere which I had missed terribly in the more northern Iraqi capital with its rough, fierce faces, its tribal customs, its harsh manners, and its condescension to the people of my country.

At the airport in Baghdad I hid my dollars, even though I had brought them into Iraq with me and had not earned them there. The PLO driver told me they would be confiscated. I also hid my Egyptian money and the Arafat cassettes. You are not allowed to take recordings or recording materials in or out of Iraq. It was the PLO man who showed me how to conceal them, and it was thanks to the PLO that I was able to leave Baghdad at all. You need an exit visa to depart from Iraq, and I didn't have one. As I passed through customs, I quickly hid the precious cassettes when I was searched by two women in a tiny room. Some of the money was found, but when I told them I was a journalist, they let it go.

I was never so glad to see Cairo as I was that evening coming back on the 11:30 P.M. flight from Baghdad. As soon as we hit Egyptian soil, there was a rush for the door and the waiting bus. The men inside acted as if they had been let out of an army barracks. They were free now. Some sang, some chatted loudly, and one man even said, "To hell with Iraq," as loud as he could. As we waited for our baggage to descend from the plane onto the conveyor belts, I asked a worker who was standing beside me if he was glad to be back in Egypt. He was a man in his late forties, shabbily dressed in faded gray trousers and a threadbare beige woolen jacket. He wore no tie. "Egypt is the mother of the world," he said sincerely, almost emotionally. "You know," he said, "if they wouldn't think me crazy, I would prostrate myself and kiss this ground we are standing on."

JANUARY 30

There is a massacre going on in the Middle East. It calls itself the Iran-Iraq war. When I was in Baghdad last week, I saw an airy ghost town of a city with mock-Abassid modern architecture of blocks of uniformly built apartment houses built by government subsidy for the supporters of the regime of Saddam Hussein. The streets of Baghdad wind themselves round decrepit, old, off-white buildings and dreary shopping streets with nothing but government-made clothing and goods in them. Everything is state controlled in Iraq, and the people have very little to say about this war, as well as the rest of their political life—for it is a centralized government. Saddam Hussein's presence is everywhere—in posters on the street banners, on stickers in shop windows, and high on the top of buildings. His is the only picture. There are no ads of any kind and no other faces to be seen—anywhere. It was the same thing in Tehran. Khomeini's face was the only one to follow you around, and, there too, even in 1979, even before the Gulf war, the streets were full of uniformed soldiers. But one of the few differences between the two cities is that in Baghdad one sees crippled soldiers and maimed men walking the streets, and there are signs of the war even in its clean, well ordered, though poor, façades. A taxicab driver did not know where one of the largest hotels in the city was, and when I asked him why not, he confessed that he was from the southern port of Basra, the war front of Iraq, and that he had been there on combat duty for six years. Seven wounds later, he had been given a couple of months in Baghdad to recuperate. His wounds include a bayonet in the back and bullets from a

Kalashnikov. He said that his village had been leveled, that his sweetheart and her family had all been killed, but he would not tell me more. When I naively asked him to show me old Baghdad, he took me to a building right in the center of Baghdad that had been leveled by an Iranian missile. "This used to be an old building," he said, half-dazed. As I watched him, I realized that he was still in shell shock. When I asked him what he thought of the president, he refused to comment. Did he want the war to go on? He was silent for a minute . . . and then shrugged.

FEBRUARY–JULY 1987

FEBRUARY 1

Mursi Saad al-Din

Editor, Cairo Today

Mursi Saad al-Din is one of Mrs. Sadat's closest aides and a former spokesman for the Sadat regime. Now he is the editor of an English-speaking magazine, *Cairo Today*. When we met he was still the smooth, charming, flirtatious man I had known. He kissed me affectionately, as one does a relative. I had known Mursi since I was fifteen years old, when his wife used to teach me English literature at a British school in Cairo. Our paths had crossed and crisscrossed many times in the past twenty years, and though we were then on opposite sides of the fence, we always remained good friends. He had been teaching with Mrs. Sadat at South Carolina University. Mursi remained loyal to the regime. "Be careful what you write," he warned very affectionately. "And don't say bad things about the Iraqi regime. You never know."

"You mean they might assassinate me," I said.

He smiled at me pityingly. "You have no political background. You should show me what you write."

Later, as he got up and kissed my hand and walked out of the Hilton coffee shop, urbane and elegant in his British wool double-breasted blazer and gray flannel trousers, I thought to myself: There goes one of the last living relics of the Sadat days. For Mursi epitomized the very crème de la crème of Westernized Egyptians. A dying breed.

FEBRUARY 2

Press conference at a wood-paneled, chandeliered room with oriental carpet and Arabesque sculpted ceiling at the Marriott Hotel in Zamalek. The hotel is the converted palazzo of Prince Lufallah, a relative of King Farouk's, and is full of ottomans and gigantic oil paintings, brass ornaments, marble staircases, and wall-to-wall gold mirrors. The occasion of the press conference is a production of *Aida* at the Luxor Temple in what used to be called Thebes, the ancient capital of Egypt.

"EGYPT LOVES YOU. COME SEE FOR YOURSELF," reads a large placard behind the banquet table flanked by chairs for the various producers and promotors at the conference. The whole idea occurred to an expatriate Egyptian, Fawzi Metwalli. As one foreign correspondent put it, he woke up one morning and thought of a way of making a lot of money quickly. From Vienna, where he lives and owns a petroleum company, he gets an idea—Why not stage *Aida* in its original location, the location that Verdi himself dreamed it would be staged in? Right in the ancient temple of the ancient capital of Thebes? A masterful wheeler-dealer, he contacted the most famous open-air opera company in Europe, the Arena di Verona, and asked them if they would stage it—complete with Placido Domingo as Radames. Yes, they would. An English stage manufacturer then was contracted to build the 5,000-seat auditorium which will seat the spectators who will be flown from all over—Italy, Spain, Greece, Switzerland and Denmark among others, and a Viennese architect, Hans Krebitz, was put in charge of the technical aspects of the production, which will have eight to ten performances.

The significance of this production for the promoters and producers is not "Guerra, guerra, guerra," but Peace, Peace, Peace.

FEBRUARY 3

Shimmering lights, purple, magenta, amber, orange, and green, were reflected in the pitch black Nile River. The joyful sounds of Beethoven's *Spring Sonata* filled the waterfront banquet hall at the Meridien Hotel. For in Cairo, February is spring weather. Beautiful women with dark skin and black hair and kohl eyelids sat listening to the music, wrapped in their minks and imported cashmere coats. Diplomats flashed silk suits and ties and gold rings on their fingers. The breathtaking, sensuous view, which served as the backdrop for the pianist and violinist from Vienna, contrasted with their sober, professional, polished playing. A replica of an Pharaonic Nile barge, decorated with beads of colored light bulbs, glided by majestically. The audience of hundreds listened in hushed respect to this imported music filling that room in the midst of the Nile. The noises and agonies of the city seemed far, far away.

The Austrian Cultural Center attracts sophisticated and Westernized Egyptians to such concerts regularly. The concerts are also free of charge and open to the public at large. Yet the audience tonight looked like the kind of audience that was hand picked. Of course, there were the familiar faces of the music lovers I used to see at such concerts in the sixties, when they were held in little chambers in tiny cultural centers around the city. But what was new was a whole class of the infitah of the affluent, monied people who came into their own in the Sadat days and who took pleasure in flaunting their fur coats and diamond earrings. Queen Farida, divorced wife of King Farouk, sat in the front row as if presiding over the affair; she wore a fur-trimmed hat and Parisian-style clothes. For me she evoked another age. Yet she was not out of place in this gathering of people who had turned out to be seen more than anything else. There was an atmosphere of "Let's enjoy it while we can—the future is unknown." Baghdad and the meeting with Arafat were fresh in my mind, and that reality superseded this present one of enjoyment and affluent living. As the concert concluded with a piece of Mozart, I wondered how long we were going to be given such entertainments, such tantalizing jewels of Western culture. For how long before the reality outside becomes all-powerful?

MARCH 1
Connecticut once more

A bleak landscape of gray winter skies, snow, and bare branches. Long lines at the supermarket on Sundays. People here look stiff and do not laugh too often. Everything is quiet. No traffic noises, no dogs barking. A total nothingness.

How I yearn for the sunshine and movement of Cairo. Once in a while, someone will ask politely: "Where have you been? We haven't seen you for almost half a year."

"I was in the Middle East," I reply.

"Oh," they will exclaim indifferently.

Snow has fallen over the red-brick buildings of the state university in New Haven where I teach my theater classes.

Bundled-up students scurry in and out of buildings. It is bitterly cold. The parked cars are covered in white. When they pull out, they skid on thc slippery pavement.

My office is located in a large circular building which houses two theaters. The offices of the faculty are tucked away in the basement of this building.

An elderly, peroxide-blond secretary guards the department offices from a small cubicle at the entrance. The walls of the basement are gray; so is the linoleum floor.

The first office on the right is for the adjuncts, temporary faculty: impoverished Ph.D.s or M.F.A.s who perform their teaching duties anxiously, so as not to tread on the feet of the formidable tenured faculty.

The second office on the right is occupied by the burly chairman of the department. Originally from Nebraska, he is a six-footer who looks like a polar bear. If you don't get out of his way, he may trample you. He has bushy white hair and thick horn-rimmed glasses and the booming voice and muscular, sturdy body of a man who works with his hands. The students call him by his first name, but they fear him. He does not believe in reading plays in class. He teaches classes in technical theater. He is a rarefied stage carpenter who roams about with a big bunch of clanking keys at his waist.

The third office to the right in this bureaucratic basement belongs to the second in command. His name is on the door but, even though I share this office, my name is not. The office has many bookshelves. They are filled with his books. I have no such shelves. Mr. Jones, my colleague, a middle-aged man with Oxford and Yale credentials, wears tweed jackets that are too short and baggy pants that are too long. He is the only intellectual in this department.

In addition to sharing his office, I share his ideas. He gives Shakespeare and Oscar Wilde precedence over shows like *The Best Little Whorehouse in Texas* and *No, No, Nanette.*

The third and final office is occupied by the scene designer, who also directs the musicals of the department. With a potbelly and a thin voice, he has a mechanical walk. Most of his time is spent in the costume rooms surrounded by young men who construct over-elaborate costumes which never look appropriate on the student actors and actresses.

I once suggested to my colleagues that we should put on a third-world play. This was my thinly disguised euphemism for an Egyptian play.

The polar bear chairman looked at me with the contempt which, in America, is reserved only for people who have just stepped off the boat.

JULY 29
London, Kensington High Street

The corner kiosk still parades every conceivable Arab newspaper and magazine. Women in black chadors, with a child in hand, walk by nonchalantly, contrasting sharply with the elegant, red-brick Victorian apartment blocks around. Men dressed in loose white galabiyas and red kufiyehs chat loudly with one another in Kuwaiti or Saudi Arabic. Shish kebab and rolled stuffed grape leaves are displayed in the front windows of small Iranian restaurants, where dark young men with piercing black eyes gaze at you as you walk by. Local shops display signs that Arabic is spoken here. Occasionally at traffic crossings a Rolls-Royce will flash by, displaying a Saudi or Kuwaiti emir and his retinue in the back seat.

In the elevator of the De Vere Hotel, a small hotel with a view of Kensington Gardens, Arabic is heard more often than not. More often than not, these Arabs will smile in recognition and say, *"Marhaban"* ("Welcome").

AUGUST 1987

AUGUST 6
London

Cecil Hourani is an Arab cultural ambassador at large. A Lebanese professor who taught both in Lebanon and in the West, he is equally at ease in both worlds. Among other things, he ran a theater festival in Carthage, Tunisia, where companies from all over the world performed alongside Arabic troupes. He lives in London now and collects Arab artists and intellectuals, encouraging them and spurring them on.

Cecil is a gray-haired man in his sixties. His eyes are dark and cunning. He is soft-spoken and suave. The accent is charming, sophisticated. His brother, Albert, however, has no such accent. His English is pure Oxford. He is professor of Middle Eastern history at St. Antony's College in Oxford. He has lived most of his life in England. To me, both brothers look European, even British. It is only when you start talking to them that you realize that they are Arabs. Not many expatriates live the Arab experience as they do.

Cecil Hourani has a home in Beirut, which he lives in part of the year. The violence of the Lebanese civil war has never scared him away from his beloved country. I feel a great empathy for him. We are both Christian Arabs who cannot tear ourselves away from our Arab roots. Besides, Cecil Hourani belongs to a rare breed of Middle Easterners who are perfectly comfortable with and have mastery of not only the Arabic language, but the French and English as well. Cecil married a Lebanese Druze lady who studied at Smith College. His daughter Zelfa was also educated in the West and works as an editor for a London publisher. Yet when Zelfa marries, it will be to someone who is totally acceptable to her family.

The Houranis were the first people I contacted when I arrived in London. "Let's have lunch," he had suggested over the phone. The rendezvous was arranged in a Lebanese restaurant in the Kensington area. I arrived early. It was a small but elegant place. The white tablecloths contrasted with the intricate wooden arabesque screen panels which decorated the walls. Here and there, paintings, perhaps by Lebanese artists, were displayed. In a corner, a table upheld a large brass Turkish canister surrounded by coffee cups. But what struck me most was that one could only hear Arabic and French spoken. The waiter who was approaching my table smiled as if in recognition. I ordered a glass of wine in French and sat back feeling at home in this world of the Levant.

Presently the Houranis arrived. As we made the rounds of the Middle Eastern salads, the taboula, the humus and the other varieties, we chatted. A man in a blue blazer approached Cecil with an Arabic greeting. It was the restaurant owner. He was gracious. His welcome invoked Arab hospitality.

"I am glad you are still writing about the Middle East," said Cecil as we sat down to our meal. Later, I made him promise to arrange a meeting with his brother, Albert.

AUGUST 10

Albert Hourani

Historian, Professor of Middle Eastern history, St. Antony's College, Oxford

Albert Hourani is very British-looking and has silvery-white hair. He seemed busy, so we plunged right into the topics of my research. Professor Hourani synthesized most of what I had been hearing on Islamic fundamentalism and the Palestinian question. One of the many books he has written is *Arabic Thought in the Liberal Age,* which deals with the nineteenth century and early twentieth century. It deals with all these movements of thought that responded to the expansion of Europe and that tried to reconcile the traditions of the Arabs and of Islam with the new ideas that were coming in mainly from England and from France.

Professor Hourani talked about his book at length—the subject of which still fascinates him: how Muslims, pious, orthodox Muslims like the nineteenth-century thinker Mohammed Abdou, were able to reconcile Islam with Western ideas. This type of thinking, he asserted, went right through to Nasser and to his (Western-inspired) idea of Arab nationalism.

"But things have changed now," I volunteered, as we sat in the foyer of the De Vere Hotel in London, "and Islam is becoming an orthodoxy, and there is even a rejection of Mohammed Abdou's liberal thinking."

"Yes. The Islamic fundamentalists regard Mohammed Abdou as someone who made too many concessions to the West. They even regard him as a creature of European imperialism."

"What exactly is fundamentalism?" I asked him.

"When one talks about fundamentalism, one can mean more than one thing by it. You can mean Muslim and conservative. The Saudis are conservative in the sense that they have to make changes, but they want to go slowly, they don't want to go fast. The people in power in Iraq are different again. I wouldn't call them fundamentalists. I would call them traditionalists. That is to say, they are not trying to go back to the real or imagined world of the Prophet and his generation. They accept Islam as it has developed, the whole Shi'a tradition of Islamic thought and jurisprudence."

"What is Shi'a?"

"The Shi'a are those who believe that the succession of the Prophet lay with the line of the imams beginning with Ali, who was his son-in-law and his cousin, and continued through the line of his descendants down to the twelfth imam, who disappeared but who reappeared in the fullness of time as the mehdi.* The imams are to the Shi'as infallible interpreters. They are the deposit of truth. And, in their absencc, the only authority lies with those who exercise 'Ijtihad'—the 'mujtahids,' the great scholars. And that gives the scholar a leadership in Shi'a community which the scholars in the Sunni community do not have. The role of the Azhar [the oldest Muslim theological seminary in the world] in Egypt is not the same as the role of the great mullahs in Iran."

"How is it different?"

"The mullahs are much more independent of the state. The Azhar is not independent of the state. The great Shi'a men of learning have often been independent of the state and sometimes in opposition to it. What's happening in Iran now is new and, I think, extremely dangerous. For the first time, the Shi'a men of learning are taking direct responsibility for government. For the first time they are involving the eternal interest of Islam in the fate of a particular regime. If I were a Shi'a, I would be extremely worried."

"Why?"

"Once you are involved in politics, you are involved in compromises, and you can no longer carry out the correct path. There may be, at some point, reactions against them. There are Iranians, I know, who are very worried about this because they feel that the Iranian regime is linking the eternal interests of the Islamic community with the fate of a particular regime. They are open to charges of having betrayed their principles. So that is the second kind of what people call fundamentalist."

"And the third?"

* Basically, Sunni Islam accepts the principle that the Caliphate is an *elective* office. The Shi'a sect has, from the beginning, disagreed with the principle of election. They hold that the leadership of the Muslim nation is hereditary, i.e., it belongs to the family of the Prophet. Their support was given to Ali, cousin and son-in-law of Mohammed. Ali and his descendants are called imams (leaders). They are considered *the sole source of truth*. For the Shi'a, there is no hope for a proper life except through complete devotion to the imam. Hence the importance of the imam Khomeini in Iran.

"Third is the fundamentalism of the Muslim Brotherhood, who are trying to go back to a certain vision of what the Muslim community was like."

"And what was it like?"

"I don't know. In their vision it was the only just and virtuous community that would ever be. And the only safe path for modern man is to follow the example of the Prophet and his companions."

"In other words, a lifestyle which approximated that of Muslims in the sixth century. But isn't that what they are doing in Iran?"

"I don't think so. And then there is a fourth kind of fundamentalism, which is that of Qaddafi, who believes that Islam is the Koran and that every man is the interpreter of the Koran. So there are four kinds of fundamentalists at least."

"So what you are suggesting is that fundamentalism is complex and varied—a movement which has different hues and colors?"

"Yes, I think so and, therefore, I am a little doubtful of people who believe that there is going to be one great wave of Islamic anger which is going to overwhelm the whole world. I think differences between different Muslim countries are very great. I can't quite see Egypt taking its leadership from Iran. . . ."

"But if Iran won the Gulf war, then what?"

"Then I think it will control Iraq and it will control the Iranian peninsula."*

"And then?"

"Whether it will strengthen the fundamentalist movement of the Egyptian nationalist movement remains to be seen. But, I think, Egyptian national feeling and Egyptian national unity is so deep, so strong, that there could well be a reaction in Egypt against Iranian interference. I don't see Cairo being ruled from Tehran."

* In 1989, Iran sued for peace.

"Is what is happening in Iran and other Muslim societies a reaction to the West or something similar? And why the anger?"

"I think the anger is the reflection of the last 150 years when Muslim countries were dominated by Western countries, when they were compelled to make accommodations to the West. Now they are asserting themselves—'we have something of our own'—which I find perfectly natural but not inevitable. I think it an expression not only of *anger* but of the *strength* of the Islamic community."

"Aside from these resentments at occupation, what is making them so angry?"

"I think it is through occupation and colonization—through weakness, they are in danger of losing their identity."

"But what has triggered all this?"

"The fundamentalist movement has been there for a long time, since the twenties. But there may be one of two things which may have triggered it: One is the extraordinary phenomenon of the Iranian revolution, which is one of the great events of the twentieth century, comparable to the Russian revolution. Second, it's the simple fact of wealth, which has all kinds of effects. One of the effects is to strengthen this perception that we have something of our own. I was thinking of the wealth of Saudi money, which now subsidizes Islamic organizations everywhere."

"But why are Saudis funding Islamic movements?"

"Because they believe in them. They believe [Islam] is the answer to mankind. I think there is a kind of disorientation in the Western world. The West is not so certain of itself as it was. And this idea of progress—is the West progressing? I can't say. There is so much disorientation, especially in the political sphere. If you ask what American policy is in the Middle East now, one can't say, can one?"

"Excuse me for digressing, but do you think the existence of Israel may also have kindled the resentment of the Arabs?"

"Yes, I would say so. Although my own impression is that the Arabs are much more ready to finish with the Palestine problem than the Israelis are. If they could have peace on honorable terms they would do so.

"The real obstacles in the way of peace are two: First of all, the deep division in Israeli government and in Israeli society. And second of all, the reluctance of the American government to do anything at all for that matter."

"What about Israel's continuous settlements?"

"Well, that would be part of a peace, and that is the real division inside Israel now."

"So you're saying that the ball is in the Israelis' court?"

"Yes—it is in the Israelis' court."

I could see that the distinguished white-haired historian was getting tired. It was time to ask him the question I had been stalling for some time. The question of terrorism. "What about Palestinian terrorism?" I ventured, hesitantly. "And by the way, could you define or analyze that word for me from the Arab point of view?"

"To the Reagan administration, Palestinians are terrorists. Southern Lebanon is the haunt of terrorism—'Let the Israelis go in and finish them off.' The Palestinians are a *resistance* movement, which has the same kind of justification as other resistance movements. But, on the other hand, there are smaller groups which one could call terrorists. Abu Nidal is a terrorist. But the PLO, as a whole, is *not* a terrorist organization."

"Why do you say it is not?"

"Because I think it's an institution which has a clear, rational aim, which it pursues in the same way as other organizations of that kind."

"It's similar to the Irgun maybe?"

"No. I would say, like the Haganah. It is an underground organization—a public organization which is prepared to use force to bring its problems to the attention of the world and to oppose the Israelis. It does not commit indiscriminate acts of terror against populations in the way in which the Stern gang did or the Abu Nidal group does. But I think that this obsession with terrorism and with the Palestinians is part of the

Reagan administration's confused thinking on the Middle East. I don't see any clear line of American policy there. Even its policy on Iran . . ."

"But if the U.S. had a clear policy, what in your opinion would it be?"

"Well, it has to be a policy about the Palestine problem. . . ."

AUGUST 15

Mr. X

Shi'ite businessman

He sat across from me behind an imposing mahogany desk, his gold cufflinks discernible at the cuffs of a custom-made linen shirt worn under an expensive blazer. Mr. X is a wealthy Iraqi businessman who has lived in London for over fifteen years, and he is a Shi'ite.

"Do you know?" he said, leaning forward toward me and speaking ardently, "there is a law in Iraq which dictates that any Iraqi who says a word against Saddam Hussein will be put to death. It's in the constitution. A man may curse the Koran, but he may not curse Saddam Hussein."

"What exactly is happening internally in Iraq?" I asked.

"What is happening would make your hair stand on end. What is happening in Iraq now has never happened in any other country in the world. Nobody speaks about it. Nobody is allowed to."

Speaking passionately, he informed me that there were 150,000 political prisoners in jail in Iraq—people who were incarcerated simply because they were against the Saddam regime.

"If a person as much as whispers their criticism of the president, they are executed and their bodies hung outside their doorways. This is the way we do things in Iraq," he said.

"But who is to blame for all this?" I asked.

"The Americans," he replied forcefully. "Saddam Hussein is their man. It was the Americans who put him where he is. Do you know who Saddam Hussein is?" he asked.

"Who?" I asked.

"You don't know?" he said incredulously.

"No, I don't know," I replied.

"He's a gangster. He's a killer. He has killed people with his own *hands*. He used to be at the head of a kill squad in the anti-Ba'th movement. Didn't you know all that?"

I shake my head. This was all completely new to me. "Are you implying that he's an American agent?" I asked.

"They put him in power," he replied. "When they no longer want him there, they will overthrow him. Do you realize that one billion pounds a day is spent in this way every day? And where do you think the money is coming from? Saudi Arabia, America, France, even Russia. It's the outside world that's propping up this regime and it's the outside world that wants Iraq to fight Iran."

"Are there many Shi'ites in Iraq who sympathize with the Khomeini regime?" I asked.

He looked at me with surprise and said, "We have to sympathize with Iranians now as Shi'ites in Iraq."

"Why?" I asked.

"We didn't before because we had a love of our Arab nationalism—but not anymore. When you look at Iran and see how many countries are fighting it, you must conclude that Iran is right."

"What do you mean by that?"

"There is a kind of conspiracy against Islam, isn't there? All these countries are fighting Islam."

"How repressive is the regime of Saddam Hussein?" I asked, wishing to drop the subject of the conspiracy against Islam, as I lit a cigarette.

"How repressive exactly is the Saddam Hussein regime? Did you ever hear of a country where a father is awarded an honorary medal on television because he executed his own son?"

I gasped slightly.

"Yes, he killed his son. Do you know why he killed his son?"

I shook my head.

"He killed his son because the son would not fight in Saddam's war. So he killed him! And that man is *honored* before the whole country for days. Do you know of any other country where that would happen?"

I remained silent. "Do you hate America?" I asked after a few moments.

"Yes, I hate America, but even worse than America is the Soviet Union. Because we all know that if there was Soviet influence in the Middle East they would really take over. Do you know what Nasser used to say about the superpowers? America is the beloved enemy, but the Soviet Union is the hated friend.

"In other words, we in the Arab world are basically pro-Western, we don't want Soviet influence because we believe in God. But how can we be pro-West with American foreign policy being dictated by Israel? Israel would like to see her two enemies Iraq and Iran enfeebled, and that is why it is behind the Gulf war and is even an arms supplier for it. That is why Israel is dictating this policy. If it weren't for all that, we might be pro-America in Iraq. But how can we be if American foreign policy is dictated by Israel?"

"What would happen if Saddam Hussein were overthrown?" I asked.

He replied, speaking pensively. "There would be three possibilities: the army—the continuation of the present regime, or the Communists who are very strong in Iraq, or the Islamic fundamentalists."

"Which would you prefer?" I asked.

"The Islamic fundamentalists, because then we may have a regime concerned with justice and human rights. But I don't think such an overthrow will take place because the Americans want Saddam Hussein there. He's doing their dirty work for them."

DECEMBER 1987–AUGUST 1988

DECEMBER 20, 1987
Connecticut

There are no more leaves on the trees. It is cold. The sky is ominously gray. I stay indoors. I have been working hard on my manuscript. I have had to sort out almost five hundred hours of taped interviews. Drudgery. Time for a vacation. Tomorrow I will fly to Cairo to be with my mother on Christmas. And to be with the sunshine.

JANUARY 19, 1988
Cairo

Returning to Cairo is like sinking into a warm featherbed. The air is balmy, the sunlight almost blinding. But the economic situation in Egypt is worsening, and Mubarak has gone on a tour of six Gulf countries in order to pledge Egypt's support for the defense of the Gulf states in case of Iraq's imminent fall. There was talk of some 10,000 Egyptian forces being sent to Kuwait, but this was not confirmed. There will, however, be an exchange of military advisors and a joint arms manufacturing deal between these countries.

Inflation is on the rise. A kilo of meat costs eleven pounds. Only a year ago it was seven. There have been many student demonstrations. On January 1, a Muslim fundamentalist demonstration broke out after Friday prayers and made its way to downtown Cairo. They say its object was to burn the Jewish synagogue there. The extreme right, the students, and most of public opinion are extremely angry at Israel's recent belligerence in the West Bank and the Gaza Strip. The U.S. is identified with Israel. Even though the U.S. recently voted against the deportation of several Palestinian "troublemakers" from the West Bank, this gesture in the U.N. has not eased the anger at America and her Zionist ally. The papers are full of stories, often corroborated by the BBC and other foreign news agencies, of the atrocities being committed by the Israeli defense forces against Palestinian civilians. For instance, in Gaza, the Israelis burst into a hospital of wounded Palestinians and arrested them and carried them away on the spot. They destroyed an intensive care unit, and when the patients could not be removed from their hospital beds, they took their names down to arrest them later on.

The demonstrators in Cairo are asking Mubarak to break off diplomatic relations with Israel. They chanted, "A curse on you, Mubarak" as they invoked him to do so. Meanwhile, Mubarak prepares to make a trip to the U.S. But people are heartened by his visit not to the U.S. but to the Arab states. Maybe they will help rescue Egypt financially . . .

JANUARY 21

Sheikh Yussef al-Badris is an "official" Muslim fundamentalist. He is very outspoken in his criticism of the Muslim Brotherhood. He is attempting to form an Islamic political party called after Mubarak's famous slogan "Al-Sahwa"—"the Awakening."

Sheikh Badris recently met with President Mubarak to discuss "the details." He hopes to appeal to a wider spectrum of Egyptians, who though not members of the Ikhwan, are still sympathetic to the idea of moving Egypt closer to Islamic society . . .

Meanwhile, in the south of Egypt, such as in Minyeh, the

Ikhwan are still going strong. A driver of a truck transporting beer (a state monopoly in Egypt) was beaten up and his load destroyed. Those responsible: an organization called Jama'at al-Qassas, which was rounded up and its leaders jailed by the police.

AUGUST 12

A drab academic year is finally over. Tomorrow I return to Egypt for the summer.

AUGUST 13

There is a new air terminal in Cairo. It is a circular glass and concrete structure. There are different satellites for different airlines. The floor is made of ceramic tile, and everywhere there are beautiful plants clustered around fountains spouting abundant water.

Landing in Cairo has also become an efficient procedure. There are no hassles—at least for flights coming in from the West. It's a different story if you arrive from Iraq or Algeria. They search you thoroughly to take your electronic gadgets, and to make sure you are not carrying arms. But if you have arrived on TWA, everyone smiles at you.

As I walked through passport control, I couldn't help marveling at the flowing water from the fountains. I had been led to believe that there would be a drought in Egypt this summer. I was expecting to see a shriveled Nile, famine, and electricity curfews. But the rains came. They even flooded the Sudan.

"Allah has saved us," said my mother, who was waiting with my brother for me. She looked tired, worn out. But she never loses faith in Allah and Egypt.

"There is no drought because Allah has stood by Egypt," said my brother, who is very religious. "Egypt is the gift of the

Nile," he added cheerfully, as we got into his old Volvo. "The Nile will always stand by us." It was useless to confront my family with the facts: The country's population swells by 1.4 million every ten months, and we import more than 60 percent of our food.

As we drove through the city on the brand-new overpasses that crisscross above dusty slums and new high-rises, my heart sank. "I have a reservation at the Meridien Hotel," I announced. My mother looked at me with irritation. "It will take ages to clean my apartment! And," I added, "I can't stand the heat. I must have air conditioning." My apartment does not have such appliances.

"We can see you live in America," said my brother sarcastically.

Nonetheless the Meridien it was. As we walked into the lobby, I thought to myself: This must be paradise. The cool air scented with perfume and flowers was intoxicating. Outside it had been 107 degrees in the shade.

With some persuasion, my mother agreed to move in with me. By the time we had unpacked, it was evening and the setting sun enveloped the Cairo landscape with a deep red. I stepped out on the terrace which jutted right into the water. Dusk was settling into darkness. A warm breeze welcomed me on the opposite bank; across the water the Sheraton Tower loomed over various little cafes and casinos. Neon lights winked on and off: TOSHIBA . . . MARLBORO. Western music filtered from across the water. The melody mingled with the distant sound of traffic noises and human sounds. I closed the terrace doors and returned to the air-conditioned room.

Much later I opened the terrace door and stepped out again. The dark water glistened with a kaleidoscope of colors. A gaudily decorated tourist ship, modeled after a Pharaonic boat, swayed in the water. The sound of tambourines and cymbals and flutes accompanying a belly dancer (I think) shot up loudly. Then the sounds receded as the boat moved on, leaving only an echo . . .

AUGUST 15

People still look as if they have been forged from the neighboring sandy Mokattam hills. They are not covered in dust. They are forged of dust. Some of them look crusty. But all of them look as if they are about to crumble.

They still sell jasmine buds, strung on sewing thread by smiling men. In the street, they hang them loosely on their necks and arms. And when the car stops in traffic, the smell is intoxicating. If you can still buy jasmine flowers in Cairo, then things must be all right, I tell myself as I drive along in the August heat. I look around again. Nobody smiles.

There are many weddings taking place. On TV most of the soap operas deal with the problems of finding a flat and car to get married with. An Egyptian feature film on TV told the story of a woman who couldn't have children. She had a breakdown. But few are talking about the young woman professor who hanged herself recently. She was teaching at one of the large campuses here. Some said she committed suicide because she couldn't get used to Cairo. She had spent six years in the United States.

What is everyone talking about? Inflation and inflation. The price of meat, of gas, and of electricity. My hotel is full of Arabs from Kuwait and Saudi Arabia. They breeze in and out of the air-conditioned halls and elevators with women and children. They look cool in white flowing galabiyas; their perfumed wives stand submissively at their sides. The women are all veiled, from head to foot. "I wish I could jump into the pool as you do," said one Kuwaiti woman wistfully.

"Do women have freedom in your country?" I said, trying not to sound satirical.

"Of course," she said.

"Can there be more freedom than this . . . ?" she asked, waving her hand at a woman passing by in a short skirt and no veil.

Carter flew in and out of Cairo yesterday. He had talks with the Palestinian representatives here. My friend, Said Kamal, was on TV with another spokesman for the PLO. "We wish to reassure our friends here and abroad that we are not weak, that the PLO is strong," said the man. "And we will succeed in building our state."

There was a cease-fire between Iran and Iraq yesterday. The guns are silent for the first time in eight long years. But for how long, asked one of the editors of a government paper.

In the evening a tepid breeze caresses the worn-out old city. "The heat is God's wrath on us," a Christian woman told me. "Do you know how many Copts have converted to Islam this year?" she asked in hushed whispers. I shook my head. "Fifteen thousand," she murmured, looking around lest someone overhear us. "These are bad times," she said sadly.

"But the government is clamping down on the Muslim extremists . . ." I reminded her.

She looked at me sorrowfully and shook her head. "They are everywhere," she said. "So much so that our Muslim friends shun us. It's never happened before. Things have changed," she added.

AFTERWORD—1989

JULY 15
Cairo

I am like an icicle that is thawing in the sunshine. I look out at the impervious Nile flowing beneath the fourteenth floor of the Meridien Hotel in Cairo and I melt. The shrill noises of the city filter across the water, pierced only by the muezzin's call to prayer: "Allahu-Akhbar, Allahu-Akhbar."

At night the electronic synthesizer from the Gezira Sheraton echoes across the water with the latest American pop hits.

In the daytime, the crowds: throngs of people pushing each other to cross streets; the buses are packed and the overhead bridges jammed. There are one million babies born every seven months. Egypt's budget deficit is estimated at $50 billion.

The U.S. is still helping out: This year Egypt will get $200 million in loans in addition to the year's $2.6 billion in aid. The U.S. also provides Egypt with 27,000 tons of white flour. Yet one government clerk told me the other day, "Mr. Bush is starving Egypt. He doesn't give Egypt enough aid." When I asked him why, he replied, "The Americans are fighting Islam, just like Israel is. That's why."

AUGUST 3
The Islamic New Year

The city seems emptier. . . .

Anyone who can afford it has gone to the Mediterranean seashore to escape the stifling heat. The papers are full of the news of the abduction by the Israelis of the Shi'a spiritual leader Sheikh Obeid and the retaliatory murder of Lieutenant Colonel Higgins. It is about the first time, since my arrival, that everyone is talking about international events and not domestic problems. Like the nineteen wives who recently murdered their husbands.

AUGUST 4

The people I have talked to are upset about the abduction of the thirty-two-year-old Muslim spiritual leader. They consider it an attack on Islam and they remind me that there are 150 Shi'a prisoners in Israel in detention camps.

AUGUST 5

The Egyptian government has officially denounced the assassination, by Hisbollah, of Colonel Higgins. Dr. Butrus Butrus Ghalli was quoted as saying that the only solution to terrorism in the Middle East is the recognition of the Palestinian people's rights to self-determination. I remind my readers that both Sunni and Shi'a Muslims are in accord when it comes to liberating occupied territories.

Another paper I read claimed that, according to "security sources," Sheikh Obeid was responsible for the kidnapping of Colonel Higgins of the U.S. Marines while Higgins was on duty in Lebanon in February 1988.

When will both sides ever understand each other's point of view? When?

AUGUST 7

I am reading the Israeli novel *The Yellow Wind* by David Grossman. In 1987, to mark twenty years of occupation, the Israeli news magazine *Koteret Rashit* commissioned Gross-